Lectures on the Law and the Gospel

LECTURES ON THE LAW AND THE GOSPEL

STEPHEN H. TYNG

SOLID GROUND CHRISTIAN BOOKS
BIRMINGHAM, ALABAMA USA

Solid Ground Christian Books
PO Box 660132
Vestavia Hills AL 35266
205-443-0311
sgcb@charter.net
www.solid-ground-books.com

LECTURES ON THE LAW AND THE GOSPEL

Stephen H. Tyng (1800-1885)

Taken from the 1846 edition by Robert Carter, New York

Cover image is taken in the Utah – Arizona desert, by Ric Ergenbright. See his work at ricergenbright.com

Cover design by Borgo Design
Contact them at borgogirl@bellsouth.net

ISBN- 978-159925-195-0

LECTURES

ON THE

LAW AND THE GOSPEL.

NEW EDITION, REVISED AND ENLARGED.

BY

STEPHEN H. TYNG, D.D.

RECTOR OF ST. GEORGE'S CHURCH, NEW-YORK.

NEW-YORK:
ROBERT CARTER, 58 CANAL-STREET
PITTSBURG: 56 MARKET-STREET.
1846.

Entered, according to Act of Congress, in the year 1843,
BY STEPHEN H. TYNG,
In the Clerk's Office of the District Court of the Eastern District of Pennsylvania.

THE LAW AND THE GOSPEL
by Ralph Erskine

The law supposing I have all,
Does ever for perfection call;
The gospel suits my total want,
And all the law can seek does grant.

The law could promise life to me,
If my obedience perfect be;
But grace does promise life upon
My Lord's obedience alone.

The law says, Do, and life you'll win;
But grace says, Live, for all is done;
The former cannot ease my grief,
The latter yields me full relief.

The law will not abate a mite,
The gospel all the sum will quit;
There God in thret'nings is array'd
But here in promises display'd.

The law excludes not boasting vain,
But rather feeds it to my bane;
But gospel grace allows no boasts,
Save in the King, the Lord of Hosts.

The law brings terror to molest,
The gospel gives the weary rest;
The one does flags of death display,
The other shows the living way.

The law's a house of bondage sore,
The gospel opens prison doors;
The first me hamer'd in its net,
The last at freedom kindly set.

An angry God the law reveal'd
The gospel shows him reconciled;
By that I know he was displeased,
By this I see his wrath appeased.

The law still shows a fiery face,
The gospel shows a throne of grace;
There justice rides alone in state,
But here she takes the mercy-seat.

Lo! in the law Jehovah dwells,
But Jesus is conceal'd;
Whereas the gospel's nothing else
But Jesus Christ reveal'd.

INTRODUCTION.

In the autumn of the year 1831, the author delivered a course of lectures upon the Law and the Gospel, to the congregation of St. Paul's Church, Philadelphia, of which he was at that time the Rector. The Editor of a collection of works called the Christian Library, requested them for publication in the series of volumes which he was preparing for the press. Thus they were first printed in the year 1833. In the same year a second edition of them was printed, in a separate volume. These were circulated and sold with a rapidity which was wholly unexpected. God was pleased to make them useful to the awakening and instruction of his children, to an extent, which has both astonished and humbled the writer. Many precious instances of conversion by their instructions through the divine power of God the Holy Ghost, have been brought to the knowledge of the author; for which he desires from his inmost soul to give the praise and glory to the God of all grace. Some of these have been of persons who are now preaching the blessed truths, which God has been pleased thus to reveal to them from his holy word. But these two editions have been for some years wholly dispensed abroad,—

and the writer has been repeatedly urged to publish another edition. The simple reason which has delayed it, has been the deepening conviction in his mind of the importance of the truths which are here taught, and his unwillingness to print the Lectures again, without such a revision and enlargement of them, as he could find no time to give. This he has at last accomplished, after much delay; and yet he feels, as he sends out the present work, more deeply humbled than before, with a consciousness of its unworthiness, and a reverence for the great and glorious truths which he has attempted to proclaim. He believes this book to contain the Glorious Gospel of the Blessed God,—stated in simplicity and clearness, in perfect accordance with the instructions of the Holy Scriptures, and the Liturgy, Articles, and Homilies of the Protestant Episcopal Church. He trusts that the Glorious Jesus, whom he worships as his Lord and his God, will be pleased to use the work, for the manifestation of his glory, the bringing of the vessels of his mercy to an acknowledgment and obedience of the truth,—and the guarding of his Church against the vital and dangerous errors, which these days have again brought forth. This Glorious King of Sion, the author would crown with all the powers of his heart and soul,—and he begs the readers of this work,—while they remember him in prayer for which he affectionately asks,—to unite with him, in adoring and glorifying, God, the Father, the Son, and the Holy Ghost, one God, world without end. Amen.

CONTENTS

LECTURES ON THE LAW.

	PAGE.
LECTURE I.—The importance of an accurate knowledge of the Divine Law,	13
LECT. II.—The practical influence of a knowledge of the Law,	26
LECT. III.—The Spirituality of the Law,	39
LECT. IV.—The present use of the Law,	52
LECT. V.—The convincing power of the Law,	67
LECT. VI.—The condemning power of the Law,	82
LECT. VII.—The Law a guide to Christ,	98
LECT. VIII.—Christ, the Righteousness of the Law,	113
LECT. IX.—The Law, the Christian's Rule of Life,	126
LECT. X.—The worth of Man's Obedience to the Law,	140
LECT. XI.—The Salvation of the Gospel confirming Man's Obedience to the Law,	155
LECT. XII.—The Perfection of the Divine Law,	171

LECTURES ON THE GOSPEL.

LECT. I.—The Object of the Gospel,	187
LECT. II.—The Gospel Way of Salvation,	201
LECT. III.—The History of the Gospel,	215

CONTENTS.

	PAGE
LECT. IV.—The Wisdom of the Gospel,	229
LECT. V.—The Power of the Gospel to Save,	243
LECT. VI.—The Power of the Gospel to Condemn,	258
LECT. VII.—The Grace of the Gospel as a Divine Gift,	271
LECT. VIII.—The Glory of the Gospel as a Revelation of God,	286
LECT. IX.—The Glory of the Gospel from the Method of its Publication,	300
LECT. X.—The Glory of the Gospel from the Subjects which it proclaims,	313
LECT. XI.—The Gospel Magnifying the Law,	324
LECT. XII.—The Guilt and Danger of Rejecting the Gospel.	338

LECTURE I.

THE IMPORTANCE OF AN ACCURATE KNOWLEDGE OF THE DIVINE LAW.

Open thou mine eyes, that I may behold wondrous things out of thy law.—PSALM CXIX. 18.

BY the law of God, the sacred writer here means the whole revelation of the Divine will to man. He designates this divine revelation, in this psalm, by the various words, "Statutes, commandments, testimonies, judgments, precepts and law." They are all employed, to describe that connected and perfect system of instruction, which is contained in the "Holy Scriptures, given by inspiration of God." In dwelling upon these communications of the will of God, the psalmist speaks the language of a heart that fervently loved his holy commands, and rejoiced to contemplate the excellence and purity of his character. In the extent of spiritual application which he perceived in these commands,—in the ardour of his prayers that they might be engraven upon his own heart; in the sorrow which he felt at witnessing the transgressions of them by others; in the eagerness of his desire to understand more clearly their excellence and perfection;—he has displayed his view of their importance, and the mind of the Spirit, in reference to the worth of a full understanding of them, to man. And we must unite with the same affectionate and earnest spirit, in the petition which he has set before us, "Open thou mine eyes, that I may behold wondrous things out of thy law."

In our natural ignorance of the things of the Spirit of God, and in the sinful aversion of our affections from them, there is a veil of thick darkness concealing from us the blessed truths which God alone reveals. We discern them neither in their meaning, nor in the extent of their influence. We confine our views of the Divine precepts, to their application in the letter to our outward conduct, and do not perceive the extent of their demands upon the thoughts and intentions of the heart. And neither as the standard of required obedience, nor as the measure of actual guilt, are we willing to consider, or able to comprehend, that the divine commandment is exceeding broad. This veil of spiritual ignorance, the Holy Ghost alone can remove. He must enlighten our blindness, and unfold to us, the secret and unsearchable truths of his own word. And to him, therefore, we direct our prayer for illumination and guidance, in the good, acceptable, and perfect will of God, that we may be led, on the one hand, to obtain a full knowledge of our sin, and on the other, of the sufficiency, and application to ourselves, of the glorious, appointed Saviour; discerning the things which are freely given to us of God.

The law, of which I purpose, by the divine help, to speak, is that one great moral law of God, all the commandments of which, are " holy, just, and good ;" an obedience to which, " is more to be desired than gold, yea, than much fine gold ;" the purity of which is, to a holy mind, "sweeter than honey, and the honey comb ;" by the guidance of which, the " servant of God is warned ;" and in the " keeping of which, there is great reward." This law is a revelation to man of the will of God. It is a transcript and publication of his holy and perfect mind. It is the rule of angelic obedience. It was the guide given to man at his creation. It is the law, obedience to which, would have given him eternal life; the violation of which, subjected him to condemnation. It is the law, which has been fulfilled for the sinner's justification, by the Lord Jesus Christ, the constituted Mediator of the new covenant;—which is written again upon the heart of the justified and restored man, according to the provisions of this covenant, by the Holy Spirit;—and in cheerful and permanent obedience to which, he is to glorify and honour his redeeming Lord, in his eternal and heavenly kingdom. This is the law of which I speak; the law which requires in every intelligent creature, supreme love to God, and unqualified submission in the spirit of love, to all his commandments.

An accurate knowledge and understanding of this divine law, lies at the very foundation of true religion, and of all instruction in the things of God. By this alone, can we be taught to appreciate and accept, the gracious provisions of the Gospel of our Lord Jesus Christ; in whom, God has been pleased to do for us, what the law required, but could not do; and by whom, he has laid open for us unsearchable riches of grace, meeting all the demands of the law, "magnifying it, and making it honorable," so that he is revealed, as "the end (or perfection) of the law for righteousness, to every one that believeth." The importance to us, of a clear and distinct intelligence of this subject, cannot be overstated; and we may well take upon our lips, and utter from our hearts, the psalmist's prayer, "Open thou mine eyes, that I may behold the wondrous things of thy law."

I. Here we gain *all just conceptions of the character of God.* His divine perfections are shining here. By his own revelation of himself alone, do we know any thing of him. "In his light, we see light." His holy law is a description of himself; the utterance in words, of his perfect, but previously concealed mind and will. Whatever be the character of our views of his law, will therefore be the description of our views of himself. The nature of his mind will be estimated by us, by our impressions of the nature of his commands.

1. Our apprehension of the purity and extent of the law of

God is the measure of our conception of the *holiness* of his own character. If we perceive this, reaching to every thought, as well as to every word and act of our being; requiring in us a perfect purity of mind and heart; demanding the spotless preservation of God's perfect image upon our souls; allowing no deviation, even inadvertently or in ignorance; accepting only an unfailing adherence to every precept, from the beginning, to the end of life; passing over no stain of sin without immediate condemnation; we shall look upon the Being from whom it has proceeded, and of whose mind it is the copy, as a Being of infinite purity and holiness; one who cannot regard iniquity but with abhorrence. But if we are satisfied with any inferior, or more limited view of the law, than this, we shall find ourselves detracting in the same degree, from the holiness of its author, and necessarily conceive of him, as a Being less opposed to sin. If we imagine that he will relax in the strict application of his commands, that he will suffer man to depart from the standard of absolutely perfect obedience, with impunity, we certainly impute to him a connivance at transgressions, and lay a serious stain upon the excellence of his character. In the same proportion, our reverence for him becomes diminished; our fear of his inspection is destroyed; our dread of his judgment passes away. He has become, in our view, in this uncertainty of his annunciations, or in this feebleness of his authority, altogether such an one as ourselves. And in reducing our conceptions of the extent of his law, we have destroyed our ability to appreciate, or to reverence the holiness of his character.

2. Our apprehension of the certainty and solemnity of the law of God, will be the measure of our conceptions of his *justice*. It is here that we are taught what is the justice of God. If we realize how strong and awful are the sanctions which he has appended to his law, and by which its obligations are enforced; if we see that they involve nothing less

than the everlasting happiness or misery of every child of man; that they are dependant upon a single defect of whatever kind in the obedience of man; that they can never be withdrawn, or satisfied by man, or mitigated in their power, or cease to operate, throughout eternity; that they can never qualify or yield in a single point, the fearful testimony, "the soul that sinneth, it shall die;" we see how fixed and unerring is the justice of that Being who has given and established this law. We behold him here, "a just judge;" "a judge who doeth right," "a great and dreadful king." But any lower view of the fixed sanctions of the law, will necessarily lead to a lower estimate of the divine justice which has been manifested in them. If we suppose that God will arrest or mitigate the operation of his law; that he will overlook the imperfections and wanderings of those whom he has placed under it; or that he will punish them only in some limited degree, which man may be able to bear; that everlasting death will not be the wages of sin; that the threatenings of divine anger against the unrighteousness of men, will not be executed in the fulness of their denunciation;—we become accustomed to low and derogatory ideas of the divine justice, and reduce the king of heaven, from the throne of unapproachable excellence, and unchanging truth, to some inferior position, both in government and character. Being ignorant of the stability and strictness of his law, we form no honorable conceptions of his justice in himself.

3. Our accurate knowledge of the demands of the law, is the source of all proper conceptions of the divine *mercy and love*. Here only, do we see the depths of the compassion of God for fallen men. When our guilt in transgression, appears to us, great beyond all our ability to measure or calculate; when we feel ourselves exposed to a judgment and condemnation commensurate with our innumerable offences; when we see our sins to be more in number than the sands

upon the sea-shore; when we are convinced that each of them deserves the eternal wrath and vengeance of God, and that we are lying under this just wrath, as an everlasting load; we shall be able in some degree, to appreciate the mercy, which has provided, unsought by us, the means of full forgiveness; we shall adore with wondering gratitude, the compassion of that offended Being, who, instead of executing upon us the vengeance which he had threatened, has himself originated a remedy for our souls condemned, entirely suited to our wants and adequate to our necessities; by which he may restore the guilty to his favour, and to life eternal, without compromising the honour of his law, or the truth of his character, but with the everlasting and increased glory of both. With such a view of the law, we shall appreciate the boundless extent of the love, which can pardon so much guilt, relieve from so much misery, and exalt and justify creatures so unworthy and so polluted. But any inferior conception of the demands of the law, reducing our estimate of the guilt and danger of transgression, will just so much reduce our estimate of a mercy which will appear to be in the same degree less needed, and to have accomplished a less important and less considerable deliverance. A ruined sinner, conscious that he has been ransomed by amazing grace, from eternal death, and rescued like a brand plucked out of the fire, will feel abundant cause to magnify the love and mercy of God forever. He has had much forgiven, and he will love much in return. But one who thinks he has had less to be forgiven, will necessarily love less also;—and in the very proportion in which he limits his view of the penalties he had incurred, and the dangers to which he was exposed, will he also diminish his conceptions of the mercy of which he has been made the less unworthy object.

All our apprehensions of the moral attributes of God will be thus regulated by our knowledge of his law, and our views of its demands. And in reference to them all, it will be found indubitably true, that loose and superficial conceptions of the one, will produce low and ineffectual ideas of the other. "God is known by the judgments which he executeth," and our estimate of the character of them, will be the standard by which we shall judge of his attributes, and government and claims.

II. In an accurate knowledge of the divine law alone, do we gain just views of *the character and work of the Saviour of mankind:*—And our conceptions of the demands of the law, and our estimate and apprehension of the wonderful mediation by which the Lord Jesus Christ has fulfilled it, will always be found in exact proportion to each other.

1. We shall here see, that our *necessity for such a Saviour*, arises from our condition under the judgment and condemnation of the law. We shall behold ourselves as transgressors of the divine commandments; as shut up under a just sentence of condemnation for sin, to eternal death; as utterly incompetent to make the satisfaction, which must be made, before we can be released, from the bondage under guilt, and the exposure to righteous anger, in which we are held. This condition makes our need for some "daysman," who can take our burden upon himself, and can speak in righteousness, mighty to save. The breach between us and God which our guilt has caused, must be made up, and we cannot do it. We can neither restore to God, the honour we have taken from him; nor regain for ourselves, the image of his holiness, which we have lost in sin. We must therefore have a Saviour who shall be able to bear the curse and condemnation under which we are lying, and to restore the union of our souls with God, which we have broken and cast away. The violated law holds us in bondage;—our lost condition under it, demands a Redeemer who is mighty;—and it is only as we understand the extent of our need, that we can appre-

ciate the indispensable necessity to us, of such a Saviour as God has revealed.

2. Then our estimate of *the nature and worth of the atonement* which the Lord Jesus has made, will be regulated by our knowledge of the law, which has required it. Whatever is our view of the extent of the necessity, will be also our measure of the nature of the offering by which it has been met. A knowledge of the claims of the divine law will convince us, that our sins are wholly innumerable, and our guilt, inconceivably great. Every deviation from the line of perfect obedience has brought upon us a curse, an everlasting curse, under the righteous judgment of God. This judgment which is according to truth, can never be satisfied, with anything but the full punishment denounced upon the offender, either in his own person, or in that of an adequate surety. The death which the law has threatened, must be endured, before a satisfaction can be made. And the knowledge of the law which displays to us, this death, as the wages of sin, will also show to us, the really satisfying nature of that offering, by which our Blessed Lord "has redeemed us from the curse of the law, by being made a curse in our stead." As our convictions of our own guilt are extended and accurate, we shall exalt and value the work of that glorious Saviour, who hath borne our iniquities, and put away our sin by the sacrifice of himself. And in the same degree, in which we reduce our apprehensions of our necessity, and of the condemnation which our sin deserves, shall we also depreciate the worth, and destroy the character, of that gracious atonement which has been made and accepted in our behalf. A clear view of what unpardoned sinners would be compelled to do and bear, will alone accurately teach, what the Lord Jesus has mercifully done and borne, for them whom he has redeemed and pardoned.

3. Our understanding of the *justification* which has been

accomplished for us by the Lord Jesus, will also depend upon our accurate knowledge of the demands of the divine law. We shall see that this law is never to be satisfied, but by a perfect and distinct obedience to its commands; that it requires every soul to possess, and to present to God, a righteousness which shall meet its highest claims; that it refuses to relax these requisitions in the least degree; that it insists upon their fulfilment in every point, and to the utmost extent. With this conviction, we shall honour and exalt the great Redeemer, who has accomplished in his own personal obedience for us, this required righteousness; and has opened, through the offering of this spotless righteousness, first to God, in man's behalf, and then to man, as his title to acceptance with God, a full and everlasting justification for every believing soul. We shall see and understand "the blessedness of the man, to whom God imputeth righteousness without works." But if our acknowledgment of these demands of the law, and of the righteousness which they require, be reduced to any inferior or partial standard; so that our own alleged sincere, but imperfect obedience may be accepted; in this false conception of the character of the law, we undermine the whole system of grace, as offered in the Gospel; we make the revealed obedience of Jesus a mere shadow of the imagination; we reduce our need of a perfect righteousness to nothing; we cancel all our obligations to him, for special mercy and abounding merit; and make him in fact, so far as the actual necessity for such a Saviour is concerned, to have lived, obeyed, and died for men, in vain. In no method can we understand, or appreciate, the glorious privilege, of having the "only begotten of the Father, full of grace and truth," as the "Lord our righteousness," but by gaining this knowledge, in a proper knowledge of the law, which he fulfilled.

4. The same course of remark would equally apply *to all the offices* of our Divine Redeemer. Our adequate concep-

tions of them all, will depend upon our accurate knowledge of the law of God. We shall not seek him as the great Prophet who alone can instruct us in the ways of God, if we do not feel our entire helplessness under the violated law; and are not convinced that our darkness and ignorance are such, as to render divine illumination and guidance absolutely indispensable. We shall not depend upon him as our High Priest, who alone can make an offering for us, and open our way into the holiest, through the veil of his flesh, if we imagine that any repentance or reformation of ours, can be availing or acceptable in the sight of God. We shall never look to him as our only prevailing intercessor and advocate with the Father, if we do not realize the utter worthlessness of the best that we can do in the service of God. We shall not trust in him as the King in Zion, who alone can give us the victory, if we have but partial apprehensions of our own weakness, and rebellion, and dangers, and see no necessity for Almighty power to rescue, or to renew us. And whatever aspect of the Saviour's work we consider, the same remark applies, the less that seems to us to be required of man for himself, the less will also appear to be demanded of his divine surety interposing in his behalf, and standing in his stead; and the less we consider the guilt and danger of man without a Saviour, the less obligation shall we necessarily feel, to him who willingly assumed and endured his condemnation. In the degree in which we are ignorant of the demands of the law, we form false conceptions of the necessities of the sinner who has broken it; and reduce our estimate of the whole work of the Son of God, who undertook to redeem him from its curse, and to magnify it and make it honourable. And if we would form correct apprehensions of the Father's love, who spared not his own Son, but delivered him up for us,—and of the amazing mercy of the Son, who came to do his will in this redemption of the ungodly, we are to acquire them, in that divine teaching which shall open our eyes to behold wondrous things out of the law.

III. These observations are equally applicable to *the office and operations of the Holy Spirit*, the comforter, who is sent to renew and sanctify the souls which the Father hath given to the Son, and the Son has redeemed by the sacrifice of himself. A correct apprehension of his divine work, for the people of God, is only to be gained, in an adequate understanding of their relation to the law, and their condition under it.

The Holy Spirit is given in the great covenant of redemption, to regenerate the sinful nature of those, whom "God hath chosen in Christ before the foundation of the world, that they should be holy and without blame before him in love;" to create them anew after his divine image; to enlighten them to discern the riches of their inheritance in Christ; and to bring them to the enjoyment of their adoption into the family of God. In precise accordance therefore, with the view which we have, of the spiritual necessity of guilty man, upon whom this work is to be accomplished, will be the estimate which we shall form, of the work itself. The less we suppose to be our natural opposition to God, and our alienation from his image, the less will there be in our view, to be done by the Spirit in our behalf. If there be not entire hostility in our fallen nature towards God, and an utter destruction of the first creation of our souls in holiness, what necessity can there be for a new creation? If the defect be partial, the remedy may be partial also. If we are not actually dead in sin, why should we require a divine and life-giving power to raise us from the dead. If we have not wholly gone out of the way of life, are not completely lost and ruined, how shall we suppose, we need Almighty grace to restore us again to the path of peace, to cleanse us from our pollutions, and to keep us in the way everlasting? If we are made to feel that our dangers and wants are extreme, that our condition is one of total corruption and depravity, as well as of condemnation and guilt, we shall see that we must have a remedy adapted to such extremities; we shall be content with nothing short of the power of the Living God, in that Spirit who is to pluck us "out of the horrible pit, and out of the miry clay, and to set our feet upon the rock," which the Father's love hath placed for us, in the atonement and righteousness of the Son.

They who gain not this clear perception of the condition of man under the violated law, see not their need of the continued special influence of the Holy Spirit, to illuminate their minds, or to sanctify their hearts. They are led to doubt, or even to deny, his personal agency in the great work of man's redemption. In connexion with this, they are often deluded by the same ignorance, to reject the whole revelation of the Glorious Persons in the Trinity,—and the various indispensable doctrines of grace which are connected with it, such as the doctrine of actual satisfaction for sin in the Saviour's death,—of the imputation of his righteousness to believers for their justification,—and of the certain preservation of them in new obedience, by the power of the Holy Ghost. They do not feel themselves to be destroyed in sin; they see not therefore their need of the free and boundless love of the Father, electing them unto life, as the origin of their hope; of the divine merit of an Immanuel to bring them in acceptance before him, and into possession of this life; and of the Almighty agency of the Spirit to enable them to know and to receive the things which are thus freely given to them of God. Multitudes thus bring down their avowed system of religion to some low and miserable standard, which in fact almost assumes the sufficiency of their own nature, and their own works to meet the judgment and to claim the favour of God. All these are mistakes which spring altogether from an ignorance of his law. Let them obtain a thorough insight into its claims and character by the enlightening power of the Spirit, and they will then see how solemnly and fatally its demands and sanctions shut them up under the condemnation and bondage of sin; they will then see, that if any one less than God himself, undertake their salvation, they must assuredly perish; they will be convinced that no arm inferior to the Lord of hosts, can rescue them from the wrath to which they are exposed, or bring to them the victory they require;—they will humbly seek, and then shall surely find, the free and great salvation, which God has so clearly revealed, and so fully offered, in the provisions of his Gospel,—and they will realize the importance of the prayer before us, "Open thou mine eyes, that I may behold wondrous things out of thy law,"— in discerning that all these advances in spiritual knowledge are dependant upon an accurate understanding of its character and claims.

LECTURE II.

THE PRACTICAL INFLUENCE OF A KNOWLEDGE OF THE LAW.

Blessed is the man whom thou chastenest, O Lord, and teachest him out of thy law.—PSALM XCIV. 12.

THE sacred writer uttered this sentiment under circumstances which well display the truth he intended to express. He stood amidst the overflowings of ungodliness. The wicked appeared to triumph on every side. They boasted of their success and power, and proclaimed their contempt of God. They derided the warnings of the divine inspection, and of their own final responsibility to God. Amidst the enormities of their transgressions, they were still self-confident and self-righteous. The psalmist beheld this wild tumult of human passions and human pride, and implored a divine manifestation of the power of God, in the execution of judgment and vengeance upon the ungodly who boasted of his absence and unconcern. And in the midst of such iniquities flowing from an ignorance of God, and his holy law, he proclaims the happiness of those who, under the teaching and chastening of the Lord, have been led to avoid the ways of evil doers, and to seek their comforts in the paths of his commandments. Under his holy discipline, they have learned the principles of truth, and acquired that practical obedience which a knowledge of his law is adapted to impart. And by its direction, they are saved alike, from the rebellion which vainly opposes the authority of God, and the self-righteousness which justifies itself in opposition to him. The text exhibits the practical influence upon man, of a knowledge of the divine law, which is the subject now before us. And while it declares the blessedness of the man who has thus been taught by God, it shews to us, that this knowledge of the law of God, is far from being a mere speculation, a dead theory in theology, but is a spring of great practical influence, which distinguishes and blesses the whole course of a sound experience in religion, and a just intelligence of religious truth.

I. *All true religious feeling* is intimately connected with a proper knowledge of the law of God. Real spiritual affections are, in a great degree, dependant upon it. Without it, man cannot have real conviction of sin, or humility, or gratitude, or zeal, or love to God. And whatever blessedness there is, in these exercises of a renewed mind, there is also, in the knowledge of the law, upon which they depend.

1. We can have no real *conviction of sin*, without an adequate conception the demands of the law, and of our own condition under it. But this is the very first step in the work of the Holy Spirit when he regenerates a child of wrath. He makes him to see his guilt, and to feel his burden, as a transgressor against God. Mere natural religion makes very partial and scanty acknowledgments of sin. It confesses the guilt of acts of transgression, but it knows nothing of the guilt of a state of sin. It mourns for crimes, but not for condition. It imagines no other method of return to God necessary, than a sorrow for the deeds of the past, and an effort of amendment for the future. But our natural condition is one of entire ruin. We are, in our fallen state, under the divine condemnation. "As many as are of the works of the law, are under a curse;" and the wrath of God abideth on them. Of the reality and extent of this guilt and ruin however, we are ignorant, until God the Spirit teaches us out of his law. "By the law is the knowledge of sin;" and the conviction which we have of our guilt as transgressors under it, must depend upon the knowledge

we have of its character and claims. If we have been taught the spotless and inflexible system of this Divine law, demanding the utmost conceivable devotion to God, and an unerring and unrelaxed obedience of his will, and denouncing the anger of God against every soul of man that doeth evil; when our eyes are opened to behold our own condition as sinners, we shall see ourselves to be wholly guilty in his sight, and our mouths will be stopped from all excuse. There will be found by us, no single feeling or thought, upon the purity of which we can rest the shadow of hope; and no circumstance which we can plead to extenuate a single deficiency. We shall find ourselves to be condemned before God, wholly and everlastingly. And our deep conviction of guilt, will bring us before him with the solemn confession, "I know, that in me, there dwelleth no good thing." But if we have only received, and have been satisfied with, general, partial, and indefinite views of the claims of the law, the same general and indistinct impressions will be transferred to our convictions of personal guilt in our transgressions of it. Our hearts will plead a thousand vain excuses from temptations to which we were exposed, or from the weakness of our nature, or from the inadvertance which surprised us,—and we shall never be led to acknowledge ourselves altogether unholy, and justly condemned. We may acknowledge that in many things we have done wrong, but we shall not see that every thing which we have done is wrong; we may confess that many of our acts are evil, but we shall not confess that the secret thoughts of our hearts are also filled with odious and abominable wickedness. We shall still have that self-righteous spirit which springs from an ignorance of the divine law.

2. As our conviction of sin, is thus dependant upon our knowledge of the law, so also is our *humility* under this conviction. The importance of this temper of mind the Scriptures largely teach us. "The Lord resisteth the proud, but giv-

eth grace to the humble." "To this man will I look, even to him that is poor, and of a contrite spirit, and trembleth at my word." "Whosoever exalteth himself, shall be abased, but he that humbleth himself shall be exalted." Humility is not merely a sense of our weakness as creatures; nor a general acknowledgment only of our character as sinners. There is not a human being who would refuse either of these concessions. But it is a real and deep consciousness of our guilty and lost condition, as justly and eternally condemned before God; a clear perception of the total opposition of our hearts to the will of God; and of the entire absence in our lives of the least conformity to his commands. It is such a sense of our wicked alienation from God, of our voluntary rebellion against him; such a conviction that every imagination of the thoughts of our hearts, is only evil continually, as makes us really abhor and loathe ourselves, and repent in dust and ashes, before a Being who searcheth our hearts, and will bring every secret thing into judgment, and set our secret sins in the light of his countenance. Such a broken and contrite spirit, the Holy Spirit gives, and God will not despise. But how rarely is such a spirit seen among men. How seldom even among those who profess to be, and who we trust are, truly awakened by the Holy Ghost, do we behold this deep sense of guilt, and this humble acknowledgment of exposure to God's just wrath and indignation. How generally in the world, is there a disposition to think, that such feelings are either wholly pretended, or else absurdly extravagant, even if they are real; and that the expressions of them are fanatical and to be avoided. But why is this?—Are these views a false estimate of the sinner's condition? Is such self-abasement unsuitable to his character and state? Surely not. But such objectors have no knowledge of the divine law. They do not try themselves, or others, by this high and holy standard. They are insensible of their own departures from God;—they do not feel themselves to be lost in sin;—and they can see no cause for such undue humiliation, under a burden, which does not appear to them to be extreme or destructive. The idea of humility, as the Holy Spirit describes it in his word, and forms it in the soul which he creates anew, never enters into the natural mind. The unconverted man cannot comprehend it. He neither possesses it, nor desires it, nor approves of it, according to its real import. It is one of the things which God teaches man out of his law, and which can be learned under no other discipline than that blessed one, by which he educates the "vessels of his mercy whom he hath afore prepared unto glory." When we have been truly instructed in the nature and extent of this law, and never till then, our convictions of sin, will be deep and definite,—and our self-abasement under them, lowly and abiding; then we shall see, and humbly acknowledge, that we are utterly destitute of all claim to mercy from God, and wholly unworthy of its exercise towards us.

3. The exercise of real *gratitude* to God, is also dependant upon our accurate knowledge of his law. Gratitude is a thankful consciousness and acknowledgment of the mercies which we have personally received from God. Its exercise must therefore necessarily depend upon the amount, and the nature of the benefits which we believe have been conferred upon us. If we are truly the children of God by faith in Christ Jesus, we shall view ourselves in the light of God's revelations of truth. We shall see ourselves to be the captives of sin and Satan, ransomed from death and hell, by the precious and perfect obedience, and amazing death of our incarnate God. We shall be in our own apprehension, altogether, as "brands plucked out of the burning;" nor can we imagine mercy shewed to any, which would constitute them greater monuments of grace than we are. With such a view of our condition and obligations, our whole soul will bless our Redeemer and Lord, for "the unsearchable riches" of his

grace. We shall call upon all within us, to praise his name. We shall rejoice in God who hath become our salvation, with joy unspeakable and full of glory. But alas! how far are we generally from such gratitude as this! How few are duly sensible of the vast obligations which divine mercy has laid upon them! With the great proportion of professing Christians, some faint and general acknowledgments of divine goodness, are quite sufficient to express their sense of the love which has ransomed them from going down into the pit; and they are disposed to consider stronger language and deeper emotions, than those to which they are accustomed, as excessive, and wanting in sobriety. But how false and how dangerous is such an estimate! How different is it from the mind of beings who surround the throne of God in glory! There, redeemed saints are filled with adoring admiration of the grace which has been displayed in the scheme of man's deliverance; contemplating its transcendant excellency, and praising God, for the glory which he has gained from its accomplishment. There is no coldness or formality there, because they fully discern the evil which has been remedied, and the blessing which has been conferred. And why are men on earth, cold and indifferent, but because they do not see the depths of condemnation, from which they have been rescued, or the labour which their deliverance required,—or the amazing love, which led a divine Saviour to undertake it? Did they behold, in the mirror of God's holy law, the burden and bondage, from which they have been ransomed, and the inestimable worth of the offering which must be made, and which has been made for them, they would surely have far other feelings towards that Glorious Immanuel, who came down into the abyss of their ruin, and put away their punishment, by enduring it himself. A just knowledge and estimate of the claims of the law which have been fulfilled by him, would lead to a high appreciation of the love which he has exercised, and the obligations, under which we are placed. But an ignorance of the law, in the very same proportion, reduces our consciousness of the mercy of the law-fulfiller, and our gratitude for the work which he has finished. The measure of our praise to God, is one of the things therefore which he must teach us out of his law.

4. From the same source of instruction, will spring all true *zeal* for God, and for his service and glory. Thus are our hearts to be taught a thorough and affectionate engagement in his service, as our Redeemer and King. Who is there among the Lord's people, that feels this zeal for God, in any measure correspondent with the standard which the Holy Scriptures have established. There, we are represented, as bought with an inestimable price, and are called upon with intense gratitude for this amazing mercy, to glorify God in our bodies and spirits which are his. With an adequate sense of our obligations to God, the language of our hearts would be, "what shall I render unto the Lord for all his benefits?" No services of ours would appear an adequate return to him. All that we could do for such a Lord, would be as nothing in our eyes. All that we should suffer for him, would be light and gladly borne. Our time, our talents, our property, our influence, our whole life, would appear to be of value in our eyes, only as they could be made humbly subservient to the advancement of the divine glory. The whole world would seem to us, in comparison with the cross of Christ, in the strong expression of Archbishop Leighton, "one grand impertinence." But how little of this spirit do we feel! How little of it, do we see in others! How little is it loved and approved among men, even in the measure in which it is manifested! How infinitely below this "reasonable service," is the standard of the multitude, who still value themselves upon the usefulness and excellence of their lives among men! But this deficiency must also be traced, to the one cause, of which we have already spoken so much. Humility, gratitude, zeal for

God, all rise or fall, as our views of the divine law, and the divine redemption which has fulfilled, and honoured it, are deep and accurate, or superficial and defective. We can never acquire an entire devotedness of heart to God, as redeemed creatures, until we apprehend the full extent and worth of the redemption which we have received. If our views of the great purposes and blessings, for which, and the great dangers from which, we "have been apprehended of Christ Jesus," are low and limited, our own efforts in pressing forward to "apprehend" these mercies, and to obey him who hath conferred them, will be equally limited. To walk as Christ walked, will appear a bondage in our view. To tread in the steps of holy apostles will seem unnecessary. To glory only in the cross, and to rejoice if we are counted worthy to suffer shame for Christ's sake, will seem a state of mind only necessary and adapted, for persons in peculiar stations of trial and duty. But no inferior state of mind is adequate to our real obligations,—or will be acceptable to him. If we would be Christ's indeed, we must live, not unto ourselves, but unto him who died for us, and rose again; purifying ourselves, even as he is pure, and striving to be perfect, as our Father who is in heaven is perfect. This is the result of the constraining love of Christ, and of our union by faith to him. And it is only as we are taught out of the law of God, that we are truly taught our need of Christ,—or are led to seek our complete salvation in him.

II. The practical influence of a knowledge of the law, is displayed in the fact, that all our *scriptural hopes*, are dependant upon it. The importance of a distinct and well defined Christian hope, cannot be estimated too highly. " Ye are saved by hope." The prayers of the Apostles for those to whom they wrote or ministered, in relation to this subject, are repeated and various; that the eyes of their understandings might be enlightened, to discern the free and unspeakable gifts of God in his Gospel, to comprehend the nature and worth of the hopes and privileges which were thus bestowed upon them, and to be able to give to others, a reason for the hope which they possessed, and which they were to offer to the acceptance of all. It is by this blessed hope, which personally appropriates to ourselves, the gracious promises of God in the Gospel, and enables us to realize as our own, things which are unseen and eternal, that we are sustained in trial and duty, and made to press forward to the prize of our high calling of God in Christ Jesus. But clear views of religious truth are indispensable to the enjoyment of a rational and consoling hope of eternal life. And while Satan is deluding the multitudes of the unconverted, with false and unfounded hopes, and by the influence of these, is persuading them to reject the invitations of the Gospel, and to remain contented in a state of sin, the falsehood of his devices is only to be ascertained by a thorough examination of the ground, upon which these hopes profess to rest.

All false hopes connected with the interests of the soul, arise from an ignorance of the divine law. When a sinful man is found actually claiming everlasting life from the justice of God, on the ground that he has done his duty, has been guilty of no harm to his fellow men, has injured no one, and defrauded no one, what but total ignorance of the law of God, can have veiled his mind with an expectation so unfounded and deceitful? While he sees not that his very best acts stand in need of pardoning mercy, as much as his vilest sins; that the least transgression of his life entails upon him a necessary and everlasting condemnation; that his heartless prayers, and his omissions and failures in required duty, will condemn him as certainly as any of the acts which appear to him more sinful; upon what does his false confidence of security rest, but upon a total misapprehension of the nature of the divine claims and requisitions of God's perfect law?

When another man proclaims his hope to rest upon the unbounded mercy of God, mercy which is over all his works, while he rejects from his heart, the clear and ample provision of mercy which is offered to sinners in the Gospel, what but an entire ignorance of the divine law is the foundation of this delusive expectation? When a judge is seated on the bench, could the clearest evidence of guilt against the criminal, be affected by his assertion of a previous dependance upon the mercy which he hoped to find in the day of trial? The hour of trial is the time of law, not the time of mercy. In the present life, there is abundant mercy freely offered to the vilest sinner; nay, pressed by his offended, but gracious Creator, upon his attention and acceptance. But it is, as it must be, mercy in God's own way, and according to the plan of his own wisdom. When the time of final adjudication and recompense has come, the reign of mercy has come to an end, and the season for its exercise has passed by forever. The principles of just and equal law must then govern every determination. The Judge of all the earth must do right. The man who is there, with sin previously unpardoned, must endure the death which is the wages of sin. He therefore who now pursues the path of voluntary transgression, and still trusts in the mercy of his Judge, for a future and final pardon, is destroyed by his ignorance of the law, or by his voluntary contempt for its demands. The claims of this holy law must be satisfied and honoured. It does not, it cannot allow the name of mercy. Without the shedding of blood, it offers no remission. Until its penalty has been paid, and all its demands have been met and answered, it is utterly vain to think of charming its denunciations of wrath to rest. The mercy of God is displayed in his gracious method of making satisfaction to the law for the sinner's soul. But it can never act in setting aside the demands of the law upon man, while they are still unsatisfied, and all hope which is founded upon such an expectation, is delusive and false.

When others speak of a vague and indefinite hope which

is resting partly upon their own works, and partly upon the merits of the Saviour to make up for the deficiencies of these, the same ignorance of the law is at the foundation of their false confidence. They avow their trust in Christ. But they can give no reason for this trust. They have no clear idea of what he has done, that should lead them to this confidence. They give no evidence that they have been really brought by the Holy Spirit, to renounce themselves, that they may win Christ, and be found in him. They have probably no distinct emotion or conception connected with that faith in Christ which they avow. For even while they proclaim this hope, they do not, and will not, accept the salvation which is offered in the Gospel, upon the terms which are there displayed. They will not renounce all works of their own, as at least, a partial ground of hope. They will not empty and humble themselves to enter the kingdom of heaven, at the same gate with publicans and harlots. This is too humiliating. Their proud hearts must have something wherein to boast themselves. If they cannot make their own lives, the sole ground of their justification, they will rely upon them in part,—or they will make them the reason, for their confidence and hope in Christ. They will not suffer themselves to be stripped of all self-preference, and self-respect. They know not how to glory only in the cross of Christ. They have never experienced or understood the condemning power of the law, nor felt the burden of guilt which it lays upon the sinner's soul. And they are in the possession only of a hope, whose whole foundation is ignorance of the curse which has been laid upon transgression, and of the endurance of that curse by the Son of God, as the ransom for those who believe in him.

All these false hopes spring from the same source. They are entertained and cherished in the mind, because it has never been chastened by the Lord, and taught by him, the wondrous things of his law. Man cannot live without hope. And Satan, perfectly aware of this fact, blinds his mind to the true hope which God presents, and urges upon him in its stead, these refuges of lies. He keeps him in ignorance of what the Lord God hath spoken, and thus deludes him to an embracing of these unfounded and impossible expectations, as his confidence in the day of the Lord's appearing.

A Christian hope is founded immediately upon Christian faith. It is a personal application, of the objects which faith discerns, and an appropriation of the treasures, which faith discloses in the divine revelations. The faith which justifies the soul, brings us simply to the Lord Jesus Christ, as the great end and fulfilment of the law, for all who believe. It teaches us, our own condemnation under the law, and leads us, emptied of all confidence in our own works, to rest ourselves wholly, upon his past and finished work of substitution in our behalf. If we attempt to blend in any measure or degree, anything of our own, with the work of Christ's redemption, we make utterly void, all that he has done and suffered in our stead. Christ has thus become of no effect to us; and so far as we are concerned, he has died in vain. The law presents two distinct claims as made upon every sinner, which must be met and answered, before he can have a hope of acceptance with God. It denounces death as the punishment of sins past; and it requires a spotless obedience as the title to future reward. It thus guards the way to the tree of life with a flaming sword which turns every way in opposition to the sinner's approach. The answers to these claims can never be found in the sinner himself. But faith discerns them both, and in their utmost possible value, in the sinner's Saviour. God hath set forth his Son, to be a propitiation for sins past, and to declare his righteousness, in the justifying of the ungodly. In this abundant provision for the pardon of sins past,—and for the everlasting justification of the pardoned soul, faith discerns a full foundation for hope. It perceives the law to be completely satisfied and honoured, and the hope which it offers in this satisfaction of the law by the Lord our righteousness, is sure, reasonable, and satisfying to the soul. It rests upon a clear perception of what Christ has done, and of what the law required to be done. And all the blessedness which there is in such a hope, becomes the portion of those whom the Lord chasteneth, and teacheth out of his law.

These views sufficiently display the practical influence of a knowledge of the law. Ignorance of it, and false apprehensions of it, are the root of all the superficial views and statements of doctrine, with which the Christian community is filled. An understanding of it, is of vital consequence in the great concern of your soul's salvation. O, seek from God, the instruction out of his law which he imparts. Let his Holy Spirit deliver you from darkness, and lead you to a knowledge of his truth in this all-involving concern. Let the dayspring from on high, guide your feet into the way of peace. Seek wisdom from above,—practical, experimental wisdom, and seek it with all your hearts:—that you may not walk in the blindness of your minds, with your understandings darkened, through the ignorance that is in you. Give your earnest attention to an understanding of this vital portion of the truth of God; and under his guidance, your affections will be sanctified and elevated, your minds opened and instructed, and your hearts led to embrace the everlasting consolations which are laid up in his dear Son. Thus will you gain a hope which maketh not ashamed; a hope founded upon the finished and unchangeable work of Jesus Christ the Lord; and believing in him, and loving him, though now you see him not, you shall rejoice in him, with joy unspeakable and full of glory.

LECTURE III.

THE SPIRITUALITY OF THE LAW.

We know that the law is spiritual.—ROMANS VII. 14.

In a contemplation of the operation of the divine law upon man, one of the first and most important topics for our remark, is its own character, and the actual extent of its demands. This aspect of it, is habitually called by us, the *spirituality* of the law. Of this, the apostle speaks in our present text. Though he describes the operation of the law, as destroying all the hopes which he indulged of merit or safety in his unconverted state, and thus, as working death for him, he proclaims it to be in all respects, holy, just and good; and producing death to a sinner, solely in a just action upon his unholy character and guilty life. He confesses that man in his natural state is carnal, and a slave to sin, and declares that all the apparent ill effects of the operation of the law upon him, are to be attributed to this fact alone. The law itself is spiritual and holy.

I. But what law is it, of which the apostle makes this assertion? We must answer, it is exclusively that great moral law, which is now before us, as the subject of this series of discourses. The assertion cannot be applied to any other law, without much qualification.

The *Judicial* law which was appointed for the Israelites, though it was founded upon the moral law of God, was but the peculiar statute law of that nation. It never had, nor was it designed to have, the least authority over any other of the families of men, unless they became incorporated by their own profession as members of the nation of Israel. In no sense, but in its origin from God, was it a spiritual law. Like all other laws for the mere outward government of man, its requisitions and prohibitions took cognizance merely of outward acts; and recompensed obedience or disobedience, respectively with temporal protection, or bodily suffering and death. This law cannot be said to be annulled or repealed in regard to other nations, for it never had authority over them. The limits of its application were the natural and the adopted children of Israel. What its permanency of authority over them may be, it does not come within my present purpose to consider.

The *ceremonial* or *ecclesiastical* law which was appointed for the same people, enjoined the rites and observances of a form of religious worship, which was established for them alone. This cannot justly be called a spiritual law, though its ordinances had an important spiritual meaning, and were certainly designed to instruct the believing mind in spiritual things. St. Paul calls it, " a law of carnal commandments," which made nothing perfect; and speaks of its ordinances as "carnal ordinances" imposed upon the people of Israel for a time. St. Peter calls it a yoke which neither they, nor their fathers were able to bear. It was a system of shadows, under which were represented to the mind endowed with spiritual discernment, the great truths and realities of the Gospel. In itself it could make nothing perfect. It was like the judicial law of Israel, confined in its application to the members of that one nation, and was intended to lead them to that blessed seed of Abraham, in whom all its figures and appointments were fulfilled.

The great *moral* law of God, was embodied in the national institutes for Israel ;—though in itself entirely separable, from all that was merely local and temporary in its authority over them. It is of this divine system of precepts, that the psalmist says, "the law of the Lord is perfect, converting the soul; —and pure, enlightening the eyes." It is to this, that the apostle refers, when he declares in our text, as a principle which was to be considered beyond the reach of doubt,—" We know that the law is spiritual." This was ordained to life. Obedience to its precepts would have conferred life upon man; —and it is only as the result of man's own transgression, that it is found to be unto death. This law is spotless and holy; and every commandment which it imposes, is holy, just, and good. It was comprized, in the ten commandments which were written upon tables of stone, by the finger of God. It was communicated to Israel, on Mount Sinai, with a majesty which well became its importance and character. The peculiar laws of Israel as a nation were subsequently proclaimed in many successive communications. This was a special revelation of the will of God, upon which all other precepts were founded. It was comprized by our Lord Jesus Christ in two commandments, embracing supreme love to God, and universal love to his creatures. It is declared by St. Paul in its one fundamental principle, when he says, "love is the fulfilling of the law."

This great law is the law of heaven, and to it every heavenly being is subjected. It was published first on earth, when it was written upon the heart of man at his creation. Its governing principles and power were obliterated then, by man's transgression,—and it was published again, written by the finger of God, upon tables of stone, at Mount Sinai. It was added then anew, to display the holy character of God; to exhibit the sinfulness, and the abounding extent, of man's transgression;—to manifest the universal necessity for the promised seed, who should fulfill its obligations, and bear its penalty for man. It was accordingly announced before the peculiar, private institutions for Israel were imposed, because it was the foundation of all other commands; and their acknowledgment of the authority of this, was a concession of the right of God to impose upon them any subsequent precepts, which should be according to his will. It displayed most clearly the impossibility of man's attainment of life by any obedience of his own, and thus shut them up for all their hope, to the faith which should be revealed, when in the fulness of the time, God should send forth his Son.

The character and extent of this holy law is described in our text. It requires entire submission to the will of the Creator; and is as obligatory upon Gentiles as upon Jews:— and as binding in heaven, as upon earth. Of this, is the declaration of our text so solemnly and distinctly made, "We know that the law is spiritual." This attribute of the law is a fundamental truth;—as evident as the same attribute of God, of whose holy mind and character it is a perfect transcript and expression. The spirituality of the law which it declares, we are now to consider.

II. "We know that the law is spiritual."

1. It is spiritual in its *origin*. It flowed from no human or inferior source, but immediately from the mind of that High and Holy Being, who is himself a spirit,—and whom no eye hath seen, or can see. It is in its principles and precepts, but a copy in words, of the will and character of God. A perfect conformity to its commands, would be a perfect conformity to the holy character of God. It was first proclaimed, when the first creature was formed. Then the will of God was first declared, as the rule of government for the beings whom he had made. In the heavenly world, it is binding upon pure spirits alone, and the love for God and for each other, which moves innumerable holy beings there, is the fulfilling of this law. There its origin, and operation, and fruits are all spiritual. Ten thousand times ten thousand spotless spirits admire, reverence, and love it, as the mirror, in which

the infinitely glorious perfections of the Deity are continually beheld. He speaks, and it is done; he commands, and his will stands fast.

This law was communicated immediately from God to man. It was written in his mind and heart at his creation, by the Spirit of God. When man first opened his eyes upon the beauties and benefits, with which his Divine Creator had been pleased to surround him, this spiritual law upon his heart, led him to lift up his immediate offering of pure and perfect love to the Lord of all, and to delight in every act of homage to his will. This same holy law has been written since by the same Spirit in the soul of every child of God among redeemed men, in the hour in which he was brought back from his death in sin, to a life of new obedience to God. And all the renewed servants of the most High, perceive and admire its perfections, and delight to fulfil its holy commandments. The purity and excellence of the law, which the Spirit of God thus teaches man, when he writes it upon his heart, is one of those things which the natural man discerneth not, and is not able to understand. In its origin within his soul, it is ever and wholly the work of the Spirit of God. By the same Spirit, it was revealed to holy men who spake as they were moved by the Holy Ghost, as the authors of those Scriptures which were given by inspiration of God,—and in the precepts of which, this holy law is recorded for the government of man. Whatever period or occasion of its revelation, we may particularly consider, the spiritual origin of the law is the same. It is written by the finger of God, and from himself proclaims his mind and will.

2. The law is spiritual in its *demands*. It is wholly a mistaken view, which limits these divine revelations to the letter of the precepts,—or to the outward conduct of men. The external acts to which the divine precepts refer, whether they are of sins forbidden, or of duties commanded, are

surely included in their intended application. But they cannot be understood as the limits of this application. These precepts refer as certainly to the desires and purposes of the heart, and the thoughts of the mind, as they do to the open conduct of the life. They lay the hand of their authority upon the inner man. They distinctly reveal to man what God requires, and they demand the unqualified and uniform obedience to every precept, in the heart which he searches. If man were in a condition shut out from the possibility of outward breaches of divine commands; nay, if he were without the body, with which they are perpetrated, the law of God would still impose upon him, the same obligations, and make the same demands. The principle of obedience, is that to which the law directs its notice and its operation. It requires every where total and unbroken submission to the will of God. The changes of occasional relations to other created beings, cannot alter the obligation of this simple principle of entire subjection to the will of God. The demands of the law are in their extent, spiritual. The thoughts and purposes which lead to outward violations of these precepts, are as really violations of them also, as are the results to which they tend. When the law forbids a single transgression, it equally forbids every thought, and occupation, and feeling, which would naturally lead to its commission. And when it commands a duty, it equally enjoins every circumstance and habit which properly conduces to its performance. Even more extensively than this,—in the very prohibition of a transgression, it requires the contrary duty; and in the injunction of a duty, it forbids the opposite sin. The commandment of God is thus exceeding broad, and like a two-edged sword, divides asunder, and discerns, the thoughts and intents of the heart. It goes thus directly to the hidden fountain of the character, and requires the inward cleansing of the soul in entire conformity to the purity of God. If it were possible, that any one had been perfectly obedient to God, in every feeling, desire, and act of the whole life, and in but one single thought had rebelled against him, that sinful thought would annihilate the worth of the whole obedience, with which it was connected. The man has thus become a sinner, and having offended in one point, is guilty of all, or wholly guilty, in the judgment of the law. This was the case with the first transgressor, in whom a single sin destroyed the whole covenant of life, under which he had been placed. The character of man has changed, —but the law has not. It is still equally spiritual in its demands, requiring in every heart, a submission to God, uninterrupted by a single insurgent feeling, a purity of character, uncontaminated by a single stain, and a zeal of devotion unrelaxed by a single wandering purpose. The law of God has no partial operation for the earth. It requires the same character throughout the universe. That which angels have always been in heaven, it requires men to be, from their birth, and forever. Its searching precepts go directly to the heart, and are to be obeyed there, in a perfect exhibition of the mind of Christ, and a perfect exemplification of the holiness of God. This is the spiritual character of the law in its demands. Uniform love with all the heart, and that forever, constitutes the only fulfilment of its precepts.

3. The law is spiritual in its *operations*. It was originally ordained to be a covenant of life ;—its designed operation was, in an unceasingly holy and animating guidance of man, to lead him to a perfect conformity to the will of God. It was a pure and sacred friend and supporter of its subjects. It taught them, what their Creator required of them; and warned them of what he had forbidden. It checked them in every temptation to transgress; it encouraged them in every path of obedience. In the keeping of its precepts, it gave them great reward. But the disobedience of man changed the whole operation of the law towards him; and gave it a

new course and purpose. It can never be the friend of sinners. It comes now with no offer of life. It remains faithful to God, though man has been unfaithful, and stands forth as a swift witness against all who have rebelled against him. With the sinner, its whole operation is to convince him of his guilt;—to judge him as thus guilty;—to condemn him to death;—and then to leave him to perish. It comes to him in the majesty of divine authority, and with distinct and undeniable accusations, for this two-fold purpose of conviction and judgment. In this work of power, it lays out before his conscience, the extent of its own claims; and places by their side, the enormity of his transgressions. It shows him what God requires;—and then it shows him what he has done. Thus laying open before him his aggravated guilt, it convinces him of the truth of its charges against him, and of the justice of his condemnation. It stops his mouth from all excuses. It compels him in deep humiliation to acknowledge himself unclean;—and then stands forth in the name of the most High, to pass a final sentence upon his soul. It proclaims the eternal wages of sin. It announces the certainty of a coming wrath. It unveils before him, an unutterable and everlasting destruction. It strips off the covering from the devouring fire. And thus, laying judgment to the line of its holy and unrelaxing demands, it destroys the hope of the sinful soul, and compels the convicted transgressor to cry out in the bitterness of his anguish, "O, wretched man that I am, who shall deliver me from the body of this death?" This is the spiritual operation of the law. Here its work ceases. It cannot go beyond this limit;—convincing the transgressor of his guilt; pronouncing his everlasting condemnation; and then leaving him to perish. This has been its actual operation upon every servant of God who has been redeemed from his iniquity, and reconciled to him. In his experience, the power of the commandment has slain and destroyed all self-confidence, all hope in any righteousness of his own; and condemned under its righteous sentence, he can say, " I know that the law is spiritual." In its origin, its demands, and its operation, this is the spirituality of the law, which perhaps these views of it sufficiently display.

III. There are certain practical purposes of great consequence, to which the consideration of this subject will properly lead us.

It is adapted to produce in us a deep humiliation. It casts out the pride and boasting of the very holiest among men, and brings down every soul in the deepest prostration before God. In regard to gross outward violations of the commands of God, you may be comparatively blameless. According to the judgment of men, you may have lived in strict conformity to the divine will. But who has rendered to God the honour which is due to him, and counted every thing else as worthless in comparison with him? When you consider that spotless line of life which the law imposes, in the different relations of man, who is not compelled to acknowledge, that his transgressions are multiplied, beyond his power to compute them? When you add to these, the unholy tempers and dispositions which you have exercised and indulged; the evil thoughts which you have allowed and harboured; the failures in duty, of which you are conscious; who does not blush to lift up his eyes unto heaven, ashamed and confounded in the holy presence of God who searcheth the hearts? And yet the mere calculation of what we have done, or left undone, would give a very inadequate view of the sinfulness of our characters. We must take the elevated and spotless standard of divine commandments, and see how infinitely short we have come of the spirit of their intention, in every act of our lives, and in every moment of our existence. We must trace the whole state of our souls from the beginning of our lives, and estimate it, by this unbending standard. And we shall see, that our whole attainments in obedience, have been as nothing, literally nothing, in comparison with our failures and our defects. The poorest bankrupt that ever lived, has discharged a larger portion of his debt to men, than we have of our debt to God. His state in his relation, is far better than yours; for you have been still increasing your debt, every hour, and every moment of your lives. The very best works of the best of men, if tried thus by the touchstone of God's perfect law, would be in themselves, but an accumulation of guilt against the day of wrath. There is in them no good thing. And the more clearly they see the excellence of the law, the more deeply will they feel humbled, under the conviction of this fact.

This self-abasing view of our own character is indispensable. We must cast aside every delusive plea of comparative innocence and harmlessness,—and judge ourselves as we are judged by the Lord. By this judgment we must abide forever; and if we come unpardoned under its power, the doom which it assigns, is absolute and unchangeable. When the book of his remembrance is laid open, the secrets of your hearts will be brought to light—your own consciences will attest the truth of the divine accusations, and the equity of the sentence which God shall pronounce. In the action of this spiritual and holy law, there can be no respect of persons. Its judgments will be severe in proportion to advantages which have been neglected and unimproved. O, that God may enable you to understand, and to consider, well, these solemn truths! May he enable you in entire self-abasement, and humility of mind, to cast yourselves in the very dust before him, under the burden of your conscious guilt!

This view of the spiritual character of the law, shows the fallacy of all attempts in man to establish a righteousness before God by works of his own. There is not a single divine precept which does not testify against our guilt before the throne of God. There is not a single precept which will relax its purity or its obligation on our account. It is a vain idea, that the Lord Jesus Christ has lowered the demands of the law, that they might be brought within the compass of man's infirmity, and he be thus enabled to comply with them. Surely there is nothing in his instructions to sanction such an idea;—He has summed up the decalogue in the blessed precepts of love,—but in neither of them, has he set aside the obligations of a single command. Has he made any abatement in their demands? Did the law require too much of man, before his coming? How was it then, holy, just, and good? Did it only require exactly what was due from man to God? How then could the Saviour reduce these demands, without robbing God of the obedience which was really due from his creatures? Nay,—how can God ever lower the holy demands of his righteous law? How can he divest himself of his glory, or give his creatures a liberty to violate his will? His law is necessarily unchangeable, like himself. It is the simple expression of his own mind and character. And the obligation to love him with supreme and undivided affection, is an immutable obligation upon every rational creature. It is a demand necessarily unalterable forever. And if any man would obtain a righteousness, by works of his own, he must obey it perfectly, in act and spirit, and that forever. Because this is utterly impossible for man, who is a transgressor from his birth, the very thought of obtaining acceptance with God, by any works of the law, must be given up by every soul of man. From this you are driven forever. If you would be saved at all, it must be in some other method than this. You must have some other righteousness, more commensurate with the holy demands of the law, and more consistent with the unchanging honour of the law-giver;—a righteousness which can magnify the law, and make it honourable. Such an obedience is fully provided for you, and freely offered to you, in the perfect and meritorious subjection of

E

the Lord Jesus to the law in your behalf. In him you may be justified and glory. But in every act of obedience of your own, you will be found wanting, and will be condemned.

The distinct understanding of this subject, is of the utmost consequence. The simple assertion of the text ought to be the language of your own experience, " *We know* that the law is spiritual." And yet, of what are men more generally ignorant, than of this vital subject? Unwilling to acknowledge themselves justly condemned, and yet unable to deny their violations of divine commandments, they would reduce the holiness of the law to their own standard, rather than seek, out of themselves, a righteousness which shall meet it. They are anxious to lessen their undeniable criminality before God, and to do this, they would charge his commandments with unreasonable strictness, and thus make him a partaker of their guilt. All this effort however, though it may delude themselves, cannot deceive him. You must settle it in your minds, as an indisputable and fundamental fact, that this spiritual, searching nature of the divine law, must remain unchanged forever. By understanding and feeling the truth of this, you will be able to comprehend the purposes which the law designs; and the uses and operations, to which it is directed by the Divine Law-giver. Such a knowledge and understanding will wean you from all vain confidence in yourselves; will persuade you to cease from man whose breath is in his nostrils; will compel you to lay aside every notion that you have anything to offer unto God: and urge you to look for, and to receive that blessed provided righteousness in Christ the Lord, which enables you to answer the utmost demands of the lawgiver upon your souls. This actual obedience of the Lord Jesus Christ, is freely offered to every penitent and believing soul. Destitute of it, you remain under an unsatisfied curse; and exposed to the just anger of God, in every moment of your lives. You are without hope or peace. The law which condemns you is spiritual, and you are carnal, sold under sin. It sentences you to death, and delivers you over unto wrath, in every single precept which it contains. It is the extreme of infatuation, to look for its possible approval, for justification and life. It will be certain and everlasting death, to venture into judgment before God, upon the foundation of any obedience of your own to its requirements.

These may appear to you, hard sayings. The Spirit of God alone, can enable you to receive them. He only can subdue your pride and vain confidence, and show to you, that by the very law to which you foolishly cling, you are inevitably condemned and ruined. O, that this convincing agency of the law by the power of the Spirit, might be received and exercised in the conscience of all who listen to me! That you might be compelled to cry out, under its weight and influence, "God be merciful to us sinners!" That you could be constrained, in this view of the unbending and impossible demands of the law of God, not only to ask in anxiety, "What shall I do to be saved?" but to renounce all hope of salvation by doings of every kind, and freely and thankfully to believe in the Lord Jesus Christ, who is himself, righteousness and salvation to every soul that seeks him. In him, being justified by faith, you have peace with God; and resting not upon your own obedience to the law for righteousness, but upon his; having fulfilled it in him, you are renewed after its image, and enabled to honour and adorn it, walking not according to the flesh, but after the Spirit. This is the divine provision in your behalf, which fully meets, and everlastingly honours, the spiritual and holy law of the most High God.

LECTURE IV.

THE PRESENT USE OF THE LAW.

Wherefore then serveth the law?—GALATIANS, III. 19.

The law of which the apostle here speaks is the moral law; that perfect rule of obedience to the divine Creator, which is imposed upon every intelligent and responsible creature. He is treating of the free and perfect justification of sinful man, according to the provisions of grace which are announced in the Gospel. He teaches the great fact, that God announced these provisions of grace, as the only foundation of human hope, and the only means of security to the guilty, long before the Saviour's incarnation, and ages previous to the introduction of the Jewish dispensation. This was the Gospel which God preached unto Abraham, who believed its promises, and was justified by his faith. By the same instrumentality of faith in the truth and power of God, all who in subsequent ages believed, were justified with faithful Abraham. But no man was ever justified by his own obedience,—or made just in the sight of God by his relation to the law; for the law brings upon man who is always a sinner under it, nothing but a curse. This is the argument of the apostle, in the comparison which he institutes between the promise of grace, giving life to faith in the divine covenant, and the law of commandments, uttering death upon every transgression. His conclusion is, that the publication of the law, which was long subsequent to the establishment of this covenant of grace, can have no influence to change the system of salvation for the fallen and guilty, which God had previously proclaimed.

But an objection is made to this conclusion, and the question in our text proposes it. If the heavenly inheritance is only to be obtained by grace through a free promise to the guilty, and not by man's obedience to the commands of the law, "wherefore then serveth the law?"

The point to which this question is directed, is very precise. It is not, what was the original use of the law when man was innocent? Or, what is its abstract purpose with beings who are not guilty? But, what could be the design of publishing it again, under a dispensation of grace already revealed? If man is to gain no justification by his obedience to it, why is it thus proclaimed to him? The objection seemed perfectly just to the reason of man. He could understand the simple proposition, if you do this, you shall live. But he could not understand the proposition, you are still to do it, but you cannot live by it. The objection is still frequently urged, if our obedience is not to justify us, why are we to obey? Why may we not live in sin, that grace may abound? We will consider this objection, in the subject now before us—*the use of the law under the dispensation of grace.* Why was it added? Why is it still proclaimed and insisted on?

The distinct assertion of the Holy Scriptures is, "by the works of the law, no man is justified in the sight of God." The objection of man's reason to this, is, then the proclamation of the claims and demands of the law is unprofitable and vain. But as Luther says, "the consequence is nothing worth. Money doth not justify, or make a man righteous, therefore it is unprofitable; the eyes do not justify, therefore they must be plucked out; the hands make not a man righteous, therefore they must be cut off. This is naught also, the law doth not justify, therefore it is unprofitable. We must attriute unto every thing, its proper effect and use. We do not therefore condemn or destroy the law, because we say it doth not justify. It hath its proper office and use, but not to make men righteous. It accuseth, terrifieth, condemneth them. We say with Paul, that the law is good, if a man do rightly use it, that is to say, if he use the law as a law." It is the preacher's duty to proclaim faithfully, the requisitions and threatenings of God's holy law, which are unceasingly violated by man. But many who listen to him, will strongly object to this continual republication of the law. They oppose, both the exhibition of its demands and penalties, which are suspended as a violated covenant, over the unconverted and unbelieving ; and the strict enforcing of its holy precepts as a rule of life upon the professed servants of God. Some are unwilling to hear anything from the pulpit which alarms and terrifies the conscience—and others desire and resolve to be satisfied with a standard of conduct, far inferior to the holy commandments of God. Both are ready to urge the objection of the text. And to both, the only proper reply is, a more distinct and persevering publication of the very law to which they object, as absolutely indispensable to awaken the conscience, convert the soul, and sanctify the character of man. In proportion as this, in its due measure and place is faithfully done, will the grace of the Lord Jesus be precious and powerful in the hearts of those who receive the truth; and the ministry of his servants be made effectual in calling in the number of his people. "To preach justification by the law, as a covenant," says Bishop Hopkins, "is legal, and makes void the death and merits of Jesus Christ. But to preach obedience to the law as a rule, is evangelical; and it savours as much of a New Testament spirit, to urge the commands of the law, as to display the promises of the Gospel."

This important subject, what is the present use and design of the law under a dispensation of grace? I wish to consider, in a general view, as involving many important particulars, which we shall afterwards consider separately. "Wherefore then serveth the law?" We answer, it has a twofold use and operation, upon the disobedient and unjustified, and upon the pardoned and accepted sinner:—upon wicked men who are still without Christ;—and upon renewed men who are adopted into his family and kingdom.

I. The use of the law with the *unconverted and unpardoned*. The Apostle says "it was added because of transgressions." It was man's iniquity which made its publication necessary. And its operation is temporary, "until the seed come, to whom the promise was made," until Christ as its end and fulfilment is adequately revealed. The object of God in the operation of the law, is merciful and gracious. "The Scripture hath concluded all under sin, that the promise by faith of Jesus Christ, might be given to them that believe." Harsh and terrifying, as the denunciations of the law appear to the ungodly, they are designed to be, and ought to be improved, for the deliverance and spiritual life, of those, against whom they are uttered. As a general answer to the question of the text, is the assertion of the Apostle, "it was added, because of transgressions."

1. It was added, to *restrain and limit these transgressions.* It finds man in his fallen condition, seeking out for himself, many inventions of disobedience. The whole world under the influence of his depravity, lieth in wickedness; and in captivity to Satan, lieth under the wicked one. This was the condition of men, after the publication of the grace of God to man, in the promised redemption by his Son. Men had filled the earth, with the habitations of darkness and cruelty. The chosen seed had corrupted themselves exceedingly. And God proclaimed again his holy law, with terrible majesty, to bridle and restrain the wickedness of mankind. It denounced judgment and wrath. It spake in thunders. It alarmed and terrified the ungodly. It threatened a devouring fire, and

everlasting burnings. This was because of transgressions; that some limit might be set up, in the fears and apprehensions of men, to the scornful triumphs of human wickedness. For this purpose has it operated always, and is it always to be proclaimed. God thus reveals his wrath against all ungodliness and unrighteousness of men, and proclaims to them, that such shall not inherit the kingdom of heaven; to drive men back, from the wickedness, to which their deceitful and depraved hearts would lead them. It is for this end, that the Apostle declares, "the law was made for the lawless and disobedient, for the ungodly, and for sinners, for unholy and profane, and any other thing that is contrary to sound doctrine, according to the glorious Gospel of the blessed God." The abounding of human wickedness, even amidst the denunciations of flames and vengeance which the law so solemnly pronounces;—shews what would be the character and condition of man, were he set free from the bonds which it thus fastens around him. Fear of the awful consequences which must come upon guilt, is the prevailing motive which restrains and controls the passions of ungodly men. It holds back in uncounted instances, the arm of murderous revenge, and bridles the accomplishment of covetous and licentious appetite. And it cannot be doubted, that if the secret, dark, and majestic frown with which the law speaks to the consciences of the wicked, could be withdrawn, and the fear which it awakens, could be hushed, the main restraint upon the depravity of man would be broken, and the chief guardian of the peace of human society, would be destroyed. As the prevailing principle, it is the selfish fear of man, which allows men to live in mutual security and peace; not his fear of human condemnation merely, but a secret, conscious, though undefinable fear of the wrath and judgment of God. And one very important present use of the law is thus to bridle and restrain the wickedness of man.

2. It is added *to bring to light, the transgressions of men*. The Apostle says "the law entered, that sin might abound;" and again, "I had not known sin but by the law, for I had not known lust, except the law had said, thou shalt not covet;" nay, he farther teaches us, that the operation of the law upon the corrupt nature of man, was actually to increase his secret desires to transgress, though it bridled his outward acts. "Sin, taking occasion by the commandment, wrought in me, all manner of concupiscence." Man, without this operation of the law, is extremely ignorant of his own character. Sin within him, appears dead. He has a vain confidence in his own righteousness, and imagines that there is some merit of good works in himself. The law is added, as the instrument, to bring his secret character to light; to shew him the transgressions within his heart; to reveal those awful things, which our blessed Lord declares, come from within, out of the heart of man, and defile his character and life; to exhibit to him, the blindness, and hardness, and impiety of his own mind in the sight of God; and to make him feel himself to be guilty, and worthy of condemnation before God. It lays down before him, its holy standard, its unrelaxing demands, its solemn denunciations upon disobedience against them. It brings man up to the view of this standard, and to the sound of these denunciations; and his unsubdued heart rebels against them, and manifests at once, the secret character which had been covered before. Thus the Saviour brought out the secret character of the self-righteous young man who came to him, to bid for eternal life. He had no conviction of sin. He "knew nothing by himself." But the Lord Jesus spread before him, the holy demands of the very law, in his obedience to which he so confidently trusted; and his secret sin was set in the light of God's countenance before him. He saw himself refusing an entire obedience, though he had professed his willingness to do any thing; and he went away

sorrowful, not for his sins, but for the mortification of his pride, and the overturning of his previous hope. This is an essential operation of the law; man's secret wickedness must be brought to his view. That transgression which saith within his heart, there shall be no fear of God before my eyes, must be listened to and acknowledged. Until this has been done, his pride, and self-confidence, and neglect of God, and rejection of the grace of Christ, will all remain, in a perfectly satisfied and self-righteous temper, nor will the preaching of pardon and salvation in the Lord Jesus have the least effect upon him. Until this divine Saviour is sought for, and accepted in his heart, the law must be proclaimed, to bring to light, the secret transgressions of which he is wholly and willingly ignorant.

3. The law is added, *to convince man of these transgressions.* It brings out his hidden wickedness to view, that inward thought of his heart which is very deep, that it may compel him to acknowledge himself a sinner, condemned before God, and lost in guilt. His own blinded reason would persuade him, that if he be not outwardly, a transgressor against men, this is sufficient, and he ought to be accepted by God. But God brings in the power of his law to bear upon his secret character, that sin may abound in his view. This is the hammer with which he breaks the rock in pieces, and makes the proud sinner feel himself, and acknowledge himself, to be worthy of the condemnation and wrath of God. He that was before self-righteous, and alive without the commandment, now feels himself shut up to death, by every precept; without hope, a vessel of wrath fitted to destruction. He looks upon the holiness of the law, and is convinced of sin. He looks upon the just authority of the law, and is convinced of wrath and judgment for sin. He looks upon the majestic and unalterable truth of the law, and is convinced, that there remaineth nothing for him, "but a certain fearful

looking for of judgment and fiery indignation which shall devour the adversaries." In this work of conviction, "the law of God" says Luther, "hath properly and peculiarly, that office which it had in Mount Sinai, when it was first given, and was first heard by them that were washed, righteous, purified and chaste. And yet notwithstanding, it brought down that holy people into such a knowledge of their own misery, that they were thrown down even to death and desperation. No purity, nor holiness could then help them; but there was in them, such a feeling of their own uncleanness, unworthiness, and sin, and of the judgment and wrath of God, that they fled from the sight of the Lord, and could not abide to hear his voice. 'What flesh was there ever, say they, 'that heard the voice of the living God speaking out of the midst of the fire, and lived?' So it happeneth at length to all self-justifiers, who being drunken with the opinion of their own righteousness, do think when they are out of temptation, that they are beloved of God, and that God regardeth their works, and that for them he will give them a crown in heaven. But when that thunder, lightning, and fire, and that hammer which breaketh in pieces, that is to say, the law of God, cometh suddenly upon them, revealing unto them their sin, and the wrath and judgment of God, then the self-same thing happeneth unto them, which happened to the Jews standing at the foot of Mount Sinai." Ungodly men are thus convinced by the law, made to feel, and to acknowledge their guilt; and are ready to hear the glad tidings of divine mercy and forgiveness in the Gospel.

4. The use of the law with the ungodly, is through the knowledge and conviction of sin which it produces, *to prepare them, and lead them, to seek for and hear the mercy of God in the Lord Jesus Christ.* The Apostle speaks of this, when he teaches the peculiar provision of mercy from God, and safety for man, to which God would thus make his law subservi-

ent. When the promised seed has come, and the Saviour is accepted in the heart; when the blessing which comes by faith in Jesus Christ is received, the law condemns no more, and men are no longer shut up under its power. Its purpose is, as a light, to reveal, not mercy and grace, not righteousness and life, but sin and death, and the wrath and judgment of God. Its immediate effect is, to increase the impatience and rebellion of man until it humbles him, and beats him down in desperation. It crushes his pride, annihilates his self-confidence, and shuts his mouth in conscious guilt. This is all that it can do. Thus it prepares the way for the promised seed, and makes an entrance to the heart, for the grace of God, and opens the mind to hear and learn of God, as the exalter of the humble, the comforter of the afflicted, the lifter up of the despairing, and the giver of life to the dead. Thus too, it opens the way for man's justification in the obedience of Christ, and prepares the sinner to hear the precious invitation, "come unto me, all ye that labour and are heavy laden, and I will give you rest." It is designed therefore, though speaking in wrath, to be a messenger of mercy; though proclaiming condemnation unto death, to lead to one who giveth life forevermore. It is added because of transgressions, to persuade men to bring the burden of them, which it shows to be excessive, and intolerable, to the Saviour's feet, that they may receive a free forgiveness through his blood, and be justified by his grace, and find him, to be in himself, the righteousness and life they need. These are the various uses of the law with the ungodly and unconverted.

II. The use of the law with the *pardoned and justified*. Its main purpose is to bring sinners to Christ, that they may be justified by his grace; but it does not cease its operation upon them, when this merciful security has been attained. It still has an important work to accomplish, subordinate to the great dispensation of grace which has fulfilled its demands and penalties, and added a higher seal to its holiness and excellence. When men have been brought from darkness into light,—and from the power of Satan unto God, and are made partakers of his grace, the law serves many purposes for their benefit.

1. It is the *rule of life by which they are governed.* They are made free from its penalties and threatenings, that with a new and grateful spirit they may be enabled to obey its commands. In their adoption as children into the family of God, a love for his character, and for the holiness which distinguishes it, has been implanted in their hearts. They are made to desire perfect holiness of character, which is the image of God, and obedience to his law. And though they work not for wages, and their hope rests not upon any obedience of their own, the spirit which is given to them, leads them to press forward in every path of obedience, desiring to be perfect, as their Father in heaven is perfect. That law which requires supreme love to God, and universal love to men for his sake, is now written for them, not in tables of stone, but in the fleshly tables of the heart. It is the rule by which they govern their most secret life. And though they actually come short of it in every particular, and are thus daily convinced by it of sin, it is the standard which they love, at which they aim, and by which they are governed with increasing uniformity through life. The holy precepts of the law are therefore still to be proclaimed to the people of God, that they may be made obedient and holy under their influence. By the heart-searching requirements of these divine precepts, are they to compare themselves, that they may see the attainments in holiness which must be made by them, if they would stand complete in all the perfect will of God. No lower rule of life than this, can ever be established. When the servants of God are perfectly sanctified, and awake up in a world of glory, after the divine image, they will be perfect-

ly conformed to the precepts of this holy law. And now, while they are expecting this inheritance, these commandments are the rule, according to which they become meet for it, and their obedience to them, is the necessary fruit of holiness in their renewed nature. By the guidance of these commandments, they who believe in Christ, are made careful to maintain good works.

2. The law serves *to warn and guard the justified and converted from the commission of sin.* There remains within them, a principle of corruption which leads to sin; a principle, which though it be conquered and limited, is ever struggling for the mastery, and labouring to bring them into subjection to its power. To keep them back from allowing this insurgent influence within them, which would combine with temptation without, for their entire overthrow and destruction, they have the indwelling power of the Holy Spirit who lives and acts within them, as the Redeemer's agent in bringing home his sons to glory; the many blessed motives and promises, which the Gospel proposes, as inducements to obedience; and these warnings and threatenings of the law, which guard them, and keep them back from sin. "By them," says David, "is thy servant warned." As the awful sanctions of the law are proclaimed, and its holy requirements are pressed upon the servants of God, they operate as a very powerful guard upon them in the hands of the Holy Spirit. They are a wall of fire to keep them from the indulgence of sinful propensity, and the submission to unholy temptation. "How shall I do this great wickedness," says Joseph, "and sin against God?" The fearful evils of transgression are seen; its awful nature is discovered; its dreadful effects are beheld; its solemn penalties stand forth to say "hitherto shalt thou come, and no further;" and they are all mercifully employed by the Holy Spirit, as instruments of protection to those whom he sanctifies; standing before them, as beacons upon

the rock of danger, to give timely notice to every unwary approach.

3. The law serves *to make justified souls grateful for the privileges which they enjoy.* They have been redeemed from bondage under its curse. They have been set at liberty from its prison-house. They have seen all its threatenings borne, and all its obligations fulfilled in their behalf, in the most honorable and glorious way. And as they contemplate the mercies which have been thus bestowed upon them, they rejoice with joy unspeakable and full of glory. As these great privileges are announced and set before them, in the glad tidings of the Gospel, they bless God for the consolation. But they can hardly be considered at all, except in connexion with the dangers and evils to which they have been the antidote. And as these are brought to view, in the proclamations of the law, the redeemed soul looks back upon them with peculiar gratitude, that for him, they have passed by forever. He is a partaker of a great salvation: he has received a kingdom which cannot be removed; and it is a most important object in the cultivation of his character, that he should not be unmindful of the heavenly benefit, nor ungrateful for its gracious bestowal upon him. As the law speaks out its thunders, proclaiming the rigour of its demands, denouncing the wrath of God upon every soul of man that doeth evil, the justified man rejoices yet more in the blessed assurance, that he has been delivered from all this storm and tempest, by abounding grace, and stands upon a fast shore of peace, with an inheritance forever. "Such was I," he says with humble gratitude, "but I am washed, I am sanctified, I am justified, in the name of the Lord Jesus, and by the Spirit of my God." And the preaching of the law is thus blessed by the Holy Spirit, to create and cultivate within him, a spirit of more ardent gratitude and joy.

4. The law serves to *keep the justified man in a close de-*

pendance upon Jesus. As the pelting storm drives the little chickens under the sheltering wing, do the terrors of the law drive home the pardoned sinner, to realize more completely the entire protection of that righteousness which the Lord Jesus illustrates by this very image. He sees more clearly that he has nothing of his own, and can never meet from any source within himself, the demands which are made upon him. He must have a righteousness which is not in himself; and cannot be found, except in the obedience of the Saviour for him; and the more loudly the law threatens, the more closely and earnestly does he cling to this provision; as the more fiercely the storm rages, does the bird fold herself more closely in her nest, and the dove fly the more swiftly to her window. To break up all self-righteousness, to bind sinful man merely in his own nakedness, fast to Jesus, that he may be clothed from his fulness alone, is the great purpose of the Gospel, and the great work of the Spirit, with him. The preaching of the law is made by him, to produce this blessed effect, and thus to be an instrument of grace, and religious benefit. It forces man from every covert of his own. It compels him to see that there is no protection but in that cleft of the rock which God hath provided for him. It constrains him to escape for his life to him who is able to save him unto the uttermost, crying from his heart,—

> Naked, I come to thee for dress,
> Helpless, come to thee for grace,
> Foul, I to the fountain fly,
> Wash me Jesus, or I die.

The Saviour thus becomes to him all in all. He is justified and glories in him alone, and casting out all self-dependance, he finds in Jesus, and in the perfection of his work, righteousness and peace.

These are manifest uses of the law with the justified and

pardoned. It rules and guides them in holiness,—it warns and guards them against sin,—it makes them grateful for redemption,—it binds them in a closer dependance upon the Lord Jesus,—and thus is made the means of spiritual benefit to them; as in Samson's riddle, "out of the eater, comes forth meat, and out of the strong comes forth sweetness,"—not so much by any action of its own, as by the overruling power of the Spirit, who makes all things work together for good to those who love God, and who are called according to his purpose.

III. For these two purposes, the law is added and proclaimed under a dispensation of grace. To accomplish all these ends which have been specified under them, we are still to preach the law, though Christ hath become its perfect end for righteousness to all who believe. But there remains still another reason for its proclamation, in the fact that *a final judgment must be administered to man according to its requisitions.* For his own people, Jesus has brought in a perfect and everlasting righteousness, which will meet and honour all the demands of the law in that great day. But for those who are out of Christ, who have rejected his proffered mediation, and cast away the cords of his grace, the law will come in, with the full force of its unyielding requisitions. It will demand an obedience in perfect conformity with these. It will shew them their extreme guiltiness. It will strip off the coverings of deceit. It will display its condemnation of them, as justly merited, and unquestionable forever. God has established but one standard for obedience among creatures who are accountable. Angels have obeyed it, and will live. Redeemed saints have found for them a perfect obedience, in the glorious righteousness of an appointed mediator. But all impenitent and unholy beings will be condemned by its sentence, and shut up under this condemnation forever. And the law stands among men, as the living witness of the fact, and of the principles, of this coming judgment. To persuade men to flee from this impending ruin, it announces its own character and operation,—that sinners may in time avoid, a sentence which must be eternally irrevocable. For Zion's sake therefore should we not hold our peace, until this momentous object is secured, and perishing souls are sheltered in the glorious provisions and power of the Redeemer. "It is Christ, and Christ alone that can save us. As the worst of our sins are pardonable by Christ, so the best of our duties are damnable without him." And while he hath been made sin for us, that we might be made the righteousness of God in him,—the law witnessing continually, of sin, and righteousness, and judgment, is to be made the instrument for emptying us of all self-dependence, and keeping us in him, who speaks in righteousness, and is mighty to save.

LECTURE V.

THE CONVINCING POWER OF THE LAW.

Now we know, that whatsoever things the law saith, it saith to them that are under the law, that every mouth may be stopped, and all the world become guilty before God.—ROMANS, III. 19.

The purity and perfection of the divine law become open to our view, in proportion to our serious and candid examination of its character. The psalmist contemplated it, as the highest standard of perfection. "I have seen an end of all perfection, but thy commandment is exceeding broad." To every mind enlightened like his, by the Holy Spirit, the same conclusion is equally distinct and certain. There is a length and breadth, in the excellence of this revelation of the divine character, which transcends the power of human investigation. It is in all respects, and in the highest degree, holy, just, and good. To those who have always been obedient to its precepts, it is ordained to life; designed to confer the highest happiness, and to open a path, which is unmingled pleasantness and peace, for those who walk in it.

But a holy law abides not transgression;—a just law condemns the disobedient; a true and faithful law offers no hope to sinners. It speaks in righteousness, but it has no power to save. Its whole operation upon the ungodly, is to enlighten, to convince, and to condemn them. But its operation is indispensable for their deliverance from the curse which itself imposes. Until they are thus dealt with, hardly as it appears, sinful men do not desire, and will not ask for, the salvation which God has mercifully and freely laid up for their acceptance in his own dear Son. This varied operation of the law, in its successive particulars, I propose now to consider. And I would speak in this discourse, of the power of the law, in *enlightening and convincing the ungodly and disobedient.*

This convincing power of the law upon the conscience of the sinner, the apostle displays in the language of the text,— "Now we know, that whatsoever things the law saith, it saith to them that are under the law, that every mouth may be stopped, and the whole world become guilty before God." "The things which the law saith," its holy precepts, its solemn sanctions, its awful sentence, constitute the instrument of its power. They are the hand which grasps, and the arm which conquers, the soul of the transgressor. The extent of their just and awful operation, is to "all those who are under the law." Are they obedient? Have they never transgressed? Its holy precepts are a means of life, and the measure of their reward of blessedness, and speak to them only in peace. Are they transgressors? Its solemn threatenings and denunciations are the measure and seal of their condemnation and death. The character of those who are under the law determines the nature and tendency of the things which the law speaks. Among a world of fallen transgressors, its influence upon all, is only, that every mouth may be stopped, and the whole world be manifested as guilty before God, and come under his judgment, condemned to a punishment, from which the law itself offers no escape. This is the necessary tendency and end of the work of the law upon the guilty. It saith the things which it contains, for this very purpose, "that every mouth may be stopped," every excuse be silenced, every soul consciously condemned,—and all brought under judgment, without merit or claim,—to be rescued and blessed, if rescued and blessed at all, entirely by undeserved mercy on the part of God, whose holy commands condemn them. This convincing power of the law is displayed, either in the salutary awakening and conviction of the sinner in his day of grace, that he may be brought to Christ for life; or in the final arousing of his conscience in the day of judgment, to a perception of his everlasting condemnation. In either case, the effect of the law is the same. It stops the mouth of every transgressor, and compels him to acknowledge himself guilty before God, worthy of death, and without a hope of life, or a right to ask it.

The convincing power of the law in the day of grace, is the aspect of this operation of which I now speak. The law is the great instrument in the agency of the Holy Spirit, to convince men of sin, and of the wrath which is denounced against sin. In his hands, it is living and powerful, and sharper than a two-edged sword, piercing even to the dividing asunder of the soul and spirit, and is a discerner of the thoughts and intents of the heart. In this process of saving conviction, the law is to be considered as the instrument of the Holy Spirit. In itself, it is to the conscience of the sinner, as a mere dead letter. Like a deaf adder, he stops his ears against its commands and its accusations. But this refusal to listen to the voice of God, yields under the power of the Spirit. When he lays hold of this hammer of the word, he wields it with a resistless force, and breaks down all the strongholds of man's pride and self-confidence, and crushes his rebellious spirit into the dust of humiliation under conscious guilt and ruin. Without this spiritual application of the law, the sinner may be alive and boastful in himself. But when the commandment comes, with the attendant power of the Holy Ghost, sin revives in all its hideous features, and destructive power, and shews itself without disguise, to the conscience compelled to behold it. Then, the sinner dies. He sinks under the clear apprehension of his guilt, and an undeniable conviction of the judgment which it impends over him. He lies powerless at the Saviour's feet; and is made willing in the day o f his power to yield himself to the freeness of pardoning love, and to the new-creating power of divine grace.

I. We will consider this conviction, under the aspect of *the things, of which the law is made to convince the sinner.* "Whatsoever things the law saith," exhibit the various facts of which it convinces the transgressor.

1. It saith "do this, and thou shalt live;" "But whosoever keepeth the whole law, and offendeth in one point, he is guilty of all." By this holy and unyielding demand, it convinces the sinner, of the *fact*, and the *guiltiness* of his past transgressions. The law claims from every being who is under it, an entire, perpetual, and spotless obedience. Its precepts describe the holiest of possible character, in the condition of a creature, and require of man, a perfect fulfilment of this. In the exercise of its convincing power, it reveals this true character of itself, to the sinner's understanding, and makes him to see, what the Lord God requireth of him. It compares the history of his own life, as it is known to himself, with the strictness and purity of these demands. It thus brings out to his view, the obliquity and defects of his past course; laying down its perfect and unbending rule upon the crookedness of all his conduct, and giving him a knowledge of his sin. It gives him a knowledge of the nature of sin in itself, and of its existence, in an aggravated degree, in his own character and life. Man has no disposition to seek, or even to receive, the information which the law thus imparts. His heart is ever ready to reply to its inflexible demands and solemn judgments, "not so, that be far from thee, to condemn the righteous with the wicked." But while it makes these charges of guilt against the transgressor, it makes him also to understand and feel their justice. His mouth is stopped from all denial, and from all excuse, of his innumerable acts of disobedience. The law searches into his secret character, and shews him to be, by the corruption of his nature, and by

the voluntary habits of his life, a being extremely depraved and guilty,—with the whole head sick, and the whole heart faint. It charges him with having spent the time which divine forbearance has allowed him upon the earth, in an open neglect and defiance of the God, in whose hands his breath is, and whose are all his ways. It accuses him of presumptuous sins, committed against warning and knowledge;—of repeated relapses into them, against all his protestations, and vows, and prayers; of rushing by all the admonitions of God, and the strivings of the Spirit of God, in his determination to transgress. It accuses him of sins of inadvertence and ignorance, utterly without number; of allowing days to pass in a long succession, wholly without a thought of God, or a consideration of his holy will; of crowding together the greater portion of his life, without reflecting upon his conduct, or feeling concerned whether he did well or ill. It accuses him of secret sins, of corrupt desires, of unholy thoughts, as countless as the ocean's sands; sins, which however concealed from the cognizance of the world abroad, are open and naked before him with whom the sinner has to do; sins which though they pass him, like the motes which play upon the sunbeam, and elude all his efforts to pursue, and examine them, are all recorded in the everlasting remembrance of God. It accuses him of the habitual omission of holy duties; of neglect of the worship and acknowledgment of God; of restraining the voice of prayer, and refusing the offerings of praise. It accuses him of vast deficiencies in the spirit of those duties which he has undertaken to perform; of dulness, formality, and hypocrisy, in his apparent approaches to the throne of God. It accuses him, in addition to all acts of omission or commission, of that which these acts infallibly indicate, a corrupt nature, a state of mental rebellion,—a fountain of aversion to God in his heart; a state of character and life, in which every feeling and purpose partakes of the universal bitterness, and is guilty and worthy of condemnation; from which there has proceeded no good thing. These are the charges which the law makes against the transgressor, as it lays out before him, its holy and perfect precepts, every one of which in its application to him, concludes him under sin. Under this operation of the law, man becomes consciously condemned, and without hope. The law has brought him to a knowledge of his sin, and made his offences to abound in his view. And under this reviving power of sin which it brings to light, he dies to all prospect or means of finding acceptance with God in any character of his own.

2. The law saith, "Cursed is every one that continueth not in all things which are written in the book of the law to do them." "The soul that sinneth, it shall die." By this solemn denunciation and sentence, it convinces the sinner, of his exposure to the wrath of God, and of his necessary condemnation to eternal death. God has been pleased to guard the violations of his law, with the most solemn and terrible sanctions. He has promised everlasting life, as the attendant upon everlasting obedience;—and he has denounced eternal death, as the inevitable recompense and wages of continued sin. He has proclaimed an unspeakably awful curse upon every soul of man that doeth evil. And because every soul of man, has done evil continually from his birth, this curse in all its terrors, is lying upon every human being. The condemnation of the ungodly, is not a future, contingent matter, but an actual, present condemnation. The transgressor is condemned already. And though like a convict in his cell, he has a respite allowed him, before the execution of his sentence, his case is to be regarded, as altogether disposed of. No new process of authority is required for his punishment. His time is fixed; and his sentence is fixed; and he is to be let alone merely, until the hour appointed, shall arrive. The state of an unconverted sinner is thus, a state of present condemna-

tion under the just wrath of God. He may be ignorant of the awful condition in which he stands;—he may choose to deny the allegation altogether. But this is one of the things which the law saith, and its convincing operation upon the sinner's conscience, is to make him acquainted with the solemn and all-important fact which is here announced; to make him know that he is condemned, and that the wrath of God abideth on him. It shews him, that though prosperity and wealth, and ease and honour, may be allowed to decorate his passing hours on the earth, his final destiny, while he remains under the operation of the law, is nevertheless, unalterably determined. There is a curse rolling onward upon his guilty soul, which will sink him into eternal ruin. The law convinces him of his real character as a sinner before God, and fastens the acknowledgment upon his mind, that there remains nothing for him in this character, but the fearful expectation of judgment and fiery indignation which shall consume him as an adversary of God. It shews him that all his past blessings and comforts in temporal things, are no proofs of God's acceptance, or favour for his soul; but that though God has thus far sustained him with much forbearance, he has been still, a vessel of wrath, fitted to destruction. In the hour of his conviction, it lays open before him, the solemn fact, that he has been the enemy of a God who hath said, " vengeance is mine, I will repay." In the certainty of this fact, it shews him too, that he is with the utmost reason and justice, condemned to eternal death; and that it would be altogether right and just in a Holy God, to cast him from his presence forever, and to refuse the exercise of any mercy upon his soul. Laying down before him, the long catalogue of transgressions, to which reference has been made, and attaching to each, the sentence of everlasting exclusion from the presence of God, it solemnly bids him to look at his condition, and ask himself, what hope there is, that he can escape the damnation of hell?

While the law reveals this dreadful condemnation, as the portion of the guilty, it only makes known, a fact which was before equally certain, but of which man was before ignorant. It saith, "there is none good, no, not one; they have all sinned; they have all become abominable." Then it saith, "cursed be every one that sinneth against God;" "let wrath come upon them, and let them go down quick into hell, for I have seen iniquity among them." In man's native carelessness and blindness, he is entirely ignorant of the condition in which a violated law has placed him. The convincing power of the law unveils his eyes to this danger, and compels him to behold it. But though under this operation, he groans in anguish, he is no more in condemnation, than he was before, when he was thoughtless and gay. He has now simply been made to see, and to consider, dangers to which he was before voluntarily blinded; and the sight of his previous actual condition, over which he has long slept in total unconcern, like the sight of the precipice, which the lightning's flash displays to the midnight traveller, immediately beneath his feet, fills his mind with anguish and despair. Sin hath revived. The wrath which it merits is proclaimed. And the sinner, weak and hopeless, dies.

3. "Moses describeth the righteousness which, is by the law, that the man which doeth these things shall live by them." "The soul that sinneth, it shall die." These also are things which the law saith; and by them, the Holy Spirit convinces man of the utter impossibility, that he should ever be justified by any works of his own. "By the deeds of the law, shall no flesh be justified in his sight, for by the law is the knowledge of sin." The law gives no other knowledge than this. It proposes, in its very nature, but two possible methods by which a creature can be just with God; and they are equally, beyond the reach of a creature who has committed a single transgression. In the one method, it offers life,

to those who have perfectly obeyed its precepts. In the other, it presents liberty to those who have fully endured its penalties. Under which of these, can there be hope for sinful man? He can never obtain acceptance by his obedience, for it is vitiated by his corrupt nature at the very commencement, and he cannot live an hour without sin. There is an inseparable imperfection and defilement in every duty which he performs. He cannot be justified by making satisfaction for his disobedience, for no satisfaction can be received short of the entire penalty, which is everlasting death; so that hoping for life by recompensing divine justice for past transgressions, is but to hope for salvation by being damned. Here is a twofold impossibility, that sinful man should ever be justified, upon any ground of his own merits, which the law demonstrates to his conscience, beyond the power of denial. The convinced sinner sees this hopeless state. He is compelled to acknowledge his guilt, and to confess his just exposure to punishment. And he is compelled to cast aside every hope of working out any righteousness for himself. A knowledge of pardon and life must come to him from some other source. The revelation of a mighty and gracious Redeemer, who as the sinner's surety, hath obeyed the precepts, and endured the penalties of the law, and hath thus brought in an everlasting righteousness to be disposed of according to his own will and gift, and who offers it freely to those who believe in him, exhibits this provision, and gives this knowledge, rationally and perfectly. But the law can never give it. Its entire work is conviction, condemnation, and punishment, for all who have sinned. It has justification for none. The purpose of its convincing operation is to exhibit distinctly this fact. And when it has brought the sinner to this despair in himself, by shewing his unspeakable dangers, and his inability to find a remedy for them, by any thing which he can do or suffer, it has finished its work. There it must leave the transgressor in this "horror of great darkness," until the very same Spirit who by the ministry of the law has thus convinced him of sin, shall by the gracious ministry of the Gospel, convince him of the perfect and sufficient righteousness which is laid up for him in Jesus Christ the Lord, to be made his own by faith, freely, through the grace of God.

These three points exhibit the convincing power and operation of the law. This three-fold conviction, of guilt, of wrath, and of hopeless despair, the Spirit of God produces, by "the things which the law saith." Until this conviction has been produced, the preaching of Christ is ineffectual upon the sinner's soul. He will never turn to Jesus with a godly sorrow for sin, and embrace the blessed offers of mercy which his Gospel presents, until he has been thoroughly awakened to perceive, and to acknowledge, the facts of which the law convinces him. He will still wrap himself in his own carnal confidence, and see no need of looking after any other righteousness than his own. He will think himself whole, and will therefore refuse the divine Physician. He will be ignorant of his danger, and will still reject the proposal of salvation. This work of the law is therefore indispensable for man's spiritual security. He will not fly to him who hath redeemed him from the curse of the law, by being made a curse for him, until he feels himself to be under that curse. Then, when the hammer of God hath broken his stony heart, the blessing of the Gospel comes to him, as the oil of joy for mourning, and the garment of praise for the spirit of heaviness.

II. We may consider this conviction under the aspect of *the persons to whom it must be applied*. "Now, we know that whatsoever things, the law saith, it saith to them that are under the law." In the connexion in which this passage stands, its evident principle and purpose, are to prove the guilt of those persons who were in the possession of the greatest spiritual privileges. The Jews, who were in every sense "under the law," were ready so acknowledge the broadest statements of guilt, and the most solemn denunciations of wrath, as truly and entirely applicable to the Gentiles. But they denied their equal application to themselves. The argument of the Apostle opposes this assumption, and demonstrates the just application of all that the law said, to those who were under the law; so that if it uttered aloud, the charge of universal guilt, and denounced as its result, universal wrath, it certainly addressed, in each case, those to whom its holy precepts had been communicated. While we apply this assertion peculiarly to the moral law, we must unequivocally assert its application to every human being. All mankind are born under the inflexible obligations of this sacred law; and the things which it saith, it saith to the whole family of man. If they applied to Jews to whom had been given all the privileges of the oracles of God, as entirely, as to Gentiles who had not received these specific revelations; they apply to those to whom the divine oracles are still granted, as entirely, as to the heathen who are without this knowledge of God. As extensively as the authority of the precepts of the law reach upon the earth, do its charges of guilt, and its denunciations of punishment also go. And if there be not an individual man who is released from the obligation of loving God with all his heart, there is not an individual who is not justly accused of transgression, and justly condemned to punishment, for having refused to fulfil this universal obligation. "All have sinned, and have come short of the glory of God." There is no man who can say, " I have made my heart clean, I am pure from my sin." The proper operation of this convincing power of the law, is therefore upon every human being. Its broadest accusations, and its most fearful denunciations belong to every one who hears me this day. And none can have the least prospect of security, by pleading exemption from the charges which it makes. "What things soever it saith, it saith

G*

to" you. And whether it comes in the power of the precept, or in the terror of the denunciation, it fastens its iron grasp upon your souls, and will hold you to eternity, unless there come to your rescue, a power of grace stronger than the power of its wrath. It speaks to the very best, and least offending of you all,—and it must be heard. It would convince you of sin. It would shew you your entire need of a Saviour. It would compel you to throw away all deluding and destructive pleas of comparative innocence in yourselves. It would bring you in the acknowledgment of a bitter sense of guilt, to cry aloud for mercy. It would send you to the blood of an Almighty Redeemer, as the only fountain which can be opened for sin, and for uncleanness. There would it lead you and leave you, as the instrument of the divine Spirit for conviction of sin. But if this gracious operation of the law be by any of you, foolishly resisted and denied, it will operate yet farther, to convict you before the bar of God; to compel you there to see your exposure to divine wrath, and eternal woe; and to draw from your own mouths, speechless in your defence, an overwhelming confession, that your damnation is just. For one or the other of these purposes, either for mercy in a day of grace, or for condemnation in a day of wrath, the convincing power of the law must be felt and understood by every soul of man.

III. We may lastly consider this convincing power of the law, under the aspect of *the result to which it leads.* This the apostle declares,—" that every mouth may be stopped, and the whole world become guilty before God." The mouths of unconvinced sinners are not stopped. Their complaints against the unreasonable strictness and severity of the divine commandments are frequent and vehement. The natural minds of men constantly rebel against the authority and declarations of the Most High God. They do not and cannot acknowledge, that they are bound to such devotion as his demands appear to require—or that they are justly chargeable with guilt, for failing in that, which is so repugnant to their dispositions, that its fulfilment amounts to an impossibility. They are found inventing a thousand excuses and pleas, for their security from punishment. Temptation, ignorance, heedlessness, weakness, are all urged as reasons by them, why they should not be dealt with upon a system of such severity, but should have some milder government, and receive a more extensive toleration. But all these excuses and complaints arise from a want of that conviction which it is the province of the law to impress. When by the power of the Holy Spirit with this ministration of the law, they are convinced of sin, their mouths are sealed against all excuses forever. The justice and holiness of God become so apparent, that they feel no right to complain, although they are condemned. The aggravations of their guilt are so clearly manifested, that no excuse occurs to their remembrance. They are cast down before a God of immaculate purity, with a spirit torn and bruised, acknowledging the truth of every accusation, and proclaiming the entire justice of every woe which he has denounced. Whatever may be the character of others, each individual will feel, that for himself, shame and confusion of face belong to him, and that God is righteous, though he taketh vengeance.

If this conviction be not awakened in the souls of men in their day of grace, while it may be salutary and effectual, it will certainly come upon them, like a giant aroused from his sleep, in the day of judgment. Confusion will cover them in that awful day, when God ariseth to shake terribly the earth, and to repay vengeance and recompense to all his enemies. Then will every impenitent and unprofitable servant be speechless, though he be bound hand and foot, and cast into outer and final darkness; while the universe will unite to proclaim the abiding and unchangeable spotlessness of the Judge who thus solemnly condemns the guilty.

But not only will the law thus stop every mouth, it will also bring "the whole world guilty before God,"—or under the condemning judgment of God, convicted of sin, and destitute of all claim for the exercise of mercy. This holy law now announces its requisitions and proclaims its sanctions, that in this bringing of a guilty world under the judgment of God, it may make room for the exercise of abundant grace, and make ready the souls of sinners, for the pardoning love of God. But when this mercy is rejected, its purpose in the same annunciations, is to open the way for the future display of the spotless justice of God in the exercise of his power of condemnation and punishment. It brings the whole world, and every individual transgressor of the world, under the divine judgment. Nothing can be demanded by any but the wages of sin which is death. In passing by every sinner, and leaving them all to perish, God would not be unjust. In pardoning and saving the remnant he hath chosen, he is infinitely gracious and merciful. When the sinner is truly convinced, he has this view solemnly and deeply impressed upon his mind. He feels that he is under a righteous condemnation, and that there can be no reason found for the exercise of any pardon or compassion towards him, but in the unsearchable riches of the love of God. He looks in this condition to no other source, for the rescue he needs, but the free and unmerited grace of God the Saviour. Oppressed and condemned, he begs him to undertake for him. He throws himself upon the sufficiency and kindness of that wonderful counsellor, who has himself become the end of the law, that he might bring in an everlasting righteousness for guilty man,—and in the acceptance of whose work of merit, God can be just, and the justifier of all who believe in him. When the law works the same conviction in the conscience of the sinner, in the dreadful day of retribution, the same result of conscious desert of condemnation will be produced. The whole world will come under the condemnation of God. He will be exhibited undeniably righteous while he judgeth the earth. And while not a sinful being has any claim to mercy, and the hardened and impenitent are justly condemned,—the freeness and fulness of his divine redemption will be gloriously displayed. For every convicted soul that in a day of grace, has fled from the law to Christ, mercy will rejoice against judgment. The pardoning love of God, and the condemning righteousness of God will meet together. And he will rejoice forever over a people who under this condemnation, have looked unto him from the ends of the earth, and found in him, a complete salvation.

LECTURE VI.

THE CONDEMNING POWER OF THE LAW.

The Law worketh wrath,—ROMANS IV. 15.

This single sentence presents the whole subject of the present discourse. It exhibits the *condemning power of the divine law,* as exercised upon transgressors of its precepts. The Apostle announces it as a fundamental principle, from the acknowledged certainty of which, he derives and establishes other conclusions. The blessings which the heirs of the divine promise receive, he says, can never be from the law, because "the law worketh wrath." To give life to sinners, as their inheritance, is in direct opposition to its very nature, and a thing impossible for it to do. It is as if he should say to the man famishing with thirst, fire cannot relieve your necessity, for fire produceth heat, it can never quench thirst, it will make the evil which you suffer, still the worse. It is but the amazing ignorance and blindness of guilty man which makes this assertion necessary.—Yet it is necessary. We have still to warn multitudes of self-justifying men, who persist in looking to their own obedience, as their ground of hope before God, that life cannot come to them by the law, for it is no property of the law to give life to sinners, "the law worketh wrath." This is its nature; and this is its whole operation upon guilty men.

My present purpose, is to exhibit this peculiar power and property of the law. It stands forth in faithful solemnity, to warn blinded men against itself. And we are to listen to its declaration to transgressors who are seeking salvation, "it is not in me." We are to speak of that aspect of its character which occasions it to be called "a fiery law," a "ministration of condemnation," and a "ministration of death." This is the only aspect of the law, which can be presented to transgressors. For innocent and obedient beings it is ordained unto life. This was its design and tendency towards man in his unfallen state. Had man remained obedient, the law would have wrought for him an inheritance of life eternal. But when man became a transgressor, however unimportant in his own estimation, was the comparative fact of his transgression, his whole relation to the law, and the law's whole relation to him, was changed. Henceforth, its operation was wrath alone. "By one man's disobedience" in one command, "many were made sinners." "By the offence of one, many died, and judgment came upon all men unto condemnation." This violated law was the covenant, under which every son of Adam was born, and under which every succeeding descendant of his has come into the world. It has worked wrath for all. It has rolled down its sentence of condemnation, from generation to generation. Remaining unchanged in its demand for perfect obedience, it has uttered forth an unchanging curse upon all who have come short of it. No mitigation of the awful penalty for disobedience, or of the demand for entire submission can be made in favour of any child of man. Every unconverted and unpardoned man remains therefore, of necessity a child of wrath, and under the burden of the two-fold obligation, of a penalty which cannot be satisfied, and a requisition which cannot be fulfilled. The Lord Jesus Christ having become the end of the law for righteousness to man, offers the only refuge from the everlasting wrath which the law thus works. And every sinner who rejects the offers, and the dominion of Christ in the Gospel, abides of his own choice, under a covenant which works, and can work nothing but wrath.

Mr. Simeon forcibly presents this view of the subject before us in an illustration like the following. "Tell me then, ye who desire to be under the law; do ye not hear the law? Does it say anything to you, but 'do this, and thou shalt live?' Does it set before you any alternative, but 'cursed is he that continueth not in all things which are written in the book of the law, to do them?' Has it any other terms than these? 'Do this' this wrath-working law proclaims—'do it all; all without exception; continue in it from first to last, and you shall live. But a curse, an everlasting curse awaits you, if you offend in any one particular.' Plead what you will, these denunciations are irreversible; its terms cannot be changed. You may say, "I wish to obey;" and it answers you, "tell me not of your wishes, but do it." "I have endeavoured to obey." "Tell me of no endeavours, but do it, or you are cursed." "I have done it, in almost every particular." " Tell me not what you have done almost, have you obeyed it altogether?" Have you obeyed it in all things, if not, you are cursed." "I have for many years obeyed it, and but once only have I transgressed." "Then you are cursed. If you have offended in one point, you are guilty of all." "But I am sorry for my transgressions." "I cannot regard your sorrow; you are under a curse." "But I will reform, and never transgress again." "I care nothing for your reformation: the curse remains upon you." "But I will obey perfectly in future, if I can find mercy for the past." "I can have no concern with your determinations for the future; I know no such word as mercy; my terms cannot be altered for any one. If you rise to these terms, you will have a right to life, and need no mercy. If you fall short in any one particular, nothing remains for you, but everlasting destruction from the presence of the Lord, and the glory of his power." This illustration of the subject before us, is by no means more striking, than it is accurate.

St. Paul says, "as many as are of the works of the law," or looking to their own obedience to the law, as their foundation for hope, "are under a curse." But this description includes the whole of those who have not voluntarily renounced their own righteousness, and fled to the shelter which the Gospel opens in the obedience of the Son of God for man. There is no human being who has ever obeyed the law. He alone, in whom dwelt all the fulness of the Godhead bodily, has offered a perfect obedience, which is for the justification of those who believe in him. All men have sinned, and come short of the glory of God; and therefore every soul without exception, is guilty before God, and condemned already. They are under a curse which the law cannot relieve, and which if the only possible remedy, by faith in the obedience of Christ, be rejected, must remain on them forever. This is a simple statement of the demands of the law, and of the actual condition of sinful man under its sentence. It is utterly impossible, for an apostate being, to rise to its demands, or to remove its sentence. It worketh therefore, only wrath; and warns men to seek elsewhere, for a hope of life, which it hath no power to bestow.

I. We will first consider the *fact* which the text declares. "The law worketh wrath." This is the precise statement of its operation. It is the instrument of bringing man under the just and inevitable anger of God. It produces this effect, both in *the obedience which it demands,* and in *the sentence which it denounces.*

1. In the *obedience* which it demands. If it were a mere outward system, and not a spiritual law; if it referred wholly to open and gross transgressions in men, it would rather encourage them to cleave to it, and to endeavour to meet its

claims, that they might hope for the life, which they would thus deserve. It would not then be the instrument of wrath, nor dissuade men from abiding by its terms. But " we know that the law is spiritual." Such is the exceeding breadth of its requisitions, the extent and perfection of the obedience which it claims, the heart-searching power of its demands, that it charges man with guilt, not merely in open violations of its precepts, but in the deficiencies of that obedience which he professes to render, the secret worthlessness of the best actions of his life. If at any time, he really loves God; the law asks, " does this love rise to the full measure of the precept which requires it?" Is it with all the heart and mind, and soul, and strength? If not, then even this best attainment has a stain of guilt, and there is sufficient reason for its condemnation. The same remarks may be made in reference to all efforts of man to fulfil the commands of God. The defects in his obedience are sin. The law cannot receive the disposition in place of the act,—or accept the desire instead of the duty. It makes no toleration for the sincerity of the wish, or the effort, if there be not a faithful and entire fulfilment of the command, in the utmost extent of its terms. It allows no deviation, no weariness, no deficiency, even for a moment, or under any circumstances, to the very end of life. It presents as its standard, the utmost perfection of character, and denounces as the only alternative to this, the death which is the wages of sin. This perfection of character it will have, or it will receive nothing. If man can fulfil this demand, it is well. If he cannot, the law worketh wrath in every precept. But this obedience, man can never render. And therefore in the inexorable character of its claims, the law brings inevitable condemnation upon the guilty, and thus lifts up its voice in a faithful warning against the indulgence of hope by a compliance with its terms. It urges men to fly from itself to him who is a Prince and a Saviour, who has fulfilled its righteousness, and is able to give repentance and forgivness of sins. The flaming sword which guarded the entrance of Paradise, keeping man from the way to the tree of life,—and the terrors of Mount Sinai, with the fence which was placed around it, and the strict prohibitions which were given against any attempt to break through and gaze, all marked the impossibility of gaining access to God, and life with him, by any way which the law could open. Moses beheld this terrible exhibition of its holiness, when he said "I exceedingly fear and quake." And when self-confident men are awakened to a view of the same character of the law, in its extreme opposition to themselves, such will be also the feeling which will take possession of them. Yet every man who rests his hope on any aspect of a righteousness of his own, shuts himself up to fulfil all the law's demands, or to abide by its eternal penalty. His salvation must be of works unmixed with grace. If he fail in any compliance, he has no hope. He may not realize this condition. Alas, he does not, or he would not abide in it for a single hour. But his vain and ignorant mind shuts him up to this dreadful necessity. And when his life is compared with the law, by which he has chosen to abide, every precept in it worketh wrath, and pronounces condemnation against him.

2. This condemning power of the law is still further manifested, in the *sentence* which it passes upon the guilty, and of which it forewarns them with the utmost fidelity. In this too, it urges man to flee from all attempts, and all hope, to obtain life, by any personal satisfaction for his offences. The penalty of disobedience in every single instance, is death. But death, whether of the body, or of the soul, is a state from which there is no return, but by the direct and immediate interposition of divine power. When man is dead, he is forever dead, unless the Almighty Being who made him, shall restore him again to life. The death which comes upon a sin-

gle transgression, is therefore, everlasting death. There is no sanction or penalty less than this, presented in the law. It reveals this, the death of the soul,—the everlasting separation from God, under his condemnation, the indignation and wrath, tribulation and anguish, which make up such a state, —as the consequence of transgression,—and of every transgression. It exhibits all mankind as guilty before God, and announces this, as the necessary result of their guilt, and leaves them under it. It is vain to imagine, and absurd to speak, of a *temporary* death, as if there were power in the dead, to restore themselves to the condition they have lost; or of a *correcting* and *purgative* death, as if there were in the nature of a curse, and an accursed condition, an influence to purify and renovate the character of its subjects. This death is *punitive;* and so far as the law is concerned, it is *final*. Its victims are passed over, and reckoned no more among the living. Certainly God has provided a remedy, and offered it in great mercy to man. But this remedy is not in the law, or in man's obedience, or in God's change of purpose. It is in the perfect work and righteousness of Christ, "both God and man," which is offered freely to man's acceptance, as the exercise and revelation of divine mercy; and by which the law is honoured, its victims are released, and man is made secure. In this righteousness, man lives forever. But in works of his own, and under the operation of the law, the curse which is upon him, abides forever, and his death is an everlasting death. While the law proclaims its simple, uniform, irreversible sentence, it asks of guilty man, "Who can dwell with the devouring fire? Who can dwell with everlasting burnings?" "Hast thou an arm like God? Canst thou thunder with a voice like him?" "Can thine heart endure, or can thine hands be strong, in the days that I shall deal with thee? I the Lord have spoken it, and will do it." The law thus brings up every soul of man before an unchangeable God, under the charge of guilt. It lays its penalty of eternal death upon each. It requires their endurance of this penalty. It can offer no possible mitigation or redress. Thus it worketh wrath—wrath only,—wrath forever. And the sinner might as reasonably seek for shelter and rest for his body in a burning fiery furnace, as hope for life and salvation for his soul in his own compliance with the demands of the law.

When God brought the Israelites to the land which he had promised them, he required their united and cordial assent to this terrible condemnation of the law. The Levites proclaimed from Mount Ebal, "cursed is he that continueth not in all the words of this law to do them." And all the people were commanded to say "Amen," be it so, it is right and just that it should be so. But how very few among those who listen to this solemn language of the divine law, are prepared to unite in this divinely appointed testimonial. They are far more ready to think, that such exhibitions as have now been made of its character, are overstrained and unjust. They cannot believe on the one side, in this perfect holiness of the divine commands, or on the other, in the actual and deep guiltiness of their own character. But, search the Scriptures whether these things are so. Ask and see, what the Lord God hath spoken upon this subject. Under his guidance and instruction, but one sentiment would pervade the minds of men. The whole world, conscious of their guilt, would be ready to cry out in a thorough acknowledgment, and approbation of the truth, "amen, amen." It is the blindness and ignorance of man alone, which hides the all-important truth from him, and persuades him to rest upon the miserable works of his own performance.

3. But while the law worketh wrath, both in the holiness of its precepts, and in the solemn fidelity of its threatenings, this condemning power is to be further considered, as an *eternally abiding power.* In man's first transgression, con-

demnation comes upon him. This was the fact with the first human transgression. That transgression was not only a personal act, but also the act of a representative for men,—and the condemnation which came for it, came upon all men for whom he stood. But this involuntary and inherited condemnation, which was received from the first Adam, has been removed, by the equally extensive redemption, which has been wrought for men by the second Adam, in the merciful work of the Lord Jesus. And every member of the family of man is thus released from all condemnation, other than that which s for his own guilt. Still the principle remains the same. Man's first transgression brings him into condemnation before God. The law condemns him to wrath, and there he abides. Its power is an eternal power, and holds the soul that comes under it forever, unless some satisfying provision of grace furnishes relief. It gives strength to sin, to hold the sinner in captivity, in this just condemnation. The sinner who is now condemned, is condemned forever. The wrath of God abideth on him. But who can adequately speak of this power of the law to condemn? No frail man can understand, or describe it! It stretches out, into all the dark and dreadful scenes of an eternal world, where the bitterness of anguish for folly past, the hateful and rebellious spirit which present guilt produces, and the perpetual exclusion from all the light and comfort which the presence of God imparts, display in fallen angels, and in condemned men, the wrath which the law works forever. Of all this misery, the present transgressor is even now, the legal and certain heir. His first offence binds him over to this. And though divine forbearance lingers out his life, that offers of mercy may plead with his soul, the law has settled its eternal relation to him; and he remains, if he refuse the mercy which is offered in the Gospel, under its power, in everlasting condemnation. This is the condemning power of the law. It is holy, just, and good. All life must come from an obedience to its precepts. But disobedience delivers over the sinner to its penalty, in everlasting death. It hath become the adversary to the transgressor;—and "the adversary delivers him to the Judge, and the Judge delivers him to the officer, to be cast into prison." "Verily, verily I say unto you," says our divine Redeemer, "he shall by no means come out thence, till he hath paid the uttermost farthing."

II. Having considered the facts of this condemning power of the law, we may consider more particularly, *our personal connexion with it.*

Every child of man is born under a curse, in the relation, in which this whole fallen family stands to an offended Creator. And though every child of Adam is also a partaker of a free redemption from this curse, in the death of Christ for all, yet every man who goes forward in a single step of voluntary rebellion, assumes again the whole burden of this curse upon himself; justifies by his own act the disobedience which deserves it, and comes again under the curse before God. And yet, every unconverted man, though in this condition of ruin, having never renounced his rebellious course, nor sought for pardon and security in the appointed Redeemer, is hoping and attempting, to gain eternal life, by his own obedience to God. There are but two possible methods of salvation for man; by grace and by works,—or by God's merciful favour, and man's own right. Between these two man must choose, and he does choose, for himself. All men who are ignorant of God's righteousness, and refuse the free offers of his grace in the Lord Jesus, are attempting to work out a righteousness for themselves. Their whole hope of salvation therefore depends upon their ability to do it. This personal connexion, all unconverted men have with the solemn subject we have considered. The moment that men turn to any thing which they have done, as their ground of hope, the reason for their acceptance with God, they choose the law for their covenant, and become debtors to fulfil all its demands. They throw themselves upon the simple alternative of perfect and perpetual obedience, spotless from the commencement, and spotless forever; or chains of everlasting darkness. This is the condition and stand, of all who are not in the covenant of grace, spiritually united to Jesus the mediator of this new covenant.

There are many varieties among this large class of persons. Some are looking for their justification, altogether to the character of their own works. They cannot understand why good works should be required of men, if they cannot furnish them, an acceptance with God. When the divine assertion is made, that " by the works of the law, shall no flesh be justified," it seems to them, to set the necessity of obedience entirely aside, and to encourage man in all transgressions. Such persons throw themselves entirely upon the works of the law. They agree to abide simply by its terms. They expose themselves therefore to the utmost of its demands,—and they voluntarily assume the whole burden of wrath which it must bring upon transgressors. Their everlasting condition must be determined by its principles alone, and their destruction becomes inevitable.

Others do not professedly renounce all relation to the Saviour of men. They acknowledge that we must be indebted to him, at least in part, for our salvation. They assert their partial dependance upon him, and perhaps they desire to cultivate it. They would connect the merits of his atonement with the supposed worth of their own obedience. The entire impossibility of such an expedient they do not perceive. They do not understand, how the one makes void the other. They do not attempt to determine exactly where or how, they are united together. Where that point in human works is fixed, in the attainment of which they may be acceptable to God, none having done as well as they could: or what measure of uniform sincerity shall be received, none being entirely so,—God has not defined, and they pretend not to know. They blindly assume this ground. But in doing it,—they equally with the others reject a redemption which is wholly of grace, and throw themselves entirely under the power of the law, unable to produce the obedience which it demands, and compelled therefore to bear the wrath which it works.

There are others who refine upon this system, but are still persuaded they must do something for themselves. They enter into a kind of compromise or agreement with the Lord of all, that they will render him obedience, if he will bestow upon them salvation. They make their promise of amendment the reason for his forgiveness. They do not expressly unite their merits with his,—but they make their obedience the reason for which his merits should be bestowed upon them,—or the reason why they may have hope in him,—and the foundation upon which they expect him to be merciful unto them. They do not remember, that they have no obedience to bring him; that there is nothing in them but guilt;—that they have no good thing of their own. Thus they rest not a simple dependence on the sovereign and conquering power, and the all-sufficient merit, of a divine Saviour. They are not prepared to embrace with thankfulness, a salvation wholly without money and without price; or to glory in Christ alone.

Even beyond this, error upon this subject is often found. Men are willing in terms to ascribe all the glory to Christ; but they want some evidence, some warrant in themselves, for their trust in him. They are not willing to take the recorded freeness of the provision, and the openness of the promise, for their simple warrant for trusting wholly and joyfully in Christ. Either they profess themselves afraid to trust in him, because they are so vile, and therefore they will reform and amend before they venture to hope in him,—thinking that he cannot receive such sinners as they;—or they have comfort and hope in him, because they never were inordinate transgressors, or because they find in themselves the evidence of a change of mind and character which indicate a true repentance. But both the principle, and the result of all these delusions are the same. They grow out of a spirit of self-righteousness; and they throw the sinner wholly back upon the claims of the law. Salvation must be all of grace, or all of works. And any attempt to blend the two in any measure, destroys the whole idea of grace; for as far as man has any thing to offer, the Saviour is required to offer so much the less. It exposes man to the one simple demand of the law, under the alternative of its endless wrath in his failure to meet it.

This is your simple connexion with this condemning power of the law. If you do not come in entire and unqualified self-renunciation,—as poor, and outcast, and perishing, to the single atoning sacrifice, and the perfect obedience, of the Lord Jesus Christ,—you must stand by the law, and meet its alternative requisitions. If you are not willing freely to accept the work of a perfect surety, offered in the covenant of grace,—you must in your own persons, fulfil the utmost demands, or bear the eternal penalty, of a covenant of works. These terms cannot be altered. They must be fully and completely met. O, that a view of them might lead you to seek to be found, only in the Lord Jesus Christ,—not having your own righteousness which is of the law, but the righteousness which is of God, by faith,—and to count every thing but loss, for Christ's sake!

III. But if this connexion of ourselves with the condemning power of the law be a fact,—if it be true, that it works wrath to an extent so unlimited, what deep humiliation of soul becomes us all, in view of its holy and unrelaxing claims! What an amount of curses it suspends over the head of an unpardoned sinner! We have seen that they are not our outward transgressions alone, which expose us to the righteous anger of God. The wrath of God is revealed against all ungodliness and unrighteousness of men. And every omission and defect in duty, as well as every act of positive disobedience, must have its just recompense of reward. If it should be granted therefore, that our lives are blameless in the eyes of men,—still our iniquities will have grown over our heads, and have become wholly innumerable. In comparison with many of our fellow men, our characters may appear exemplary and worthy; but in the sight of God, there is no respect of persons. If he should behold in us, less outward gross iniquity,—he may see far more than an equivalent for this, in secret spiritual sins, by no means less hateful in his sight. Certainly we are not understood as saying, that gross outward transgressions add nothing to the guilt of man; but that in the absence of these, God may see secret transgression in the heart, more than sufficient to make up for the absence of them. Our true humiliation will be produced, by beholding the defectiveness of our best services. Look upon this deep deficiency in duty. Behold it in its aggravated character, as against a God of infinite love and mercy; against a Saviour who has assumed our nature, and laid down his life for us;—against a Holy Comforter who has been pleading with our hearts, to guide us in right paths, and to lead us unto true repentance. Behold it also, as persisted in, against abundant light and knowledge; against vows and resolutions and promises;—against divine judgments and mercies; and continued in without repentance or shame, for many years. Behold it as a cruel rejection of the boundless love of a crucified Redeemer; as a bold and violent determination to stand upon our own ground, and to abide by our own merits. Shall we not see in all this, adequate reason for humiliation? Shall we not see, that the law justly works wrath against us, and that our guilt must sink us into everlasting perdition, unless God shall wonderfully interpose, and cause his grace to superabound, where sin hath abounded so fearfully? If we fairly consider our own characters as thus displayed, we shall see, that to call ourselves the chief of sinners, is not merely an humble expression of the lips, but is the real character of our souls. The very best man among us, knows far more evil in himself, than he can know of any other,—and sees a depth of guilt in his own heart, concealed from the view of other men, which is sufficient to overwhelm him in everlasting condemnation.

If you fairly bring up your characters to this divine standard, you will feel compelled to cry for mercy, like Peter sinking in the waters, "Lord, save me, or I perish!" Others may be amazed at your distress, and think it unnecessary; but you will know the plague of your own heart, and feel compelled to lie down before God, in the deepest self-abasement. O, that you could be brought to this state of mind! and have it as a settled principle in your minds, that by the deeds of the law no flesh can be justified. Listen to this law, though it condemns you. If its warnings are alarming, they are still indispensable; and it is far better that you should be warned in season, that your house is built upon the sand, than be suffered to remain in a false peace, until you perish beneath its ruins. It is a fatal delusion which shuts your hearts against the acceptance of a Saviour, who is the completion of this fiery law, for righteousness to your souls. This is the only hope presented to you. And while the law drives you thus away from itself, humbled, guilty, and condemned, it does not thrust you upon an ocean of uncertainty, to find by chance, and where you can, a remedy for your disease, and a satisfaction for your want. It acknowledges a righteousness in your anointed substitute, adequate to its utmost demands.

It bids you seek to him, and live. It assures you that he can preach glad tidings, though it cannot. It acknowledges its own weakness, and proclaims his power. And it bids you flee from the wrath which it must work forever, to find an everlasting righteousness in him.

LECTURE VII.

THE LAW A GUIDE TO CHRIST.

Wherefore the law was our schoolmaster, to bring us unto Christ, that we might be justified by faith.—GALATIANS, III. 24.

The subject presented by this text is of great importance, and peculiar interest. It displays the instrument by which a sinful man is directed to a Saviour's feet, and the vast benefit which he gains by following this direction. However severe and searching may be the method of guidance, the result to which it leads is most desirable and important; and the very severity which has led to this result, tends to enhance the comfort which is derived from it. The chill and darkness of the night which has passed, make the beams of the rising sun more welcome and more delightful. So the deep anguish and darkness, through which the law leads the convicted sinner in its awful denunciations, make the consolations which abound in Christ, who has met all these denunciations, the more sufficient, and the more precious.

The apostle speaks of the law in our text, as a guide to Christ. He has shewed its total inability to give life to a fallen man, and the absolute necessity of that gracious redemption which God has revealed in his own Son. He describes the condition of all, in whose hearts, these glad tidings of redemption have not been received, as one of necessary and entire ruin, from which there is no other way of escape, than that which is here laid open. The law bringing a curse upon transgressors, and offering no pardon for sin, shuts them up, destitute of all hope, but the blessed one which is offered in this covenant of grace. It imprisons them under its curse. It demands a full satisfaction for their guilt. It rejects all their offers, and all their pleas. It allows no method of escape, but that which grace has thus opened in the accepted satisfaction of a Saviour. It becomes thus a guide to Christ. All men as sinners against God, are shut up in this imprisonment. Their eternal ruin in it becomes inevitable. They cannot live by any works of their own. They cannot endure the certain penalty of their transgressions. They cannot escape from it, by any power which they possess. In the midst of this darkness and despair, the Lord Jesus Christ is revealed as the great object of faith, offering freely as the gift of divine grace, that which man could never obtain by any worthiness of his own. When this door of grace is opened, and this messenger from God, proclaiming an entire satisfaction for sin, looses the chains of sinners, and bids them go in peace, they are no longer shut up under the law. If they hear the voice, and follow the guidance of the revealed Saviour, they are under grace, and can come no more into condemnation, but have passed from death unto life. If they refuse his offered mercy, then, " this is their condemnation, that light has come into the world, but they have loved darkness rather than light, because their deeds were evil."

The apostle speaks of this guiding power of the law, both as a dispensation, and as a personal instrument. As a dispensation, it held all mankind in bondage, until Christ was revealed among men, in the fulness of his grace, as its end and satisfaction. In him the righteousness of the law was perfectly fulfilled. The demands of its covenant were entirely answered and satisfied. The world which it had condemned, became a redeemed and purchased world, by the propitiation which he had made for the sins of men. When this great object of promise and faith had come, and had completed his work, the dispensation of the law was satisfied, and honoured;—and the world for whom he lived and died, came under the provisions of the covenant of grace. Each subject of the violated law, had liberty offered him in the completing Gospel; and whosoever would, might take of the water of life freely. As an instrument for personal guidance, the law still remains, in its record, and in its application, a schoolmaster to bring sinners unto Christ. The Holy Spirit uses it for this purpose, and by it, he leads the souls of sinners, to embrace the blessed and glorious hope, which is offered to them freely, in the obedience and death of the divine Redeemer. This *personally guiding power of the law* as a divine instrument, is the subject of the present discourse. We may consider first the *method* by which the law fulfils this office,—and secondly, the *purpose* for which it is done.

I. We will consider the *method* in which this guiding power of the law is exercised. "It is our schoolmaster, to bring us unto Christ."

1. By *completely shutting us out, from every other hope.* The demands of the law must be fully answered, before it can allow any hope of life. They can never be set aside. They are as unalterable as the character of God himself. The law is holy, its commands cannot therefore be abated. It is just, its sanctions therefore cannot be mitigated. It is good, and it must remain eternally good, whatever may become of those who have transgressed, and therefore dislike it. Its direct purpose and tendency in all that it requires, is to promote the honour of God, and to advance the happiness of men. If it becomes to any creature, an occasion of sorrow, it is only through his own perverseness in violating its commands. This is the actual character of the law. If therefore the sinner would have hope by it, he must come up to the measure of of its requirements. He must bear the curse which it has

denounced, and obey the commands which it imposes. But when he looks at these demands; when he surveys this awful curse, and examines these holy precepts; when he is convinced of their unalterable character; he sees the utter impossibility of his ever meeting them in his own person. He has therefore no hope. He has no alternative, but to lie down, and perish forever. The idea of a substitute to fulfil these obligations for him, and of the possible acceptance of this substitute in his behalf, would never come to man under the law. But grace having revealed such a substitute, in the person of the Lord Jesus Christ, and declared that the Father is well pleased in him, the law drives man to find him. It shuts him out from all prospect of salvation in any other quarter. It speaks to him nothing but indignation and wrath. It thus forces his mind to think of some one who can fulfil all righteousness for him, and set him free from the curse which it impends over him. He hears it announcing to him if you can undergo the full punishment for sin, you shall be set free from the curse; and if you can offer a perfect obedience in holiness, you shall be justified and live. But these requisitions are as deep as hell, and high as heaven, what can he do? He hears the law again announcing, as the instrument of divine guidance to Christ, if you can find one who is able and willing to do these for you, you shall still not die, but live. It thus drives him from himself, and puts him upon the search for some such Redeemer and friend. While it absolutely shuts him out from all other hope, it hints to him, that hope may still be found, in the revelation from God, of this plan of grace; and thus it becomes a teacher to his soul to lead him to Christ. It has shut him up to this alternative; he must find a sufficient surety and Saviour, or he must lie in his prison, until he has paid the uttermost farthing. This is the first step in the personal guidance of a sinner to Christ. He is convinced that he must have a Saviour, because he cannot save himself; and his awakened conscience cries out in anguish, "Wherewith shall I come before the Lord, and bow myself before the High God? Who shall deliver me from the body of this death?"

2. The Law shews him the *character and qualifications which he must find in the Saviour upon whom he can securely rely.* He must be one competent to fulfil all the requisitions which this holy law has made; able to bear the load of infinite wrath and punishment, and capable of accomplishing, and offering a spotless obedience. He must not only be capable of doing all this in fact, but must be under no obligations to do it, in his own nature and condition, and competent therefore to undertake it in behalf of others. But this can be no created Saviour. A creature, though the very highest intelligence which God hath formed, being still limited in his power, and infinitely beneath the Being who hath formed him, would sink forever under the wrath of God. There is no material difference in this adaptation, or rather, this total want of all adaptation, between the highest created being and man himself. They are both as nothing in the sight of God. The fire of God's anger would consume the one, as easily, and as certainly, as the other. Nothing is gained for man, by shifting the work of expiation from himself, upon any other creature. The law shuts him out therefore, from confidence for satisfaction for sin, in any being, who is like himself limited in nature, however glorious and great. The highest conceivable creature can no more obey for him, than he can suffer. Every created being is already in the circumstances of his own nature, under the law, and is required to obey it, in all its commands. All that the law enjoins, he is bound to fulfil. He can do nothing therefore, which is not already his absolute duty. He can never have any thing which can be called merit in the sight of God. However exalted and glorious he may be, his obedience is all due; and when he has rendered it all, he is but an unprofitable servant; "he hath

done that only which it was his duty to do," and the omission of which would have constituted him a transgressor. He can never therefore obey for others, nor have a righteousness which would not be required to justify himself, and which might therefore be imputed to them. The law therefore shuts out every created being, from acting as a Saviour for lost man. Its claims and demands convince him, that no arm but an Almighty one, is competent for the work which is to be undertaken. It teaches him, that he can rest upon no substitute, who is less than the High and Lofty one who inhabiteth eternity, whose name is holy. If he can become the substitute for his creatures, if he can come to accomplish this wonderful work, the dignity of his nature would affix a value to his sufferings, sufficient to honour the demands of the law; his mighty power would enable him to bear the penalty and triumph over it;—and there would be a value and excellence in his voluntary obedience and suffering, which would magnify the law, and be a full satisfaction to all its claims. Whether such a plan as this be possible, the law cannot determine. But whether it be possible or not, it solemnly and absolutely shuts out every other plan, by making demands, which no one less than God himself can ever fulfil. Man must find such a Saviour, or he must perish in guilt without him. If such a door of hope can be opened, the law will hold him in bondage no longer. If such honour can be rendered to its claims, it will consent to the full salvation of the sinner, and approve of the crown conferred upon him; and the song of Moses, and the song of the Lamb shall be one forever. The law thus prepares the convicted sinner, to listen to the revelation of such a Saviour, to hear the glad tidings of the Gospel, and to receive with gratitude, its amazing communications of God's purposes and plans of grace. Having thus been taught the actual wants of his soul, he can rejoice when he hears the faithful sayings, that "God was manifest in the flesh," "made in all things like unto us, sin only excepted;" that "he hath borne our sins in his own body on the tree," and "became obedient unto death, even the death of the cross;" "hath been put to death in the flesh, the just for the unjust;" "hath been raised for our justification;" hath become "the Lord our Righteousness;" hath been "made sin for us, when he knew no sin, that we might be made the righteousness of God in him." These blessed revelations are welcomed and received with joy, because they are just the satisfaction, which the law has taught him must be made, and which it has bid him to seek for, if it can be found. By leading the mind to look for a Saviour so mighty, and so competent, and to be satisfied with no other, the law becomes a guide to bring him unto Christ, who is "God over all blessed forever." And when this door of grace is opened by the Gospel, and the light of heavenly day shines in upon his prison, he is ready to arise and follow the herald of peace and security, with gladness and haste.

3. The law shews the sinner *the way in which he must become a partaker of the Saviour's mercy, and be interested in his revealed redemption.* It exhibits to him clearly, his own real character and condition. It shews him, that he is sold under bondage to sin, and in a state of entire condemnation before God; that he has nothing of his own, to offer for his redemption, and no ability of his own to do any thing for his own rescue. It holds up to him plainly, the great and indispensable truth, that his salvation must be all of grace, the fruit of overflowing divine compassion; having no reference to any worth in him, in his state of captivity, or to any thing that he can do for his deliverer, after his release. It wholly strips him of all merit and worth, and sends him to Christ without works, and without confidence in any thing of his own. It bids him go to Jesus, as one who is lost and perishing, and not as one who is in any degree, deserving or serviceable. It

tells him to look to Christ, in the midst of his wants; seeking instruction for his ignorance,—pardon for his guilt,—cleansing from his pollution,—and free and full redemption from the slavery in which he has been held. He must think of nothing in himself, but his wants and miseries; and must expect nothing from a Saviour, but as the result of his own grace, and as the free gift of God to the condemned and perishing. He must renounce, and count as worthless, every thing that is his own; and desire and seek to have Christ made unto him, all in all, "wisdom, and righteousness, and sanctification, and redemption;"—that throughout eternity, he may praise him for deliverance from the bondage in which he was held, and glory in the Lord alone. The law assures him, that if he entertain the idea, of earning any thing by his own obedience, or of considering his obedience, as the reason of God's favour to him, he must come back under its power again, and Christ will become of none effect unto him. He must renounce all thought of this; and be content to be saved by grace alone, receiving every thing, out of that fulness which is laid up in the Lord Jesus Christ. His salvation must be wholly a gift, from beginning to end; communicated in the simple offer of it by God the Saviour; and received by him, through a cordial faith in this communication, a faith which rests every thing upon the certainty of the divine testimony, and the sufficiency of the divine power. Thus the law guides the sinner to Christ, stripping him completely of all merit and excellence of his own, and urging him to fly naked and helpless, to him, who " will clothe him with garments of salvation, and cover him with the robe of righteousness, as a bridegroom decketh himself with ornaments, and a bride adorneth herself with her jewels."

4. Then the law proclaims to the sinner, *its entire satisfaction with this provided Saviour.* It acknowledges that all its demands are met and honoured, by this glorious method of

God's revelation, in which God can be just, and the justifier of him who believeth in the Lord Jesus. It confesses to the sinner, that in the obedience and death of the Son of God, there is a way of salvation, entirely suitable to his condition and wants, and entirely honourable to the character of God;—suited to him, because it provides for a man who is wholly ruined, every spiritual blessing, as a free gift from God; bringing him a righteousness of obedience and suffering which is perfectly adequate to his need, and covering all his dangers and wants; honourable to God, because it displays and magnifies every attribute of his character, maintains unsullied the integrity of his law, exalts the dignity of his government, and manifests the wonderful extent of his wisdom and truth. The law thus entirely accepts the salvation of the Gospel, and acknowledges itself perfectly satisfied with the provision which it has made. In this way it becomes fully a guide to Christ. It urges the sinner to fly by the open door which is set before him, and to gain a participation in that everlasting covenant which is established in this offered Saviour, because there is no condemnation to them that are in Christ Jesus. It exhorts him, to receive this provided and offered Saviour, who hath done for man, in the likeness of sinful flesh, what the law could not do; to look to him alone for every blessing; not to be discouraged by any convictions of his own unworthiness; but to go to him, though the chief of sinners, that he may receive the unsearchable riches of his grace. It is thus the instrument which the Holy Spirit uses to prepare the sinner, to listen with confidence and gratitude to him who came to call sinners to repentance,—to seek and to save that which was lost,—to preach deliverance to the captives, and to set at liberty, them that were bound. While he stands at the door and knocks, the law gives up the sinner into his hands, to be led by that blessed invitation, "come unto me, all ye that labour and are heavy laden, and I will give you rest;" and to enjoy those gracious assurances, " though your sins are as scarlet, they shall be as white as snow,—though they be red like crimson, they shall be as wool." " Whosoever cometh unto me, I will in no wise cast out." Henceforth the sinner thus delivered, is no longer under the law, but under grace, and sin shall have no more dominion over him.

This is the guiding power of the law,—and the method in which it operates. By shutting the sinner out from every other hope; by exhibiting the qualifications, which he must find in a sufficient Saviour; by shewing him how he is to become interested in that Saviour's merit and work; and by acknowledging its entire satisfaction with all that this Saviour hath done for man; the law is made the schoolmaster to bring him unto Christ, "that he may be justified by faith."

II. We will consider *the object for which this guiding power of the law is exercised.* " The law is our schoolmaster, to bring us unto Christ, that we might be justified by faith." Justification before God, or to " be just with God," is the great want, of a rebel under the condemnation of his law. He must gain this blessing, or he must perish. Justification for the guilty, includes within it, a pardon for past transgressions, the effect of which is but to remove his punishment, but can give no title to reward; and a right, or title to future blessedness and security, which can arise only, from a perfect obedience of divine commands. The justified man has both these blessings bestowed upon him freely by grace,—receiving forgiveness of sins, and the imputation of righteousness without works.

If a man would be justified by works, he must be entitled by a right of his own to this forgiveness and reward. He must possess a two-fold righteousness, to present to God. He must satisfy the demands of the law by bearing its penalty; and he must honour and obey it, by fulfilling its precepts. If this can be done by man, he may have whereof to glory. He will be perfectly independent of every other being. Heaven will be his inheritance by legal right. There will be no room for the exercise of grace, because man will justly merit every thing which he can receive. God could not justly deny to him, that which has become his own, by the right and merit of his own obedience. This would be a justification by works, and would give to man, a just ground for boasting. But the law, in the exercise of its convincing and condemning power, shews this to be impossible. By the deeds of the law can no flesh be justified, for by the law is the knowledge of sin. But still, the condition of man is not changed. He must be justified, or he must perish. His need remains,—and while it is unsatisfied, he is under condemnation.

If he cannot be justified by works, is there any other method, in which he can be justified? Is there any way open, in which he may attain this desired end? The law " brings him unto Christ, that he may be justified by *faith*." To be justified,—that is, to be pardoned, and made righteous,—by faith, does not mean, that faith is received in the stead of obedience, or is regarded in itself, a righteousness for man. Faith can never be the ground or reason of our justification. As an act of man, it is as imperfect and worthless, as any other act. But it is the appointed instrument which conveys to us, and makes our own, the voluntary and perfect obedience of our great surety, a righteousness which as we have seen, answers and honours every demand of the law. This righteousness is imputed unto us, and made ours, by the free gift of God; and thus we are justified by grace. It is received by us, and accepted on our part, by faith in that testimony of God which reveals it, and offers it to us,—and thus we are justified by faith. We are justified actually, in the righteousness of Christ, which is given to us freely by his grace, and received by us thankfully, by faith in his communications, and a trust in his power. This faith works by love, and purifies the heart,—

and is manifested in obedience to God: and thus our participation in the righteousness of Christ, is made evident, by the fruits in which it results. And in this sense, we are ultimately justified by the testimony of our works, and not our faith only.

But that we may be justified before God, the law which can make nothing perfect, brings us to Christ. It sends us to ask for, and to receive, his perfect and accepted righteousness, to be counted unto us, as ours. It bids us to obtain a full title to acceptance with God, in this perfect obedience of his, which he offers unto us,—and the worth of which it acknowledges and proclaims. It strips us of every thing of our own, and directs us to become engrafted into Christ, that we may derive from his fulness, the blessings which are laid up in him for us, by the Father's grace. When we have accepted these glad tidings, and received by faith the offer of righteousness, which God has thus freely made in his dear Son, the law sets us at liberty. We are no longer in bondage. We are no longer under the law, but under grace. We are now one with Christ. His righteousness hath become ours, and we are accepted in it. All his power and love are exercised for our benefit, and in our behalf; and being justified by faith, we have peace with God, through our Lord Jesus Christ. "The law of the Spirit of life in Christ Jesus, hath made us free from the law of sin and death." Having received this inestimable gift, we are to stand fast in the liberty wherewith Christ hath made us free, and not to be entangled again by a yoke of bondage. "Being justified by faith, we rejoice in hope of the glory of God."

III. Now that you have considered the method and object of this guiding power of the law,—I would urge upon you, an acceptance of the instruction which it offers to you. Other teachers may speak in far milder terms,—and accommodate their instructions far more, to the dispositions of a carnal mind. They may tell you, of the excellence of human character, and the value of human works;—of the vast mercy of God which will not allow the condemnation of sinful man; —and of the lessened demands upon man, and the lowered standard of obedience, which the Saviour of men has introduced. If you listen to them, and abide by their guidance, it will be to your ruin. Dependance upon your own character before God, will be destruction to you forever. Whatever standard you may establish for yourselves,—when you try yourselves by it, you will find that your own system of obedience shuts you up under sin. Which of you has acted fully up to the light which he has enjoyed, and has done every thing which he believed to be required of him, in the way in which he believed it to be required? Which of you, would dare to stand by this trial,—and have his everlasting destiny fixed according to it,—even from the testimony of a single day, or a single hour of his life? Nay, you cannot imagine a standard of character, in any degree, according to your own views, honourable to God, which would not place you under immediate condemnation. What can you have therefore of your own? Or how can your salvation be in any degree, derived from your own obedience? The utmost attainments which you can ever make in holiness, are nothing before God: —nor is a single act of it, free from the defilement of sin.

But why do I speak of holiness in this connexion? Unsanctified nature in man has no holiness. All possible obedience to God results from the vital union of your souls to Christ,—in which you are justified before God. You can have no holiness of character, till you have thus renounced yourselves entirely,—and fled for refuge, to the blessed hope which is here set before you. This is the very first work of obedience demanded of you. Until this is done, every thing you do is in a state of rebellion, and every aspect of your character exhibits rebellion against God. Until salvation has thus actually visited your souls, you obey God in nothing. You are under the law condemned. But when the day-spring from on high thus comes to you,—you are alive to God, and accepted with him through his grace,—without the least reference to any fact concerning you, but the simple one, that your are found in Christ, clothed with the righteousness of God by faith.

The salvation of man is thus wholly of grace. His natural condition is entire ruin. O, may God be graciously pleased to impress these truths upon your minds, and enable you to receive and cherish them! Like the Israelites bitten by the fiery serpents,—you are incapable of restoring yourselves, to health,—or of finding a healing balm throughout the earth. Death is sweeping you off in swift succession,—and alas! whither is it bearing you? What but everlasting death is to be the result of your ruined condition? But is there no remedy? Let Moses be your guide to Christ. As Moses lifted up the serpent in the wilderness, that the perishing multitude might look upon it and live,—even so hath hath the Son of man been lifted up, that whosoever believeth in him, should not perish,—but have everlasting life. This day is this transaction renewed in your midst. Behold the Lord Jesus Christ, is set forth among you,—crucified for your sins. There is no other name under heaven, given among men, whereby you can be saved. The law which furnishes no life,—would guide you to Christ, who hath life in himself, abundantly. Behold the eternal Son of God, lifted up upon the cross;—bearing the burden of your sins;—made a curse for you;—bruised for your iniquities; presenting his soul an offering for sin! Listen to his gracious invitations. " Look unto me, and be ye saved, all the ends of the earth,—for I am God, and there is none else." "There is no Saviour beside me." Hear the Law and the Gospel uniting in the same testimony from God,—" Believe in the Lord Jesus Christ, and you shall be saved." " All that believe in him, shall be justified from all things." "In the Lord, shall all the seed of Israel be justified and glory." Obey these invitations and testimonies. Cast away all righteousness of your own,—and come to him whom God hath set forth as a propitiation for sins, to declare his righteousness, in their remission. Come, miserable, and poor, and blind, and naked, and cast yourselves down at his feet, to find and receive a free and full salvation. Fly from all self-dependance. Renounce all false views;—and come simply in your guilt to Jesus,—receiving him into your hearts by faith,—and in him rejoicing in hope of the glory of God. "He is the true God, and eternal life. Little children, keep yourselves from idols."

LECTURE VIII.

CHRIST, THE RIGHTEOUSNESS OF THE LAW.

Christ is the end of the law for righteousness, to every one that believeth.—ROMANS, x. 4.

THIS text asserts a fact of unspeakable importance to guilty man. It teaches the full scheme of divine redemption for him, as a rebel against God, and under the condemnation of his law. It comes to him in this lost condition, with the intelligence, that there is a Saviour provided for him by the love of God, in whose power and work, all his necessities may find an adequate and everlasting supply. It proclaims that all fulness dwells in him; and that the demands of the law upon man are answered and removed, by the perfect and everlasting righteousness which he has finished, and which he offers to the acceptance of all who believe in him. The Holy Spirit employs the law as his instrument, to convince the sinner of his certain condemnation in sin, and then to guide him to the Lord Jesus Christ, as the only refuge and security for his soul. He there displays to him the sufficiency and fulness of this Saviour, who has perfected an obedience which meets all the requisitions of the law, and which is freely offered, and fully applied by his power, to every believing soul. Christ is himself the righteousness of the law for man. And the man who has received him, is in possession of a righteousness, which releases him forever from condemnation, and entitles him to a glorious and everlasting reward. His actual work, finished in the days of his humiliation, and now offered to the Father in the glories of his exaltation, is the whole foundation of hope for man,—and the entire ground upon which he may appear in peace before the throne of God. This is the treasure which is offered in the Gospel,—and the simple object for trust and confidence to the Christian heart. This entire perfection of the work of Christ, in meeting the demands of the law, is the subject which is presented for our consideration in the text before us. "Christ is the end of the law for righteousness to every one that believeth." May the same blessed Spirit who applies this finished provision of grace to the sinner's soul, enable us to understand and embrace it.

I. "Christ is the *end of the law.*" The accomplishment or perfection of the law: the end to which its promulgation was directed, and the result which its operation by the power of the Spirit attains. To him, in its communication to man, it was designed to lead, and in him, all its demands and purposes have been fulfilled. Through centuries of its publication to guilty man, the law was travelling forward to reach his manifestation in the fulness of the time. And in him, it finds the actual fulfilment of all its purposes, so that it is satisfied and well pleased in him, and gives place to his gracious and holy dominion forever. Having in its dispensation to a fallen world, brought the redeemed of Christ to him, it had no further work to do; its warfare was accomplished, and its journey at an end. Having as the instrument of the Holy Spirit, brought the sinner's soul in faith to Christ, and witnessed the acceptance of him there, through the grace of God, it has attained its perfect end with him; and rejoices in the glory which it has received from this Almighty conqueror, while it delivers up to him, the subjects of his grace.

1. Christ, is the end, *to which, the law as a dispensation was designed to lead.* The full redemption which divine wisdom and love had already provided, and laid up in him, ready to be revealed in the appointed time, was the point in

view, in all its promulgations to mankind. The publication of the precepts of holiness in the moral law was to lead the hope of the guilty to him. It was not designed to open a way of safety and life to transgressors in their own obedience. Its purpose was directly the reverse. It invited none. It faithfully and solemnly warned all, to fly from its sentence, and from the attempt to gain acceptance by fulfilling it. By exhibiting the perfect spotlessness which was required in acceptable obedience, and displaying the impossibility, that man should ever accomplish it by any works of his own, it urged forward the desires of men for salvation, to some other source. The law was thus added, or proclaimed anew to man from time to time, because of transgressions,—to convince him of his guilt;—and to witness and minister from generation to generation, to the coming of that promised seed, in whom the righteousness of God should be manifested, and the hope of man should be found. It thus constrained every believer in the divine promise, to look forward to him; making him the desire of all nations;—and causing him to be looked for and welcomed, by all who were waiting for consolation, and redemption from the burden of guilt. He was the treasure which it was pressing forward to attain. He was the haven of rest, in which it desired to land its subjects in safety at the last;—and its purpose and operation would be incomplete, till he should come, in whom it had pleased the Father, that all fulness should dwell.

The rites and ceremonies which were appended to this law were also designed to lead to Christ. Every sacrifice offered with fire, from the time of Abel, pointed to him, and was but an unmeaning rite, except as the conscience of the offerer acknowledged guilt, and his faith rested upon the one great sacrifice divinely provided, and divinely promised. The purifications and washings appointed for Israel, the construction of the tabernacle and the temple, the habitual worship which was celebrated in them, and the multiplied ordinances which were appended to this whole system, were designed to lead the mind to him, in whom all righteousness should be fulfilled, and complete redemption should be found. These were all shadows, of good things to come, which were already laid up in the Lamb slain from the foundation of the world, and would be revealed in his manifestation to men. They made nothing perfect in themselves. They were like guide posts upon a journey, fulfilling their office, by directing faith to him, in whom the traveller should find actual redemption, and eternal peace. As they are viewed in this connexion, they are beautifully intelligible, and highly instructive. If they are separated from this key of explanation, they are but inexplicable and arbitrary appointments, and a yoke which none were able to bear. Christ is the end, in which they were all to meet, and to be perfected.

2. Christ is the end, *in whom all the demands of the law, are actually accomplished;* so that the law sees in him its real and entire perfection. He has fulfilled all the shadows and ceremonies which were appointed to lead to him. He has finished the purposes which they designated, and has set them aside forever. That which is perfect has come, and that which was in part has been done away. The predictions and illustrations which the types and figures of the Old Testament gave, of the circumstances, character, and work of the Redeemer of men, have been fully realized. He is the Great High Priest, the only sacrifice, the true paschal lamb, who has by the offering of himself once for all, perfected forever them that are sanctified. He has opened in himself, the real fountain for sin, and for uncleanness. And while there was nothing in sacrifices or burnt offerings which God could accept, or have pleasure therein, HE has done the will of God in a body which was prepared for him ; and having offered himself without spot to God, to obtain eternal redemption for us,

he has fulfilled the law of ordinances, and shines forth in the fulness of grace, as the perfection of all its instructions and promises.

He is the actual completion of all the demands of the moral law. Both its precepts, and its penalty, have been fulfilled and answered by him, to the utmost of their claims. The law required a spotless righteousness, an obedience which should be in the minutest point, unblameable;—and Jesus was made under the law, for the attainment of this object, and has rendered an actual obedience to every part of the law's demands. Because he was so exalted and holy, and was in himself under no subjection to the law, his obedience was perfectly voluntary and disinterested, and has thus magnified the law, and made it honourable. In his actual submission to every precept of holiness, and his entire fulfilment of them all, as the representative for man, Jesus has become the entire perfection of the law, and has glorified it in the shining excellence of his life.

And while he thus perfectly fulfilled the law, so that it had no claim upon him in the shape of any penalty for sin, he yet gave himself to be dealt with, and punished as a criminal. He received the full punishment for transgression, and died an accursed death under the condemnation of the violated law. He did no violence, neither was deceit found in his mouth, yet it pleased the Lord to bruise him, and to put him to grief, and to cut him off, out of the land of the living. But he was wounded for our transgressions, he was bruised for our iniquities, and the Lord hath laid on him the iniquity of us all. He furnished the only possible instance, in which the same being should conform perfectly to the precepts of the law, and still endure the curse and penalty of their violation. The obedience which he offered, was the one perfect obedience which the law required. The sufferings and death, which he endured, were the one condemnation and curse, which the law laid upon transgression. This actual penalty in all its sorrows, and in the full power of its vengeance, he assumed and sustained. By his infinite dignity and power, he was able to bear them, and to triumph in his suffering. "See" says Luther, "by what means, these two things, so contrary, and so repugnant, may be reconciled in the one person Christ! Not only my sins, and thine, but also the sins of this whole world, either past, present, or to come, take hold upon him, go out to condemn him, and do indeed condemn him. But because in the self-same person which is the highest, the greatest, and the only sinner, there is also an invincible and everlasting righteousness; therefore these two do encounter each other; the highest, the greatest, and the only sin, and the highest, the greatest, and the only righteousness. Here, one of them must needs be overcome, and give place to the other. Righteousness is everlasting, immortal, invincible. Therefore in this combat, sin must needs be vanquished and killed; and righteousness must overcome, and live, and reign. So in Christ, all sin is vanquished, killed, and buried; and righteousness remaineth a conqueror, and reigneth forever." "The sins of all the world," says the excellent Bishop Hopkins, "assembled and met together upon him, so that there was never so much wickedness represented at once as in his most holy and sacred person. The sins of all ages, and of all persons, were here contracted together. And all those treasures of wrath which were particularly due to each of these sins, were all emptied forth on him. As in his own person, he sustained the guilt of all, so in his own person, he suffered the wrath and curse, that was due unto all. He suffered at once, for every one, that, which else, every one must have suffered eternally in hell."

This two-fold demand which the law made upon man, Jesus accomplished in man's behalf. The hour in which he became a voluntarily subjected being, he began this unconstrained humiliation for man. And every moment of his life, was a part of his one great offering, for the transgressions of his creatures. His infinitely exalted character and rank added a dignity and worth, to his obedience and sufferings, which made them of more value, and more honourable, than would have been the personal submission of the whole human race. The law can make no demands upon man, which this Almighty Redeemer has not fully answered. He has provided a perfect righteousness, which is its perfection and end. All that it sought, it has found in him. It therefore yields the government of believing men, to be upon his shoulder, who hath ransomed them from a curse, by being made a curse for them. Its dominion is finished. Its dispensation has passed away. And Christ has become its end, for righteousness, to every one that believeth.

II. This leads to our second point, *the purpose for which Christ thus became the completion of the law.* "Christ is the end of the law *for righteousness.*" This was the only possible purpose of such a subjection. The single term righteousness comprises the whole circle of the law's demands; and the whole compass of a sinner's wants. The law could ask for nothing but a righteousness which should be a full satisfaction of its penalties, and a perfect conformity to its precepts. When this perfect submission, conformity, and endurance was formed, the law was satisfied, and could make no farther demands. It asked from man a spotless obedience. It was satisfied and honoured, when the covenant representative of man rendered the obedience which it thus required. The sinner under the solemn condemnation of the law, wanted nothing but a righteousness, which could meet the requirements of the power that held him in bondage. And though the law required this to be found in himself alone, yet the bringing in of the better hope which is offered in the covenant of grace, allowed him to find this righteousness in a surety in his behalf. But the necessity for such a righteousness for him could never be set aside. Whoever should become his surety, must become in every point of submission to the law, his substitute also. And in the attainment of this righteousness in the person of another, competent to render it, his release and liberty were made secure to him forever. The violation of the law made an atonement and expiation necessary, to honour its justice and truth, if sin should be pardoned. Whenever the Saviour came, who was to be the sinner's substitute, he must furnish this atonement, without which there could be no remission, in order to bring in a righteousness for man. The relation in which the transgressor stood to the law, made a priest and sacrifice indispensable to the righteousness which he must have. And when that priest and sacrifice appeared, there was an entire imputation of the sinner's guilt and responsibility to him. He assumed the burden. He finished the purpose for which it was assumed. In this endurance of the sinner's penalty, he made a satisfaction to the law, and thus far, brought in a righteousness for man; a righteousness which sinful man might successfully plead, for the pardon of his guilt, and the deliverance of his soul from bondage and punishment.

But the Saviour came not, merely to release man from the bondage of condemnation and punishment; he was also to bestow upon him, an inheritance of life eternal. This was to be a free gift to man, through the abounding of divine grace. But it must rest upon the perfect obedience which the law required, for life could be obtained in no other way. The precepts of the law must be fulfilled for man, as well as the penalties. To accomplish this righteousness, Jesus was made under the law; and every thing which he did and suffered as man, contributed to make up and finish this work of obedience, which the case of man required. His labours, instructions, and miracles; his pains of body, and agony and darkness of mind; his acts of obedience, and his experience of deprivations and sorrows; were all united to perfect him in this assumed responsibility; to constitute him who was Jehovah, the righteousness of man; and to render him able to save unto the uttermost, all who should come unto God through him. In his work of voluntary mediation, there is a completed righteousness, a treasure of merit, infinitely honourable to God, and altogether sufficient for man. We stand complete, when we stand in him. While the Father beheld with joy, the glorious undertaking, in which he was engaged, saying; "this is my beloved Son, in whom I am well pleased." The holy law, under which he was subjected, receives his spotless work of merit, and proclaims, "In this righteousness I am magnified and made honourable."

This satisfaction of our Blessed Redeemer to the law, is perfect and entire. It answered every claim which was made upon man, for obedience and suffering. The result was therefore a perfect righteousness, a finished conformity to the law. But it was not for himself. The law had no claims upon him. His obedience and sufferings were entirely voluntary. He fulfilled them, from no necessity of obligation, but in a free covenant of love for man. He lived and laboured, not in vain, fighting as one that beateth the air. It was for a seed that he was to see, and in whom he was to be satisfied for the travail of his soul, while they were to be justified by the knowledge of him. He thus became the perfection of the law, and in possession of a righteousness which fulfilled it, in behalf of those, whom the Father had given to him, whose nature he assumed, and whose responsibility he covenanted to bear.

III. This introduces our third point of remark,—*the persons for whom all this was done.* "Christ is the end of the law for righteousness, to every one that believeth." Faith,—faith in him, in his promises, and work, and power,—is the instrument, and the single instrument, by which sinful men are made partakers, of the righteousness which he thus possesses.

The condition of fallen man, is universal guilt and condemnation. Every individual of this family is born under the curse of a violated law, and in a state of rebellion against God. For the world in this condition, the Son of God has died. He has provided for a race universally guilty, a remedy universally applicable. He has rendered the salvation of man, consistent with the character and government of God. He has become a propitiation for the sins of the whole world. He has thus a righteousness in his possession, sufficient for all, and offered to all, as the gift of grace to them. The satisfaction of the law which was indispensable, to render the salvation of a single sinner consistent with the character of God, was equally adequate for all to whom it should be applied. Every barrier which the truth and justice of God had interposed, was thus removed, and the way was perfectly opened for the salvation, of all who should be persuaded to come thus unto God. But the actual result and limit of this divine provision is stated in our text; "Christ is the end of the law for righteousness to every one that believeth." He becomes the personal righteousness only of those, who receive him, and rest upon him in faith. "To as many as receive him, to them gives he the privilege to become the sons of God." His offering has been set forth, as a propitiation, to declare the righteousness of God, that God might still be just, and the justifier of him who believeth in Jesus. The way of safety is now perfectly laid open; and man is required to believe the record which God hath given concerning his Son. There is no difficulty in the sinner's path, if he will be persuaded to " know and believe the love which God hath to him;" if he will thankfully receive the testimony of Jesus, as infallibly true, and trust himself to its fulfilment with undoubting certainty.

"Christ has become the end of the law for righteousness." Does sinful man believe this fact? Does he cease therefore, to look for acceptance before God, to any works of his own,—and simply hope, in the righteousness which has been thus finished for him, by Jesus Christ the Lord? Does he in this faith, devote himself in newness of life, to this glorious Lord? Then Christ is the end of the law for righteousness to *him*. The righteousness which Christ has, is his. Every obstacle to his salvation has been removed. He is accepted, crowned with full redemption, and saved with an everlasting salvation, in that covenant Lord, to whom the Holy Spirit has thus brought him, and united him in confidence and love. When he thus believes the testimony of God, and receives the record, which God hath given of his Son,—he is made one with Christ; and all the merit of the work of Christ is counted to him, as his own. As Christ was clothed with his guilt, so is he completely clothed with the righteousness of Christ. For him, there is an end of the law, a perfection of its demands, and a conclusion of its dominion, in Christ, in whom he believes, and with whom he stands, by faith. This faith meets the requisitions of the law, by referring them all to Christ, in whom they have been fulfilled and completed, and pleading this fulfilment by him, as its own. And this plea is acknowledged, as wholly sufficient,—Christ is accepted, as the end of the law, and an everlasting righteousness, for the believer,—and he being justified by faith, has peace with God.

If man will not receive this offered grace, nor believe these blessed facts which God has thus announced, the simple consequence is, Christ is no righteousness for him, and there is no end of the law in his behalf. He remains under its dominion and its curse. He renounces an offered redemption, and sinks again in bondage. He refuses the merit which grace provides, and comes before God, upon the ground of his own merit and strength. He has loved darkness rather than light, and this is his condemnation. He lives and dies under a curse. He is condemned already, and the wrath of God abideth on him. He is without the possibility of hope; cast into a prison, from which he can in no wise come out, until he has paid the uttermost farthing. All this is the simple result of his refusal of that righteousness, which is offered to all who believe, and of his rejection of that redemption which is provided by the grace of God, and urged upon the acceptance of sinful man.

IV. In concluding this important subject, we may remark:

How glorious and consistent is that scheme of salvation which is presented in the Gospel! It offers simply, JESUS CHRIST,—an Almighty Saviour,—all and in all, in himself. It takes us just where it finds us, in a state of entire guilt and ruin; condemned by the holy law of God, to eternal perdition; and utterly incapable, of procuring any justification, by our own obedience. In this condition, it announces to us, a Saviour divinely great and glorious, who has assumed our nature,—to become a perfect substitute for us, and the atonement for our sins;—and who offers us in himself, everlasting reconciliation with God. God's acceptance of this amazing propitiation is solemnly proclaimed. The method in which we are to become interested in it, by a simple faith in Christ, and confidence of ourselves to him, it discloses with precision and clearness. The simple demand which it makes, is for thankful, humble, faith in Christ. The promise which it gives is, that then, he shall be our righteousness, and we shall be complete in him. The simple direction which it gives us, having thus believed,—is, to make confession with our mouth, of the Lord whom we have received, and to walk by the guidance of his Holy Spirit, in all his commandments and ordinances, blameless. What perfect consistency, unity, and efficiency, is there in such a system! How highly glorious it is to the blessed God! How unspeakably precious to guilty man! How important is that simple living faith, which it requires, and to which all its promises are made! And while superstition, and self-righteousness, and unbelief, would reject this all-sufficient Lord, or mingle up with him, the merit of works, and the assumed, undue power of ordinances,—how vastly does the obligation increase upon us, to state this divine system of grace and truth, plainly, openly, and uniformly; and to urge upon all men, a free and thankful acceptance, of what God has so freely and fully provided! How awful is their condition, who cast away this hope, and thus despise the divine character, and affront the majesty of God! For them, there remaineth no more sacrifice for sin, but a certain fearful looking for, of judgment and fiery indignation. He that hath the Son of God, hath life; but he that hath not the Son, hath not life,—cannot see life,—but the wrath of God abideth on him. This blessed hope in Christ, is set before you,—make it the anchor of your souls, sure and steadfast; and you shall find an abundant entrance into the rest, whither your great Redeemer hath gone before you.

LECTURE IX.

THE LAW, THE CHRISTIAN'S RULE OF LIFE.

Being not without law to God,—but under the law to Christ.—1. CORINTHIANS, IX. 21.

IN this expression, St. Paul describes the exact condition of a true believer in the Lord Jesus Christ. He introduces it, as a parenthesis, in the midst of a discourse upon the freedom which he claimed in his ministry of the Gospel. He declares his cheerful conformity to the various habits and prejudices, of those to whom he ministered, that he might be made the instrument of winning them to Christ,—so that though he was wholly free from the authority of men, yet he willingly submitted himself to their customs and desires, that he might gain the more. But he would not have this varying compliance with the feelings of others in things indifferent, construed into a neglect on his part, of the unvarying authority and law of God, as if he were without any abiding rule in this relation.

He felt himself entirely free from all those appointments and precepts which had been given to his nation, that had been fulfilled and ended in Christ. But to the permanent precepts of holiness, which God had proclaimed in connexion with these, he could not be indifferent. They were written in his heart, with a divine power. They governed his conduct with an unceasing constraint. His joyful acceptance, of the hopes and promises of the Gospel, had confirmed and increased the power of these precepts over his heart. He was " not without law to God," because he was "under the law to Christ." The Saviour whom he served, and in whom, he had his whole relation to God, had renewed for him, the same perfect standard of obedience, and had added new and more powerful motives to lead him to love and regard it. He thus describes the condition of every believer; entire and everlasting freedom from the law, as a dispensation of condemnation and death,—but everlasting and delightful subjection to the law, as a rule of conformity to Christ; leading to entire love to God, and universal love to men for his sake. The great salvation of the Lord Jesus, though it is founded upon a perfect satisfaction of the law, in all its penalties and precepts, as a righteousness for man,—adopts all the holy commandments of the law, as the rule of life and conduct, for those who have accepted this righteousness, and been made partakers of this salvation.

This is the condition of every justified man. He has been delivered from the bondage of the law. He is made free from its denunciations. It has no penalties to demand of him, and no judgments to inflict upon him. It has no longer dominion over him. He is not under the law. He is in possession of a divine righteousness through the gift of grace, which meets all its claims, and sets him free from its power forever. But he is not without law in his relation to God. He has been placed under a new dispensation, which furnishes new obligations to a holy obedience to God, presents new motives to this obedience, and gives him new power to put them into actual effect. He is under the law to Christ, who has bought him with a price, and perpetuated and confirmed upon him, every divine commandment. The motives to obedience are changed,—the influence and effects of this obedience are also changed,—but the rule of holiness remains the same, and in the same conformity to it, he glorifies God in his body and his spirit which are his.

The man who has truly embraced the Gospel of the Lord Jesus, has cast out all dependance upon his own obedience; and rests his whole hope of justification, before God, upon the perfect righteousness of his divinely appointed Saviour. He does not expect to earn a single hour of peace or glory, by his own holiness of character. The obedience in which he trusts, and in which he envelopes himself by faith, was long since finished. He cannot add an iota of merit to that great offering which has been once for all, made for his soul, and which has perfected his title, and his hope forever. The inheritance has been given him by promise, through grace; and he labours and strives, and obeys, from love and gratitude to him who hath bestowed it, and that he may become prepared and capable, for the enjoyment of that glory, for which he is apprehended of Christ Jesus. But as his rule of character, as the governing standard of his life,—the law hath dominion over him, so long as he liveth. By its precepts he is led to bring forth fruits of holiness unto God. And perfectly righteous as he is, in the imputed righteousness of his Lord, he labours to become increasingly holy in the spirit and character of his mind, that he may honour him who hath chosen him to be his servant.

To this view of the divine law, I desire now to call your attention. It is *the perfect rule of life to every believer in the Lord Jesus;* governing him, as the declaration of his Saviour's will; and made by the renewing of the Holy Spirit, the standard of his choice, and the path in which he delights to walk. In the work of justification, our own obedience forms no part. Our righteousness, and the righteousness of Christ our Lord, are opposites here. We have renounced the one, that we may gain the other. We are taught to " count all things loss, that we may win Christ, and be found in him, not having our own righteousness which is of the law, but that which is through the faith of Christ, the righteousness of God by faith." We are accepted in his obedience alone. We are thus accepted, when with our hearts, we believe in him. But being accepted, and having "obtained access through him, into this grace, wherein we stand, rejoicing in hope of the glory of God," the precepts of God's holy law become the rule of our life;—we are made ready and able to say, "O, how I love thy law; it is my meditation all the day."

I. The divine law is *the believer's rule of life.* It is the perfect and unalterable standard, to which his character is to become conformed. In itself it is perfectly excellent and holy. It is a description and transcript of the character and perfections of the Creator himself. A conformity to its precepts, is an attainment of the pure and holy image of God. Righteousness is an entire fulfilment of these precepts. Holiness is a conformity to the image of God in which they are thus embodied. And though man can never have this perfect righteousness in himself, the believer increasingly attains this holiness, this conformity to the perfect image, after which he is renewed by the Spirit of God. The one principle which fulfils this law, and marks this divine image, is love. "Love is of God, and every one that loveth, is born of God, and knoweth God; he that loveth not, knoweth not God, for God is love." The more we gain this love to God,—and this love to others, for his sake,—the more are we conformed to his image, and the more fully do we honour and obey him. "Hereby shall all men know that ye are my disciples," saith the Lord Jesus, "that ye love one another as I have loved you." This holy requirement of love, entire and unlimited love, was laid upon man by his Creator, as it was laid upon every other intelligent creature that he formed. No change in man's circumstances or condition, could ever alter the holy and perfect standard which God had thus set up before him. Whatever station we might occupy in the scale of intelligent being, it must be every where, equally our duty, to maintain, and cultivate, and exercise, this disposition of universal love. The obligation to this, could not be set aside, without authorizing that destruction of the image of God, which sin accomplishes, and robbing God, of the glory which is his due. When we have been delivered from the condemnation of sin, and are partakers of the mercies of God in the Gospel,—and a new heart "under the law to Christ" has been given to us, the constraint of this obligation to universal love, is immeasurably increased, by the vast privileges which redemption has bestowed, and the exalted motives which it has furnished. No being in the universe has received such benefits from God, as a sinner who has been ransomed by the blood of his dear Son. No being therefore, is under such obligations to love God with all his powers, and with an unceasing, everlasting love. This love, God requires of us, according to the blessings we have received, and the Gospel which brings his greatest blessings, his unspeakable gift to man, places this standard before us, with new authority. According to its principles, we are to serve God, in newness of spirit. In conformity to its pattern, we are to be renewed from day to day. By this increasing conformity, we become more and more like God, and prepared for his kingdom. And though we are forgiven and accepted in Christ our Lord, alone, the holy law is still our rule; and the freeness of pardon, and the fulness of our salvation, make us to love it, and to strive to follow it, yet more earnestly. The standard is unchanged; but we have received that love for its holiness, which casts out all fear of its judgments, and urges and enables us, to render the very obedience which before, we had neither the wish, nor the ability to present.

II. Our conformity to this law, was *one great object of our redemption by the Lord Jesus.* In all that he did and suffered for his people, he purposed their restoration to holiness. He did not labour, merely to rescue them from death as a punishment; but to deliver them also from the bondage, and power of sin which had deserved it. For this, he was called JESUS, "because he should save his people from their sins." For this, "God raised up a mighty salvation, that we being delivered from the fear of our enemies, might serve him without fear, in holiness and righteousness before him, all the days of our life." To have delivered a rebellious family, merely from the ruin which they deserved, would have been a partial object;—the great design was to bring back these rebels, to a state of obedience and love; to take away the spirit of hostility which had governed them; to restore them to the one great family of God; to renew the peace and harmony of a disordered universe; to stop the breach which the waters of contention had made; and to bring into one, all conflicting feelings and purposes, in Jesus Christ the Lord. This was the great purpose, for which the Redeemer "gave himself for us, that he might redeem us from all iniquity, and purify unto himself, a peculiar people, zealous of good works." He has restored redeemed man, to a voluntary submission to that holy government of God, which is the source of universal peace. He has himself received this government, as the ruler of redeemed men; and "died, and risen, and revived, that he might be Lord, both of the dead, and of the living." He cannot rule in mercy, over a world that rejects him, and still lies under the wicked one. Over them, he must rule with a rod of iron, and dash them in pieces, like a potter's vessel. But he has purchased for himself, an universal Church, an assembly of elected, pardoned sinners; that he might govern them in holiness, and present them unto God, holy, and without spot or blemish. This sanctifying of sinful men, is one great end of his redeeming, gathering, and reigning over them;—and as he sees this work advance, and sinful men coming more and more under his control, under the law to him,—he sees of the travail of his soul, and is satisfied. He rejoices over every ransomed sinner, whom he brings in triumph, to the glories of a heavenly home, renewed after the perfect image of God. He presents each one to the Father, as the accomplishment of his great design, in making his soul an offering for sin, and consenting to be numbered with transgressors. And as he sees the spotless character of holiness, impressed upon glorified saints,—and increasingly manifest in every child of God on earth,—he delights in the attainment of this great end of his manifestation in the flesh,—and his humiliation in death. For this, he has plucked rebels, as brands from the fire, and brought them home from condemnation, that they might gain an everlasting conformity to the image of God, in an obedience to the commands of his perfect law.

III. Our obedience to the law in its precepts, *is the purpose for which we are personally delivered from its condemnation.* The Son of God hath purchased us, by the offering of himself for us. He hath freely bestowed upon us, the liberty of the Gospel,—so that we are no longer in bondage under condemnation, but are in freedom under grace. But we have not been made free by grace, that we may continue in sin, but that we may walk before him in newness of life. God hath sent his own Son for us, in the likeness of sinful flesh, that the righteousness of the law might be fulfilled in us, who walk not after the flesh, but after the Spirit. While we remain under the power, and in the bondage of the law, we can never obey its holy commandments. It can offer us no assistance or strength. It cannot make us acceptable or holy in the sight of God. It acts as an hard task-master, requiring us to make brick, and furnishing us with no straw. It censures our disobedience; it condemns our defects. But it cannot repair the one, or relieve the other. But when we have embraced the liberty and life which the Gospel gives, all the help we need, is freely bestowed. We are then enabled to offer that obedience, sincere and spiritual, however partial and defective still, which we could not before present to God. The purpose for which we have been thus set at liberty from condemnation, is that we may thus obey the divine commands. There is a race to be run, and a contest to be maintained;— but it is in vain to command the culprit who is in his dungeon, bound hand and foot with chains, either to run or fight. When his fetters are loosed, and his prison doors are opened, he may be successfully urged to arise and strive. Equally unable are we to honour God in obedience, while we are held under condemnation. But Christ hath broken up this bondage wherein we were held, and hath borne the condemnation for us. We are therefore at liberty; and the object of this liberty, is our new obedience, that we may be under the law to Christ, and live unto him, who hath loved us, and given himself for us. The value and importance of the law as a rule of life, are thus magnified and displayed. It is the measure and standard, by which having been made free from the curse, we are to bring forth fruit unto God.

IV. This obedience to the law as a rule of life, is *one of the chief blessings promised in the Gospel.* It was to be one blessed result of publishing salvation in the Lord Jesus Christ, that God would put a new heart into those who received this offer of grace, and renew a right spirit within them; that he would write his laws upon their hearts, and in their minds; and cause them to walk in his statutes, and to keep his judgments, to do them; that he would cleanse them from all their uncleanness and sins, and put his Spirit to dwell within them. These promises convey an assurance of the sanctification of the people of God under the Gospel, according to that standard of holiness, of which the law is the measure and rule. When we truly accept the unsearchable riches of Christ, which are offered us in the Gospel, we are thus formed anew, in a life of holy obedience; and these gracious promises are fulfilled. The power of sin is broken in every converted heart;—and the influence of sin, and the disposition to yield to it, are conquered, in proportion as we are sanctified by God's Holy Spirit, and renewed after his image. We are thus engaged in a new obedience of the divine commands. This personal holiness of character is a covenanted privilege of the Gospel. It is not made a condition of his acceptance of us, but a result and effect of it. Our obedience to his law, is thus infallibly secured, by God himself undertaking to work it in us, and for us, by the power of his own Spirit.

> He wills that I shall holy be,
> What can resist his will?
> The counsel of his grace in me,
> He surely will fulfil.

It is his determined purpose to present his Church, at last, without spot, or blemish, or any such thing. The solemn covenant which the blessed Saviour makes, with every sinner in whose heart he dwells as the hope of glory, is, that sin shall not have dominion over him, for he is not under the law, but under grace. When he was under the law, sin had dominion over him;—but when he has fled for refuge to the blessed hope which is offered to him in the Gospel, this dominion is destroyed. His new obedience is promised to him, by God himself, and he shall be holy because God is holy. Certainly no higher honour could be put upon the law, as the Christian's rule of life,—than this constituting obedience to its precepts, one of the chief blessings promised in the Gospel; than this assurance, that in the full redemption which should be effected for sinful man by the Son of God, they should be made holy, and without blame before him in love, by divine power, according to their desire, and after the precepts of his law. In this deliverance of our souls from bondage, which he has promised, and effected, so far are we from being allowed to sin, because grace abounds, or set loose from the law, to follow the motions of unholiness in our own corrupt nature, because our salvation is free, that the very obedience which the law demanded in vain, the Gospel fully secures and promises. It thus perpetuates the law, as a rule of life, for those who receive its offered mercies; and magnifies and exalts, its holy character, and righteous authority, by enabling man to meet it fully, and to answer its demands.

V. This obedience to the law, as a rule of life, *our Lord has made a characteristic of his disciples.* "By this," says he, "shall all men know that ye love me, if ye keep my commandments." " Ye are my friends, if ye do whatsoever I command you." " By their fruits ye shall know them." Personal holiness of character, or real, spiritual obedience to the commands of God, is the mark of true discipleship to Christ. No professions of regard or devotion, can testify the sincerity of love. No sufferings in the flesh, though they amount to martyrdom for his sake, can form an accurate indication of the state of our hearts before him; if a cordial love for him, and a vigilant pursuit after holiness in obedience to him, be wanting. The only adequate evidence, that we have been freed from the condemnation of the law, and have been made partakers of real and lasting liberty in the Gospel, is to be found in our holy obedience to God, our supreme love for him, and our universal love to men, actuating us in all the relations and duties of life. Every man who has truly embraced the Gospel, will be a truly holy man,—nor can any man be a true believer, who is not so. The grace of God which bringeth salvation, has visited the believer's heart, for this very purpose, that he might be taught and enabled, to deny ungodliness and worldly lusts, and to live soberly, righteously, and godly in the world. If a man is still voluntarily a sinful man, walking in the lusts of the flesh,—fulfilling the desires of the flesh, and of the mind,—it is vain for him to profess, or to confide in, a supposed deliverance from the condemnation of the law, or an interest, in the dominion and righteousness of the Lord Jesus Christ. Conformity to Christ is the only proof of the dwelling, or of the operations, of the Spirit of Christ in the heart. Every thing is uncertain, as an evidence of grace, but the love which fulfils the law. They that are Christ's, have crucified the flesh, with the affections and lusts. Against such there is no law. Being bought with a price,—redeemed by the precious blood of Christ, a lamb without blemish, and without spot, they are delivered from the law in all its penalties, and are thus enabled, in a new and holy obedience to God, to be under the law to Christ. From them, this new obedience is required, as the evidence of their character, and of the truth of their profession, and the law as the rule of their life is adopted and confirmed.

VI. Our Blessed Lord has displayed the importance of the divine law as a rule of life for his disciples, *in the explanation and summary which he has given of its precepts.* He came, not to destroy the authority and constraint of the law, but to fulfil its requisitions, and to magnify and honour its holiness, and to confirm the obligation of its precepts. He declares the existence and operation of this rule of life to be more permanent than the heavens and the earth. He illustrated the perfectness, and spirituality, of its character and commands. He shewed that their influence extended even to the desires and thoughts of the heart. He renounced entirely, the limitations which men were disposed to affix to these precepts, in the mere outward and apparent conduct of the life. He taught that no character was desirable, or to be approved in man, but that which is conformed in sincerity and holiness to the will of God, who searches the hearts; and that no apparent character can be of any avail, while the spirit and life of true obedience within, are wanting. Thus the Saviour extended and explained the precepts of the law, adopting it, not in the letter only, but in the spirit, as the rule by which his disciples were to be governed, as the established standard of personal character in the church which he was to gather upon the earth. When he was asked to decide the controversy among the Jews, which was the chief of the divine commandments, he selected the two precepts which required universal love,—precepts which must govern as long as there are intelligent beings to love or to be loved; as the precepts which furnish a compendium of the whole law, and a key to its adequate and proper interpretation. He thus displayed and exalted it, as a rule of life for his people, and enforced and illustrated it as the standard of government, for all who should embrace his Gospel and profess to follow him. The Saviour requires perfect, spiritual holiness in all who profess his name, to be attained by the transforming power of his own divine Spirit. And though they may come far short of this in fact, yet their efforts are to be still directed to this attainment; they are to acknowledge and feel their unworthiness and guilt in every failure in it; and to throw themselves humbly upon him for pardon and acceptance, because they can have no merit of their own. But though our highest efforts and best attainments are feeble and worthless, and we are in no degree to look to our own obedience as a foundation for hope, we can never be allowed to set before ourselves, a lower standard and purpose, than perfect holiness of character, in a perfect obedience of the law, as our rule of life. We are always to seek, to have every thought of our hearts, brought into captivity to the obedience of Christ; and to exercise unceasing vigilance and labour that we may be presented before God, perfect in Christ Jesus, not only in the full justification of our persons in his righteousness, but in the perfect conformity of our lives to his example. For this end, we are under the law to Christ, and by its standard, we are created anew, through the power of the Holy Spirit, in works

M*

of holiness, which God hath before ordained, that we should walk in them.

VII. These views display the importance and influence of the law as a rule of life. It is set up, as an eternally unalterable standard. We are redeemed by the Son of God, and have been delivered from its condemnation, that we may walk according to its precepts in newness of life. Our conformity to it, is promised us in the Scriptures, as one of the blessings and privileges of the new covenant, and is made the characteristic of our union with Christ; and for this end the Saviour has illustrated and explained the commands which it imposes. This aspect of the divine law is most important. And though we are set free from its condemnation forever, by the perfect obedience, and the atoning death of our Lord Jesus Christ, we are still under the government of its precepts, as administered and enforced by Christ our Lord forever; and not one jot or tittle of it can be allowed to pass till all be fulfilled.

Let me urge you, not to lower these demands of the law in any aspect of its operation, in your views of its claims. As a covenant and dispensation, it cannot recede from one of its just and righteous demands. They have been perfectly fulfilled in the work of our Lord Jesus Christ. As a rule for personal character in man,—its requsitions are of equal force and permanence. It enjoins upon us, to attain a love for God with all our heart and strength—and to love all others as ourselves. Do not propose to yourselves, any lower standard than this, to govern you in your daily walk in life. Be not satisfied with the standard and judgment of the world around you. Be not contented with the performance of a mere round of outward duties,—or a few kind and beneficent acts. We are to die altogether unto sin,—and to live unto righteousness, with our whole heart and spirit. We are to make it our object, to have the whole body of sin within us, subdued and mortified; to delight ourselves in the law of God in the spirit of our minds,—and to perfect holiness in his fear. While the precepts of the law are our rule,—the life of Christ who hath fulfilled them is our example. We are to walk as he walked; to purify ourselves as he was pure; to be as he was in the world. Nothing must satisfy our desires and determinations, short of absolute perfection of character; longing and labouring ever, to be holy as God is holy, and perfect as our Father in heaven is perfect.

O, let us, then, be willing servants, and cheerful subjects of these divine precepts, and this perfect government! Consider the obedience which God requires of you, perfect freedom, and run the way of his commandments with enlarged and thankful hearts. When this spirit is in the heart, there is liberty and comfort,—and the commandments of God are not grievous. Let me beseech you then, to give yourselves up unreservedly unto God. While we profess the system of truth which has been here laid down, they who do not enter into, or adopt our views, will judge of them, and of us, by the manifest holiness of our own characters and lives. They must see in us, what the real tendency of the truth of Scripture is. The honour of God and of his Gospel depends much upon the character of professing Christians. And I desire that you who profess yourselves to belong to Christ, may be wanting in nothing. Strive to walk worthy of your high vocation in every duty. By abounding in every virtue, and every praise, make it evident, that you have no wish, to sin because grace abounds,— but are cheerfully and wholly under the law to Christ. In this way, are we to put to silence the ignorance of foolish men, to prove ourselves indeed the disciples of Christ, and to be made effectual instruments of doing good to others. Let us press forward unceasingly to attain the measure of the stature of perfect men in Christ Jesus,—and thus labour to honour him, who hath bought us for his glory, in our bodies and spirits which are his.

LECTURE X.

THE WORTH OF MAN'S OBEDIENCE TO THE LAW.

Blessed are they who do his commandments, that they may have a right to the tree of life, and may enter in through the gates into the city.—REVELATIONS, XXII. 14.

The salvation which the Gospel offers to man is entirely free. It is a fundamental principle in it, that it is not of works, lest any man should boast. God hath saved us, not by works of righteousness which we have done, but according to his mercy. Yet the assurance is uttered with equal solemnity and precision, without holiness, no man shall see the Lord. It becomes therefore a most important topic for us to consider, what is the worth of man's obedience? What effect has it upon his salvation? Under what aspect is this obedience required of him? Salvation from sin,—offering everlasting life, and happiness in that life,—is the great promise of the Gospel, and the object to which the Gospel leads our desires and exertions. To attain this blessing, it urges us to forget the things which are behind; to count all other things as loss; to look not at the things which are seen, and are temporal. But while it offers this salvation freely, through the grace of God, it opens but one path to its attainment,—one highway, which is called the way of holiness. This is presented to us in our text. They who do the commandments of God, have a right to the tree of life, and may enter in through the gates into the city.

The everlasting portion of the people of God, which we are thus to seek, is presented to us here, as a dwelling in a city, offering the idea of security to the redeemed soul,—and as partaking of the tree of life, presenting the image of perfect satisfaction and enjoyment. They who are walking in the way which leads to this security and enjoyment,—and are preparing on the earth, to become partakers of this inheritance of the saints in light,—are those who are doing the commandments of God,—to whom his holy law is a rule of life,—and who are renewed in holiness according to its precepts, after the image and example of Christ. While this text sets before us, the two points, of the end of glory which is to be attained, and the way of holiness through which it is to be attained,—it presents as the general subject of this discourse, *the worth and influence of man's personal obedience to the divine law.*

I. The *great end and result* to which the Christian's life on earth is to lead, is *the everlasting security and happiness of heaven,*—an abode in the city of God,—and an eternal nourishment from the tree of life.

1. The blessedness of the saints *is a glorious and everlasting abode;* a dwelling place for the whole assembly and Church of the first born, whose names are written in heaven. The Lord Jesus calls it his "Father's house." One Apostle describes it as a "city which hath foundations,"—"a continuing city,"—"whose builder and maker is God;"—"the Jerusalem which is above;" and another calls it, "the new Jerusalem which descendeth from God out of heaven." The latter writer dwells at length on the circumstances and appearance of this heavenly city;—he describes its walls and gates, and inhabitants, in expressions which are adapted to fill the Christian mind with the most elevated and glorious conceptions;—all combining the two themes of amazing splendour, and immaculate purity. The main idea suggested by this figurative description of the portion of the saints, is perfect and everlast-

ing security. Within walls and bulwarks of salvation, the redeemed soul is defended forever; and by an entrance through the gates which are opened to him, he receives a just and regular admittance to this defence. He has now, as the gift of grace, a kingdom which cannot be removed. He was once wandering abroad, as a guilty and condemned rebel. He fled from the avenger of blood, under a consciousness that he deserved to die. The violated law uttered forth its denunciations against him, and the offended justice of the law-giver demanded the punishment of his sin. The plain in which he was pursued, furnished him no shelter. His own strength supplied him no means of defence. Wearied, desponding, and condemned, he was ready to perish in his guilt, when the glad tidings of the Gospel directed him to a city of refuge,— and urged him to run thither, and be safe. Through the door which was opened, in the offered obedience and death of the Lord Jesus, whose invitations he accepted, and to whom he came for life, he sought and gained a blessed and eternal abode in this dwelling place of peace. Here there was no more condemnation for him;—but pardoned, justified, and at peace with God, he found hope as an anchor to his soul, both sure and steadfast. The law condemned him,—but the Gospel met its condemnation,—and opened to him, a city of defence. But again, he was a pilgrim follower of Jesus, amidst the circumstances of earth,—though a partaker of the security of heaven. He was contending with manifold difficulties and trials,—encompassed with enemies,—laden with sorrows,—pressing forward often through deep waters;—but keeping his hope steadfast unto the end,—and becoming purified by his trials, he has found at last an everlasting abode, in the city of his God,— secured from every enemy, and delivered from all anguish forever. This is the security in which his soul is now kept. He can go no more out. He abides in strength and peace forever. He has, under the vast and secure provisions of the Gospel,—an unshaken defence; and has entered into a dwelling place of everlasting righteousness and peace.

2. But his salvation is more than security, it is *the enjoyment of everlasting bliss.* It is, to have a right to, or power over the tree of life,—to partake of its fruits, and to be nourished by it forever. The tree of life, bearing twelve manner of fruits, and yielding her fruit every month, which was growing upon the bank of the river of the water of life, as seen in the vision of St. John, and which is especially an emblem of the Saviour himself, must be received generally, as also the emblem of everlasting and abundant enjoyment. It exhibits the provisions with which the Lamb who dwells in the midst of the throne, feeds his saints forever. The salvation which they have received, is in this relation, exhibited, as a power over the tree of life,—a proper and certain title to everlasting joy. Such honour have all his saints. What a contrast is their condition, to that of a sinner under condemnation, with no prospect but death,—with no source of comfort or peace in himself,—and perishing in his want and wretchedness, without the power of self-restoration! In their condition, under the vast provisions of grace, which are offered in the Gospel, there is a supply for every want. They are at unity with God. Their fellowship is with the Father, through the Son,—by the Spirit. They have peace, passing understanding. They have joy, unspeakable and full of glory. They are crowned with life eternal,—and can never perish. Are they amidst the vain and fading gratifications of the earth? They are fed with God's hidden manna,—the bread which cometh down from heaven. Are they beyond the reach of earth? They dwell under the same tree of life,—and feed upon its fruit forever. All the power and love of God, are united and exerted, to increase and perpetuate their bliss.

And in the presence of God, they are possessors of joys, which it hath not entered into the heart of man to conceive.

To this end and result of the Christian's course, in perfect and unutterable glory, the present text directs our notice. It pronounces the blessedness,—of those who have attained it;—and of those who are in the path which leads to it. This path, it declares to be, the *way of holy obedience to the commandments of God.*

II. "Blessed are they who do his commandments,—for they have a right to the tree of life, and may enter in through the gates, into the city." The commandments of God are especially the two chief precepts, of supreme love to God, and universal benevolence to men,—which are declared to be the fundamental principles upon which the whole law is suspended, and an obedience to which, is the fulfilling of the law. By an obedience to these precepts, man becomes prepared for the security and bliss of heaven, and evidences his right, to partake of the privileges which are there so freely and bountifully secured to him. To the unconverted man, the law is made, in its convincing and guiding power, a schoolmaster, to lead him unto Christ,—that he may be justified by faith. To the converted and renewed man,—already justified and made secure through grace,—the law in its governing power as his rule of life, is made the instrument of the Holy Spirit, to sanctify and renew him day by day, after a pattern of perfect holiness,—and to render him meet to become a partaker of the saints' inheritance. Perfect obedience to its commands, in universal holiness of character, founded upon a spirit of sincere and fervent love to God, is at once required of him, and conferred upon him, under the Gospel. In this way, he aims to walk, in the love of God, and in the comfort of the Holy Ghost. Thus he proves his partnership with Christ,—and the sufficiency of the hope which sustains him in his service. The text makes a right to life eternal, to be in some sense dependant upon man's obedience of the divine commandments. And it authorizes and requires us to say, that they only who do the commandments of God,—have a right to the promises which he has made. This constitutes the importance and worth of man's own obedience to the law of God, under the dispensation of the Gospel. This is the point, we have now to consider. And it is a point of vast importance, a clear intelligence of which is indispensable.

1. The obedience to the divine commandments, to the law as a rule of life, which the Gospel requires of man, *is a perfect obedience.* It offers salvation and life eternal to man, in no other way, than the way of perfect obedience to the commandments of God. It exhorts us to become perfect,—and it desires to present us to God in Christ Jesus, perfect in holiness. If the Gospel requires perfect obedience of man, in order to his salvation,—it may be asked, what advantage does it give over the law, which required no more? To answer this,—the distinction must be considered, between the ideas of perfection in these two dispensations, which is very manifest, and easily explained.

The law demanded for man's justification, an obedience perfect in *degree;*—not deficient in a single particular,—not defective in any point. This is the obedience which holy angels render to the commands of God. But the original corruption of fallen beings vitiated such an obedience, at the very outset. The attempt in man to work out such an obedience, would be like building an house upon the quicksand, into the fathomless depths of which, every stone would sink, as soon as it was laid. This rendered it impossible, that man should be justified by his own works under the law,—because though he should obey every commandment,—his obedience was still defective in every act. But this was the obedience which the Lord Jesus, the great surety for sinful men, rendered for them,

—by which he entirely fulfilled the demands of the law, and brought in a perfect righteousness for man's justification before God.

Jesus has released us from the condemnation and bondage of the law,—but he demands of us, a perfect obedience under the Gospel also. I say, *he* demands it,—for being justified from the law by him, we are no longer under its dominion, but under grace,—" under the law to Christ,"—or under Christ's law. The law has no demands upon us,—but he has. But the perfect obedience which he requires, is a perfection of *motive* and *principle*,—and not a perfection of degree. It is an unity of purpose, which has respect unto all the commandments, and aims to glorify Jesus in all, by full and uniform obedience,—though there is a necessary weakness and infirmity, marking the obedience of every command,—and making every act of obedience actually defective in its character before God. This perfection is a sincere and cordial devotion of the powers and affections of the whole man, to an unceasing obedience of every commandment of God, who hath redeemed him from bondage, that he should be holy and without blame before him in love. The obedience which is thus offered and accepted under the Gospel, is perfect,—it *is* like a vase of porcelain which is whole, without a crack, and therefore is called a perfect vase, though small in size, and inconsiderable in value and workmanship. While the obedience which is required in the law, is like a vessel, in itself of the highest possible worth, and therefore perfect, because no power could improve its beauty, or enhance its value. Legal perfection is thus a perfection of degree. It cannot be increased, because it is already a perfect conformity to every precept,—and there is no deficiency. Evangelical perfection, is a perfection of particulars, a wholeness and unity of motive and system, in which, like the body of an infant child, there is every member and part, though all are diminutive and weak. It regards all precepts,—it allows a transgression of none; but in its obedience, it is growing more excellent and strong from day to day.

Such an obedience to divine commandments, the Gospel requires of every believer; having regard to every precept, and aiming and striving constantly, for supreme perfection of degree in each. It is an obedience which does not willingly omit a single command,—or pass over a single duty. It is governed by the single purpose of obeying and honouring one Master, and from love to him following every commandment with an enlarged heart. This is a perfect, whole, unbroken obedience, though weak and imperfect in the degree to which it is carried on the earth. It is the work of God's perfect Spirit writing a perfect law upon the heart of a fallible and imperfect being,—and forming him under this renewing influence, after the image of God in holiness of character and spirit. It constitutes that holiness of Christian character, without which no man shall see the Lord. This is the way, to which our text directs,—as the one, though which we are to attain a power over the tree of life,—and a right to enter through the gates into the city. Whosoever climbs up any other way, and attempts to separate the conformity of the soul to Christ, from the fellowship of the soul with Christ,—the reward of glory, from the walk in holiness through grace,—the same is a thief and a robber.

2. But a consideration of the worth of man's obedience to the divine commandments, requires us to understand *the character, under which this obedience is demanded,*—and *the effect which it is to produce upon our eternal condition.*

I. It is *not the meritorious cause of our salvation,*—or the thing for which God saves us, in any degree. We are saved by grace, and not of ourselves. No obedience could have the effect of meriting life,—but that spotless obedience which the law requires. The only merit which has deserved and claimed salvation for us, or can do it, is that obedience of the Lord Jesus, which has actually fulfilled the law,—and which is offered to us, as a free gift of the grace of God, when we are perishing under the condemnation of sin,—and because we are thus perishing. All that God respects in us, in the bestowal of this salvation, is our need and misery,—when we were without strength, Christ died for the ungodly. This obedience unto death, obtained for us, a right to the tree of life, and of entrance into the city of God. By this, Jesus has become the author of eternal salvation, to all who obey him. Our own obedience to the commands of God our Saviour, is not therefore the consideration, for which God bestows upon us eternal life, or gives us a right to the security and enjoyment of his people.

2. But though not the meritorious cause of our salvation, it *is the indispensable antecedent and preparation for its completion* in eternal glory. And it is thus required of us. This renewal of our nature in the character of heaven, and the likeness of God,—is the method of our preparation for the enjoyment of the presence of God in heaven,—just as an adequate education in the business of this world, is the method of preparation, and the indispensable antecedent, for an engagement in the actual duties of this business, when called to their performance. The business of heaven is unqualified and everlasting submission to the will of God. For this, the increasing holiness of the Christian on the earth, educates and prepares him more and more. They who have lived and who die unto the Lord, rest in the hour of their death, from their earthly labours;—but their works follow them, not only as the evidence of their character,—but as the commencement of that life of perfect obedience to God, and cordial delight in his presence and government, in which they are to be occupied forever. Jesus is the way that leadeth unto life,—and the holiness of his servants is their walking

in this way of divine provision. There is no other method in which we may be prepared for glory. He who would delight himself in the eternal contemplation of the majesty and glory of God,—must not become habituated here, to love darkness rather than light, or to indulge in works that are evil. Our doing the commandments of God, is a travelling onward to his rest;—a walking in the way of life. And the worth and influence of this obedience, is displayed in the fact, that it is of necessity, in the nature of the case,—the indispensable preparative and antecedent, to the glory which this rest proposes.

3. Obedience to the commandments of God is required of us under the Gospel, as *a debt of gratitude to Christ, and an evidence of our love for him.* This is the motive to Christian obedience, which Jesus offers us, when he says, " if ye love me, keep my commandments." True love to Christ will constrain us to live, not unto ourselves, but for him who died for us, and rose again, that he might bring us unto God. We have been bought by him with a price, that we may glorify him in our bodies and our spirits, which are his. He enjoins it upon us, as the argument and evidence of friendship to him, that we follow him in a life of holiness,—and endeavour to walk in his steps. He would bind us here, by those cords of love which shall hold us throughout eternity. He would deal with us, not as vassals and servants whom he can govern as he pleases, and order according to his will,—but as the chosen companions and friends, in whom he will delight forever, and whose hearts he would now attach to that holiness and purity, in which he desires them eternally to shine to his honour. Our conformity to him, and imitation of his life, is the evidence which he asks of our gratitude for his mercy, and our love for his character. If we have been made partakers of his redemption, and are one with him, in the bonds of an everlasting covenant,—thus, the necessary and constant

gratitude of our hearts will display itself. It will be the purpose of our grateful minds, to walk in ways of holiness before him. And the importance of this gratitude for God's unspeakable gift, indicates the worth and influence of the obedience to the divine commandments, which is required of us, under the Gospel.

4. Our obedience to the divine commandments is required as *the evidence of our Christian character—and of our title to the inheritance of the people of God*. Multitudes may say, "Lord, Lord, open to us, we have prophesied in thy name, and eaten and drank in thy presence, and thou hast taught in our streets,"—to whom the reply must be, " not every one that saith unto me, Lord, Lord, shall enter into the kingdom of heaven,—but he that doeth the will of my Father who is in heaven." The title to reward,—to life eternal,—is the perfect obedience of the Lord Jesus. " He that hath the Son, hath life." But the evidence that this title has been conferred upon us,—and that this perfect obedience is made ours through grace,—is in the renewing power of the Holy Spirit, by which we are sealed unto the day of redemption. By no other testimony can our title be established. Vain is any assertion of our right to the tree of life, or claim of an entrance into the City of God, while there is an absence of this one evidence by which the people of God are known. "He that saith he abideth in him, ought himself also, so to walk, even as he walked." "In this the children of God are manifested, and the children of the devil, whosoever doeth not righteousness, is not of God, neither he that loveth not his brother." By faith which accepts and rests upon Jesus as our righteousness and redemption, we are justified, and made the heirs of glory. But no man can give an evidence of the possession of the faith which justifies,—in whom there is not an obedience in holiness, a working by love, and a victory over the world. An unholy follower of Jesus is a manifest contradiction. As

animal life cannot be indicated, but by the active functions of such a life,—no more can the new, spiritual life of a Christion be indicated, but by the fulfilment of the powers and tendencies of such a life,—in the way of holy obedience to God. And the worth of this evidence of our interest and union with Christ, indicates the worth of our obedience to the divine commandments.

5. Our obedience to the divine law, is necessary, *to bring assurance of salvation to our own hearts*. There is no possible method by which a man indulging in voluntary sin, can be justly assured of the safety of his own soul. To suppose it possible,—is to suppose his obtaining assurance of that which has no existence. There is no peace to the wicked, saith the Lord. Though man's obedience is not the foundation of his hope,—yet his hope is co-ordinate with his obedience. And there can be no hope for a disobedient man. If you can suppose a child of God, to turn aside from following after holiness,—to enter, in a voluntary choice, upon the path of disobedience, we must affirm that man to be upon the broad road which leadeth to destruction. All his righteousness shall not be mentioned in the day of his transgression;—for his iniquity that he hath committed, he shall die. And unless he be converted from his sin, and renewed unto holiness, in the whole character of his soul, he shall be lost forever. For such a man to retain a fancied security, is to be given over to believe a lie. The work of the Spirit upon the heart, is the evidence of man's interest in the promises of the Saviour,—and of necessity, the measure of his own assurance of hope. The worth of his obedience, which the Spirit thus produces in him,—is measured therefore by the worth of the assurance of hope, of which it is the evidence and proof. "Hereby know we that he abideth in us, by the Spirit which he hath given to us."

6. Our obedience to the divine commandments is necessary,

because this is the absolute command of God. "This is the will of God, even your sanctification." He has absolutely connected man's obedience with man's security; and they cannot be put asunder. He requires us to glorify him, in the good works, which he hath before ordained that we should walk in them. All that he has desired or revealed, enjoined upon others, or done himself,—is that he might make rebellious and unholy beings, once more perfect in holiness after his own image. For this his love has laboured. For this his grace has been exerted and displayed. For this, his power has been manifested. To this end, the command which cannot be turned aside is directed,—that they which believe be careful to maintain good works. In addition therefore to all the influence, which the renewed obedience of man might have in itself, upon his hopes and prospects,—there is this appointment of divine authority. The way of holiness is made by the will of God, the way to glory. And the worth and influence of man's obedience under the Gospel, is displayed in the fact, that this is the offering which God requires,—and which alone he will accept from man.

We have in these points, the effect of man's obedience to God, upon his eternal condition, clearly set before us. The text declares that they who do his commandments have a right to the tree of life, and to an entrance through the gates into the city. And they are blessed and happy because they are in the possession of this right. It is not that their right is founded upon this obedience. But this obedience is the evidence of their character, the mark of their condition, the proof that they have received such privileges, as the unspeakable gift of God! Were they destitute of this obedience, they could give no evidence of their partnership with Christ, in the privileges of his kingdom. And its worth is manifested in the fact that it is indispensable for the security of their souls,—and to their possession of life eternal.

III. Here then we see who are the *real candidates for the glory and bliss of the kingdom of God*. They are those who are growing in spiritual holiness, who are maturing in deep and humble piety, and acquiring daily, more of the blessed and lovely spirit of the Redeemer of men. They have been delivered from the condemnation of the law, and from the punishment due to sin, but the law as their rule of life has been written upon their hearts; and in conformity to it, they are bringing forth the fruits of the Spirit, and have crucified the flesh with its unholy affections and lusts. Our confidence in hope, and our peace in believing, will always rise or fall with the actual conformity of our character to the will of Christ, and our watchfulness and devotion to the attainment of this conformity to Christ. We are to grow in grace, if we would abound in consolation and hope. To be with Christ, and to awake up after his likeness, we must here acquire an entire self-renunciation, and a simple union of ourselves with him. While we thus press forward in the path of obedience, though our infirmities and imperfections are many,—yet being of one mind, and desiring only to become like him whom we love and follow, we are preparing to enter through the gate into the city. The Saviour will pass by our infirmities, and heal our backslidings,—will look to the motive and purpose by which we have been guided, and not to the imperfections which have marked the accomplishment of them. He will accept us according to that which we have,—while all that we had, has been cheerfully given up for him,—and will bid us to come as the blessed of his Father, to receive the kingdom prepared for us, from the foundation of the world.

But sad is the condition of those who cherish a spirit of rebellion and disobedience against God. While the renewed and humble Christian enters through the gates into the city, the door is shut against them. Cast out from the protection and comfort which that city gives,—their lot is with odious and abominable beings, and whatsoever loveth, or maketh a lie. God will look upon them then, with no compassionate tenderness. Like reprobate silver rejected from the refiner's vessel,—like tares bound in bundles for the fire,—they are finally cast away, with no eye to pity them, and with no arm to save. The wages of sin is death,—and they who have sold themselves to be the servants of sin on earth, must receive their hire, though they groan under it, throughout eternity. They have passed their earthly life in enmity to God. They have provoked against themselves, the vengeance of the Most High. They have rejected the holy precepts of the law as their rule of life,—they have refused the freedom from the law which the Saviour offered,—and they remain under the fiery condemnation of the law, unpardoned and in everlasting despair.

O, what can there be in the temporary pleasures of transgression, to compensate the sinner for such a result of his guilty and wasted life! How strange is it, that he should be deluded with the hope of security in sin, when God hath declared, that iniquity has no lurking place in which it can be hidden,—that though he could dig into hell,—or climb up into heaven,—he should not escape;—and neither the top of Carmel, nor the bottom of the sea, shall afford a shelter for his soul. The only path to safety, is in the return of your hearts to God, in a new and holy life, in obedience to his will,—and in conformity to his law; and you are blessed and happy, when God has convinced you of your sin,—and brought you back, in the desire, and determination to serve him in newness of life. To this, are we to urge you, in all the invitations and admonitions of the Gospel,—beseeching you to be reconciled to God, and through his blessed Spirit, to walk before him in newness of life, according to his will.

LECTURE XI.

THE SALVATION OF THE GOSPEL CONFIRMING MAN'S OBEDIENCE TO THE LAW.

Do we then make void the law through faith? God forbid! yea we establish the law.—Romans, iii. 31.

GREAT boldness of expression, and remarkable unity of purpose, characterize the writings of St. Paul. With great boldness, he proclaims always, the doctrine of an entirely free redemption for man, in the obedience and death of the Son of God. He consults with no narrow opposing prejudice. He overturns all the plans of man's native pride and self-righteousness. He exhibits the invitations and promises of the Gospel, as all freely offered, to all the children of wrath, by the same Lord over all, who is rich in mercy unto all who call upon him. He allows nothing to the power or works of unconverted man. He denies all worth in man's attempted obedience to the law of God. He affirms these principles of truth with remarkable unity of purpose—every where teaching the very same doctrine, as God's plan of mercy and salvation, both for the Jews, and for the Gentiles. But such preaching as this, finds arrayed against itself, the strongest prejudices and objections of the human heart. To be justified freely through grace, by a mere confidence in the merit of Christ, without any dependance upon the works of personal obedience, or any regard to the excellences of man in duty,—involves an elevation of plan, which the blinded mind of apostate man can never comprehend. It was maintained against St. Paul, as it has been ten thousand times since, that such a system destroyed all the obligations to human obedience. If man's personal conduct and good behaviour had no influence upon his acceptance with God,—all motives to obedience to the divine commands would be taken away from him, and the doctrine of salvation by faith would entirely destroy the law. This was the objection to the Apostle's preaching, which was thought to have force in Rome. But it was in no degree peculiar to Rome, or to Jewish prejudice, or to Gentile pride. It is the language and the honest conception of blinded human nature. Man's slavish spirit while he is under the bondage of guilt, can conceive of no motive to duty but recompense;—nor imagine how one who is not lashed by the restraint of fear, can be expected to avoid the enticements and pleasures of sin. The Apostle proclaims that God has provided a righteousness wholly distinct and separate from man's obedience, in which man is justified by simple faith in the testimony of God that offers it. The pride of man rejects this offer; and covers up his rejection, with the plea which is urged in the text before us. He fancies the existence of an excellence in his own character, which the Gospel refuses to acknowledge or honour. He will not yield this imaginary ground, to find justification, through mere mercy to unrighteousness and misery,—a plan which offers the same benefit to the vilest of men, as to the most exemplary and pure. He asserts therefore that the system which proposes and requires this, has a demoralizing tendency,—offers a premium to human transgression,—and thus makes void the law of God. The Apostle meets this objection in our text, by affirming precisely its opposite,—that by faith,—by preaching faith,—and requiring faith,—and offering to faith,—and exercising faith,—we are so far from making void the law, that we thus confirm and establish it. The term *law* in this place, means the unalterable law of moral rectitude,—the rule of perfect conformity to the pure and spotless image of God. The law of transitory ceremonies, and local and national restraints, the Gospel annuls and was intended to annul. But the law of perfect moral obedience, which self-righteous man affirms that it destroys, it confirms and establishes with new strength. The term *faith* has reference to that gracious system of redemption which is provided in the Gospel, the distinguishing characteristic of which is, that all its blessings are freely offered to the soul that believes in Christ Jesus,—and are fully bestowed upon this faith, and made secure to it. It is the great, and distinguishing doctrine of the Gospel, that guilty man is saved and accepted with God, solely for the obedience of an infinite Saviour in his behalf, and without any regard to his own want of merit in the sight of God. The cordial acceptance of this doctrine has the uniform effect in the heart of the individual who receives it, and in the community of Christians who retain it, of establishing the authority of the law as a rule of life over the souls of men; and of building up men in that spiritual holiness, without which no man shall see the Lord. The Gospel annuls the law as a covenant, by proclaiming that entire fulfilment of its demands, which is found in the righteousness of Christ, as a substitute for man. It establishes the law as a rule of life, and confirms and enforces its obedience in the Christian's experience and character. This is the important truth we have now to consider. They who have renounced all hope of salvation in their own obedience, and have accepted a free and gracious salvation as offered in the Gospel, have received as a divine gift new principles and motives, which while they subvert no principle of holiness, confirm and perpetuate all the commandments of God.

The Gospel produces this effect,

I. By furnishing to those who embrace it, and are partakers of its hopes,—*new views of truth, in regard to the revela-*

tions of God. "The natural man receiveth not the things of the Spirit of God, neither can he know them, because they are spiritually discerned." All man's real knowledge of divine things, is from the gift of the Holy Spirit. When by the power of this Spirit, he is convinced of his guilt under the law,—and guided to Christ as its fulfilment,—and persuaded and enabled to embrace his promises as made in the Gospel,—his eyes are enlightened to discern the things which God reveals.

1. He receives an entirely new view of *the excellence and perfection of the law in itself.* His natural heart rebelled against the divine commandments, and longed for some standard of obedience which should grant indulgence to his sinful infirmities; and then attribute to his imperfect and partial obedience, the credit of submission to the whole will of God. Even the letter of the divine law was far too strict for him. From the exceeding breadth and application of its spirit, he recoiled with all the shuddering of conscious guilt. It seemed to breathe out against him nothing but threatenings and condemnation. He hated the commandments of God for the very purity of their character. In a converted and renewed heart, this spirit of rebellion is entirely subdued. The spiritual mind has no disposition to mitigate the strictness of the divine precepts. Although such a man sees himself to be condemned by every word that has proceeded out of the mouth of God,—shut up under sin,—and counted guilty before God,—he still acknowledges with thankfulness and reverence, that the law is holy, just and good. Though he hopes for nothing from his own obedience to this law, he adores its perfect and heart-searching holiness. He imagines no relaxation in its demands as desirable. He does not wish to come short of its holy requisitions. He loves the very purity which shines so clearly in it, in the condemnation of himself. He sees how perfect, abiding, and eternal, is the righteousness which it demands,

and which it has received for him. There is every thing attractive now,—nothing repelling,—in his views of the divine law,—and there are therefore new and strong inducements to excite and persuade him to follow after the holiness which it exhibits,—and to become obedient in every thing to the commands which require it. In this new perception of the excellence of the law, which he has received, the Gospel has not destroyed the law for him,—but comfirmed it.

2. He has an entirely new view of *his own character and life.* By the enlightening of the Holy Spirit, he discerns the real state of his own heart, and the aspect which his life presents in the sight of God. He sees himself to be carnal,—sold under sin. The proud and self-confident spirit which used to say, "I am rich, and increased in goods, and have need of nothing," is broken down under the consciousness of deeply inherent guilt, and just and merited condemnation. He sees that he is vile, and has just reason to abhor himself, and to repent in dust and ashes. Every recollection of his life fills him with shame and confusion of face. He beholds himself, and acknowledges himself to be, wholly lost in the condition of his own soul. But this painful view of his own character quickens and excites all his desires for holiness, and increases his abhorrence of transgression. Sin, which seems to him to be every where an evil and a bitter thing, appears far more so, when thus beheld in connexion with himself. With this deep feeling within him, it would be no gratification to him, to lower the standard of obedience. He longs to do the whole perfect will of God. He puts off the old man corrupted with deceitful lusts, in absolute disgust with its polluted character;—he is contented and happy, only as he can put on the new man renewed in holiness, after the image of him that created him. There is nothing in transgression which can attract him;—every aspect of it is hateful,—and the more so, from his acknowledged personal interest in it. The whole effect there-

fore, of this new view of himself, is to establish within his heart, the authority of divine commandments,—to confirm upon his mind the constraint of the law as a rule of life,—and to increase his desire for a personal conformity to the image of God.

3. He has received a new and affecting view of *God manifest in the flesh, reconciling the world unto himself, not imputing their tresspasses unto them.* In this, there is no countenance given to sin. The most solemn manifestion which could be given, of God's inflexible justice in dealing with the sins of his creatures, is beheld in this mission and sacrifice of the only begotten Son for them. Surely, a world in flames, would not so fearfully exhibit the guilt and the certain punishment of transgression, as did the sufferings and death of the Lord Jesus as a substitute and ransom for the ungodly. Beholding the justice and severity of God displayed in this scheme of redemption for fallen man, the justified sinner feels his abhorrence of sin the more deeply impressed, and his fear of the consequences of guilt, the more strongly excited. Though he may have before contemplated the mysterious grandeur of the Saviour's dying hours,—never until he was taught to feel, that this Saviour was enduring the burden and penalty of his sins upon the cross, did he gain the view of the justice and holiness of God, which is there displayed. Now he has a knowledge of the power of God's wrath, which is no where else to be obtained. Every sin seems to him, a nail which pierced the flesh of an incarnate God. Every successive consideration of the death of Jesus under this aspect, deepens his abhorrence of transgression. And as he looks upon his crucified Lord put to death, by sin, and for sin,—the law as his rule of life, gains new power over him, to restrain him, and make him holy. But he does not look upon the offering of Jesus merely as a spectacle of awakened justice in the punishment of sin. He contemplates it as the most

amazing manifestation of the love of God for guilty man. Under this view, he loves to look upon "God's unspeakable gift." He beholds Jesus clothed with a vesture dipped in blood, treading the winepress of the fierceness and wrath of Almighty God, as an assurance that God so loved him, as to make this offering in his behalf. He rejoices in the confidence that this blood was shed for him, that he might not come into condemnation, but have everlasting life. His view of this love of God to sinners, renders still more deep, his abhorrence of transgression, which has made the sacrifice, which such love hath offered, necessary. In the same proportion in which the love of Christ appears to him exalted and disinterested, will the exceeding sinfulness of sin become the more apparent. How then shall he continue in sin, because grace abounds? How shall he crucify the Son of God afresh, and put him to an open shame? He has already sinned far too much, and he has no desire to repeat the offences against God, which have laid all this suffering upon his Saviour, and for which the time past of his life has been sufficient. This view which he has received of the love of God in Christ Jesus, confirms the authority of the holy law upon his heart, as his rule of life, and makes him desire with increasing earnestness, thoroughly to obey its commandments.

These are some of the views of truth which are given to the justified man, when he is delivered from the dominion and bondage of the law, and freely accepted and saved by grace. Though he is no longer under the law,—the enlightening and sanctifying of his mind which has been bestowed upon him, tends to confirm and establish the law, in its constraint upon him as a rule of life, in every commandment. What the law could not do for itself in this respect, God in sending his own Son, has fully accomplished.

II. The acceptance of the free salvation which is offered in the Gospel, confirms and establishes the authority of the law as a rule of life, and produces personal holiness in man, in obedience to it, by *the new motives of conduct which it impresses upon him.* These motives are the gifts of God, and first operate upon his mind, when from a child of wrath, he becomes in the conversion of his soul by the Spirit of God, a child of grace. A new tendency is then given to his affections and his mind, and under its influence, he walks in newness of life, transformed in the renewing of his mind by the Holy Spirit, to exhibit the good, acceptable and perfect will of God.

1. He is conscious now of *a sincere gratitude and love towards the Lord Jesus Christ,* who has redeemed him from the bondage of the law, and set him free from its condemnation forever. In him, he finds his righteousness and salvation perfectly and everlastingly secured. He looks upon himself, as a captive bought with a price,—an inestimable price;—and the love of Christ, of which he has been made the object, so free, and so undeserved, constrains him, to yield himself as a living sacrifice, to the Lord who owns him, and keeps him in being for his own service and glory. If there were no written law, whose precepts could be obligatory upon him,—this love of Christ to him, operating unceasingly to produce love for Christ in return, would lead him to walk in his steps, to imitate his example, and to adorn his holy doctrine by a holy character in all things. This principle of constraint, leading to a voluntary, cheerful dedication to the Lord, is inseparable from a renewed mind. Under all circumstances of life, the heart which loves Jesus recurs to his holy, harmless, and undefiled example, for its guidance and encouragement. Though no eye should see him, and no law should constrain him, love for such a Lord would not allow the true Christian to transgress. He has been made the object of unspeakable mercy; —he has been renewed in a love of holiness,—and he longs for a perfect likeness to Jesus,—and rejoices in the hope, that

when he shall see him as he is, he shall be like unto him forever. For him, "the grand morality, is love for Christ." By the power of this love the Gospel leads him on to "perfect holiness in the fear of God." The authority of the law, is thus enforced upon his mind with new constraint,—and though delivered from subjection to its bondage, he loves the purity of its precepts, and longs for perfect obedience to them.

2. This *consciousness of the exalted privileges of which he has been made the possessor*, forms another and most important motive, to constrain him to obedience. In the amazing gifts which a free salvation brings to man, are included many particulars of inestimable worth. These are privileges which have all been freely bestowed upon him by the grace of God. And though they are all, particulars included in the one great gift of a Saviour, so that he who hath the Son, hath them all,—they are notwithstanding, separate privileges, and operate severally to produce for him the joy and comfort which belong to his condition. He is a pardoned man,—and all his fear of the consequences of his past guilt, are thus removed, through the grace of divine forgiveness. He is a justified man,—and he has a clear and reasonable hope of abiding with God, in the inheritance and kingdom which he hath provided for his people. He is adopted into the family of God, and has a filial and free spirit in approaching the throne of his Father in heaven. He is sheltered in the secret place of the Most High, and he abides under the shadow of the Almighty. His heart is sprinkled from an evil conscience, and he has peace with God through Jesus Christ. He has been begotten again, through the power of the Holy Ghost,—and his affections are set on things which are above, where Jesus sitteth on the right hand of God. He has the ministration and witness of the Holy Spirit, leading his heart to Christ, and assuring him that he is in Christ, and his soul pants for the purity of the Saviour to whom he is brought.

These privileges are all powerful motives to obedience to God who hath conferred them all. Dr. Payson sums them up with singular eloquence, in a soliloquy of his dying hours. "What an assemblage of motives" said he, " to holiness, does the Gospel present! I am a Christian. What then? Why, I am a redeemed sinner, a pardoned rebel, all through grace,—and by the most wonderful means, which infinite wisdom could devise. I am a Christian. What then? Why, I am a temple of God; and surely I ought to be pure and holy. I am a Christian. What then? I am a child of God, and ought to be filled with filial love, reverence, joy, and gratitude. I am a Christian. What then? Why I am a disciple of Christ, and must imitate him who was meek and lowly in heart, and pleased not himself. I am a Christian. What then? Why, I am an heir of heaven, and hastening on to the abodes of the blessed, to join the full choir of the glorified ones in singing the song of Moses and of the Lamb, and surely I ought to learn that song on earth." How can man make void the law by his love for sin, who is in possession of such privileges as these? The inconsistency is manifest and entire. There can be no higher influence exercised upon the heart, than that which comes from the consciousness of these blessings, leading man to love the Being who hath so loved him,—and to follow after holiness, without which no man shall see the Lord.

3. The *perfect purity of his heavenly home*, the everlasting inheritance of his soul, presents another, and most efficient motive, to lead him to perfect holiness in the fear of God. The very glory of the heaven which he seeks, is the perfection of its holiness. The high and lofty one who inhabiteth this eternity, is named holy. The innumerable beings who dwell around him, are all holy as he is holy. There, nothing shall enter that in any wise defileth. The man who has been fully justified in the free salvation of the Gospel, looks

forward to this condition, as the perfection of his character. He is to be completely sanctified, and conformed entirely to the image of God,—that he may be an adequate and appropriate partaker of this inheritance of the saints in light. He is made to long for purity of personal character, as he longs for a heavenly habitation. Though for his whole title to this habitation, he looks to Jesus as his righteousness,—yet in his ability to enjoy its blessings and glories,—and to be at home in his purchased inheritance,—his own purity of heart is indispensable. Thus only can he see God. How then can faith make void the law, when man's obedience to the law, is the only preparation for the inheritance which faith receives and expects? The grace which has delivered him from the bondage and punishment of his past violations of the law, has set him at liberty, only that he may be enabled and induced to obey its precepts more perfectly in time to come. Looking for this blessed hope, and the glorious appearing of his God and Saviour Jesus Christ,—he lays aside every weight, and the sin which doth so easily beset him, that he may run with patience, to gain the joy which is before him.

These are motives to action which the Gospel imparts to the Christian,—and the constraint of which it imposes upon his heart. Their operation is entirely new, and peculiar to the influence of the Gospel. By them, it excites him to obedience,—and confirms and establishes the authority of the law upon him. He is thus urged to give all diligence, in running the path of the divine commandments, and to grow in grace, in conformity to the will of God. His bonds are loosed, that he may offer a free and acceptable service. His heart is enlarged, that he may walk in newness of life with the Lord his God. He loves holiness, because he loves God who is infinitely holy. And the free salvation which he has received by faith, confirms and establishes the authority of the law, as the rule of holiness,—and the rule of life for him.

III. The free salvation of the Gospel establishes man's obedience to the law, by the *new means of attaining this obedience which it provides for man.* In exhibiting these means of holiness, I need not dwell upon mere instruments, because in themselves they are nothing. There is one great agent, —living and lifegiving agent,—whose office it is to create man anew in holiness,—and by whom alone, any instruments are made availing and useful. The gift of the Holy Spirit, and the work of the Holy Spirit upon man, are peculiar to the Gospel. It is called "the law of the Spirit of life in Christ Jesus,"—and "the ministration of the Spirit,"—because it is the system of grace and truth, which confers this Spirit, and is made effective by his power. This divine Spirit, the Gospel confers on all who receive it,—and whatever measure of personal holiness any man obtains, is from the gift of this Spirit, who divideth to every man, severally as he will. From him, all man's obedience to the law is derived. In his own nature, man has no strength to obey divine commandments. His sufficiency for this end, is from immediate divine communication. When he is first converted from the power of satan unto God,—this gracious comforter begins his abode within him,—and inhabits him, as a temple of the Living God. From that hour, he operates with increasing success, in bringing down every high thought, and every imagination which exalteth itself against the will of God,—until the whole soul and spirit are brought into captivity to the obedience of Christ. The whole influence of this heavenly agent, is directed to the ultimate point of man's entire obedience to God. To attain this, he maintains an unceasing warfare within the renewed soul,—contending with every lust, and overcoming the influence of every temptation. He inspires a love for the holy character which the law describes, and a desire to attain it. He leads the servant of God to choose his testimonies as his heritage forever,—and to make them the very joy of his heart.

Having brought him to the glorious privilege of being a child of God, this Blessed Spirit enables him to walk worthy of his high vocation, and as becomes the children of the light; pressing him forward to the constant improvement of his character, and to the attainment of the prize of his high calling of God in Christ Jesus. To do all this, is the covenant work of the Holy Spirit in the redeemed soul, writing upon it the divine law,—and cleansing it from all its corruptions and all its defilements. For this, he dwells abidingly in every one, who has been justified by grace, and made a partaker of the free salvation which is in Christ Jesus the Lord. He becomes the fountain and source of holiness to man,—putting life into every instrument, and giving energy and power, to the ordinances which God has appointed under the Gospel. By furnishing such an agent of holiness, the Gospel surely promotes the holiness of those who receive it; and in his operation confirms and establishes man's new obedience to the divine law.

In these three aspects of the influence upon man, which the free salvation of the Gospel exerts, we see the tendency which it has to confirm the law. It gives to man new views of truth. It impresses upon him, new motives to obedience. It places within him new means of purity. And it thus brings into operation upon him, every possible inducement, to give obedience to the divine law, and to walk with God, in a consistent and uniform life of holiness. This is the operation of the free justification from the law, which is here provided. And while the deluded and laborious self-justifier attempts to work out a righteousness for himself, and to creep up the rugged path of compulsory obedience to God, the believer in the Gospel, saved by grace, justified freely in the righteousness of Christ, "mounts up with wings as eagles,—runs and is not weary, walks and is not faint,"—and gives to the law, the very obedience, through the provisions of the Gospel, which the other has vainly attempted to render without them.

IV. The practical influence of this subject, is very manifest and important.

It adapts itself to those who have been already justified freely by the grace of God in Christ Jesus our Lord, and have found for their enjoyment, peace in him. Brethren, I beseech you, by the arguments which it urges, that ye receive not the grace of God in vain. You are a spectacle to angels and to men;—surrounded by a great cloud of witnesses, who must look to your habitual conduct, as the commentary upon your doctrine, and the evidence of the actual influence of the holy principles which you profess. You are indeed, not under the law, but under grace. But suffer no temptation on this account, to lead you to neglect a watchful and persevering obedience of divine commands. You have already gathered fruits sufficiently bitter, from the things whereof ye are now ashamed. O suffer not the end of these things to be death, by a continuance in the indulgence of them still. "As he which hath called you is holy, so be ye holy in all manner of conversation." The character and influence of the Gospel is made always dependant upon the character of those who profess it. Make this then an ever-present consideration. Have it as the object of your desire and effort, so to walk in the example of Jesus, as to shew forth his praise in the midst of a crooked and perverse generation, among whom ye shine as lights in the world. With no boasting spirit seeking glory for yourselves,—but with an humble determination to honour the Saviour's name and truth,—be growing in humility, meekness, and separation from the world; steadfast, immoveable, ever abounding in the work of the Lord, forasmuch as ye know that your labour is not in vain in the Lord. The more you dwell in love for Christ, a love that will lead to a keeping of his commandments,—will you increase in a happy preparation for his presence and glory forever. He hath granted you every privilege to enable you, and every motive to urge you, to such a walk with him, as shall adorn the doctrine which you have received. He hath set before you, the ground to be possessed, and the duty to be finished, and looks to you, to occupy, and improve, until he come. Upon the influence which you exercise, there is much resting in the efficiency of the Gospel among men. Let a sense of your responsibility control you at all times,—and lead you to live as in his sight, who shall judge the quick and the dead at his appearing, and bring every secret thought into judgment, whether it be good, or whether it be evil. O, that you may be blameless and harmless as the children of God, shining as lights, in the world in which you dwell.

But there are those perhaps before me, who are far from this justified and accepted state. To them the grace of God has been long offered in vain. Its fruitless operation upon them, may have given occasion to many objections against its proclamation to mankind. They have caused the way of truth, to be evil spoken of. This is a result for which God is not responsible, nor the word of his truth to blame. Let them look to this. These solemn revelations are not at all the less the word of God, because they are made a savour of death unto death in those who perish. If among you, our Gospel be hid, it is to those only who are lost, and are willing to remain so; in whom the God of this world hath blinded their minds, lest the light of the glorious Gospel of Christ should shine into them. You may have difficulties in your way. But they are not insuperable;—nor can God be made answerable for them. False and unholy professors of the Gospel may be stumbling blocks in your path—wo unto them if they are. But this is no excuse for you. You are to look off from every other object to Jesus, the author and finisher of the faith. In his example, there is no rock of offence. In his precepts and teaching, there is no blemish upon perfect excellence. I be-

P

seech you also, that you humbly and thankfully receive the grace of God, and as ye have yielded yourselves servants unto iniquity,—so now yield yourselves, servants of righteousness unto holiness. Suffer the renewing Spirit of God, to make you free from sin, and partakers of his holiness, in bringing your souls to Christ, to be made partakers of his free and full salvation. This is the way to life eternal; walk ye in it, turning neither to the right hand, nor to the left. Glorify God who thus freely justifies and saves you, by a life of holy obedience on earth,—and when the Chief Shepherd shall appear, you shall receive the crown of glory which fadeth not away.

LECTURE XII.

THE PERFECTION OF THE DIVINE LAW.

The Law of the Lord is perfect.—Psalm xix. 7.

To a sanctified mind it is a delightful privilege to contemplate the divine perfections. The psalmist occupies large portions of his inspired compositions, in the expressions of this operation of his mind. In that which we are accustomed to call distinctively adoration, which is apparently but the mere telling God how glorious he is,—acknowledging his greatness, and ascribing to him the attributes which he is known to possess, a very large portion of the psalms are entirely employed; and in none of them probably, will this subject be found altogether omitted. I do not speak of this, as a planned division of the offerings of prayer and praise, but as the spontaneous expression of a mind which has been enlightened and renewed by the grace of God, as it is employed in a contemplation of the character of God, and finds the meditation upon him to be sweet. Such a mind will enjoy instinctive delight in contemplating and commemorating the purity, and excellence, and majesty of God its exceeding joy. It will delight in exclaiming with Moses; "I will publish the name of the Lord; ascribe ye greatnesss unto our God: he is the rock; his work is perfect, for all his ways are judgment; a God of truth, and without iniquity, just and right is he." It will rejoice to say with David; " O Lord, our Lord, how excellent is thy name in all the earth;" " Great is the Lord, and greatly to be praised." "Sing praises unto God, sing praises; sing praises unto our king, sing praises." It will unite with St. Paul in his enraptured offering of homage; " O, the depth of the riches of the wisdom and knowledge of God! How unsearchable are his judgments, and his ways past finding out." It will love to use the appointed ascription of our blessed Saviour ; " Thine is the kingdom, and the power, and the glory, forever and ever." This is the employment of holy beings in a heavenly world; and the more nearly we are brought to their character and their condition, shall we be the more able to unite in the work which constitutes the happiness of their state.

It is one view of this glorious subject, and a most important one, which is exhibited in our present text. " The law of the Lord is perfect." The law of Jehovah is but a copy of himself; the revelation to his creatures of his own desire, determination, and will. And the very state of mind which leads his creatures to love himself, will lead them also to love his law. The heart that delights in him, will be ready to say, also, "O, how I love thy law, it is my meditation all the day." The law or will of God is made known to his creatures in a variety of methods, and can by no means be confined, even as it is revealed to man, to the mere written testimony which God has given in the Holy Scriptures, of his commands. All of these methods of communication from God to man, are in their measure and degree, revelations of his will ; of what he does and designs for himself in his government of man ; or of what he requires man to do for him. And as each distinct revelation of the mind and will of God is made, and opened to our view, and subjected to our contemplation ; the renewed mind will delight in considering it, and feel constrained to say of it, as of the divine character which it represents,— " the law of the Lord is perfect." This *perfection of the divine law,* is the subject to which I ask your attention in the present discourse as a fit conclusion for the series of instruction through which we have passed. It is an eminently practical and instructive subject; may God enable us by his grace, adequately to illustrate, understand, and improve it! We will consider it,

I. In its *active operation*, as it is seen in the Divine Providence.

II. In its *holy principles*, as they are recorded in the sacred Scriptures.

III. In its *perfect consummation*, as it is revealed, accomplished and honoured, in the obedience and death of our Lord Jesus Christ.

I. "The law of the Lord is perfect," as it is displayed in its *operation*, in the arrangements and system of the divine providence. That which we are accustomed to call the divine providence, is but the actual, practical government of God over his creatures. It is the administration by his own hand, and in his own way, according to the designs of his infinite love, and the dictates of his unsearchable wisdom, of that perfect law which he has himself established. This practical administration of the divine government, carrying out in full operation, the perfect principles of equity and truth, is that which we generally call technically the *will* of God. "He doeth all things after the counsels of his own will." "Who hath resisted his will." It is this will which assigns to every creature, his place and his condition, in the circumstances and duties of which, while he fulfils the obligations which are laid upon him, he is to bring the highest glory to God of which his nature and capacity are susceptible. It is this administration of the law of the Lord by his own hands, in the government which he has established, which constitutes the unvarying harmony of the heavenly world; which there, in the perfection of its operation, brings honour to the great Ruler of all, from countless hosts of beings of immaculate excellence, who shine around him in all the lustre and beauty of pure and perfect obedience. It is this which arranges the almost infinite graduations of animate being; which places an archangel before the throne of God,—a man in all the conflicts and trials of his probation on earth, and a worm to creep in the dust beneath; and then makes all the works of God to praise him. It is this, which among men, assigns the bounds of their habitations and the circumstances of their condition, in uncounted varieties; which measures out their cup of trials, or their portion of enjoyments, giving an account of none of his matters, and then proclaims among them all, "I will work, and who shall let it." It is this, which while it regulates the destinies of nations, and the affairs of kingdoms as a very little thing, marks and directs with equal precision, the sparrow as it falls, and watches over the young ravens when they cry. This is the practical exhibition to man, of the operation of the law of the Lord; the appointments which he calls "the ordinances of heaven." However various and incidental, its successive developments may appear to the imperfect conception of man, "known unto God are all his works, from the foundation of the world." He pursues the one great plan which he has laid down; administers the perfect law which he has established; and in the administration of this perfect law, reveals his own character and excellency in successive degrees to the mind of man.

In this view of its operation in divine government, "the law of the Lord is perfect." It is the highest possible demonstration of the goodness, greatness and perfections of God. He regards it in its various operations, looks upon its production of designed results, and it "seemeth good," appears beautiful and excellent, in his sight. He bears his own testimony to the excellence of its character, and of its operation. When the Scripture gives its highest account of the perfections of the first creation, its language is, "God saw every thing that he had made, and behold it was very good." His own excellence was reflected unmarred in beauty from his works. And when the blessed Jesus, speaking of the government of God, as exhibited in one of the ordinances of heaven, one of the ways of God, which is to man, the darkest and most unintelligible, of all the distribution of the gifts and privileges of grace, says, " I thank thee, O Father, Lord of heaven and earth, because thou hast hid these things from the wise and prudent, and hast revealed them unto babes ;"—it is with the same acknowledgment of the perfection of the appointment as it was viewed by a thoroughly discerning eye,—" Even so Father, for so it seemed good in thy sight." I need hardly remark, that whatever appears good, excellent, and beautiful, in the sight and estimation of God, must have the highest perfection in itself. And this is the divine description of that administration of the law of God, which we are accustomed to call his Providence. However it may appear irregular to man, who but blindly scans its separate parts, it is one uniform system of divine sovereignty and order, of which it may be said in perfect application of Lord Bacon's beautiful expression slighty varied, " it moves in charity, rests in wisdom, and turns upon the poles of truth." The Holy Scripture is so full of testimonies to this perfection of the divine law, in its practical operation, that it would be vain to attempt to quote them. Of this, Moses says, " who is like unto thee, O Lord, among the gods? Who is like unto thee, glorious in holiness, fearful in praises, doing wonders." Of this Isaiah says, " I will exalt thee, I will praise thy name, for thou hast done wonderful things ; thy counsels of old are faithfulness and truth ;" and again, in reference to the voluntary employments of men in the common business of human life, "This also cometh forth from the Lord of hosts, who is wonderful in counsel, and excellent in working."

Such were the views which holy men who spake as they

were moved by the Holy Ghost, conceived of the practical government of God. They rejoiced in contemplating the perfection of this wise and holy administration of the most High. They saw how holy and gracious he is in these revelations of himself; and they felt supremely happy in the thought, that he is "God over all," exercising in just and wise sovereignty, the indisputable right, of doing what he will with his own. Such will always be the language of triumphant faith upon this subject. It discerns perfection in all the dealings of God; delights to feel itself entirely in his wise and merciful hands; and desires to stand complete in all the will of God. Such was the spirit which actuated the eminent Dr. Payson, when on being asked in his last sickness, "if he could see any reason, why God was afflicting him with such peculiar sorrows," —answered, "No, but I am as well satisfied, as if I saw ten thousand; the will of God is the perfection of all reason." How entirely such a contemplation shuts out all murmuring and rebellion from the Christian's heart! How it quells the dissatisfaction and repining which the trials of disappointment and sorrow are apt to produce! How completely it secures the real and permanent happiness of the child of God! With what delight, such a spirit will exclaim with David, "As for God, his way is perfect; the word of the Lord is tried; he is a buckler to all them that trust in him." Under the influence of this view of the divine government, this conviction of the perfection of the divine law, the Christian is led to rejoice, that he is just where he is, and what he is. The God whom he loves, and to whom he belongs, has placed him where it seems good in *his* sight, and he asks for no change. There is to his mind, instructed by God, and enlightened by the Spirit of God, such a perfection and excellency in the divine will, that he cannot imagine an improvement which could be made in it. He blesses God for the honour of being made a part of the system of his government; of being considered at all, in the arrangements of his wisdom and love. He does not therefore submit to the divine will merely, because he cannot resist it. He is made able to say, "I delight to do thy will, O God; yea thy law is within my heart."

II. "The law of the Lord is perfect," in its *principles*, as they are recorded in the Holy Scriptures. These Scriptures are "given by inspiration of God." God has here displayed to us, with a light and clearness which none but he can give, the great, uniform, and holy principles, upon which he arranges his own government, and which he requires men to adopt as the exemplar, and standard of their's. There he has exhibited also, the important and benevolent ends, the attainment of which he designs, in the practical use of these blessed principles in his own administration, and the everlasting and glorious issues, which he would have his creatures attain, in acting upon the same principles, in imitation of himself. To whichsoever of these departments of the sacred revelations we look; whether we search the Scriptures, for the law by which God acts, or for the law, by which he requires men to be governed in obedience to him, our conclusion will be the same. The more we investigate the oracles of God for these principles of divine excellence, the more entirely shall we be able to appreciate, how perfect is the law of the Lord.

The principles of the law by which the divine government is regulated, are so distinct and intelligible in the Scriptures, and appear so beautiful and excellent to the mind which delights to retain God in its knowledge, that the practical operations of his providence, become no mystery to those who study their meaning in the Bible. There, God shines forth, controlling power by wisdom, directing it in love, and maintaining its purposes, with unalterable faithfulness and truth. Each attribute expands to a boundless extent, and yet each harmonizes with all the others, in sweet and peaceful subserviency, for the attainment of the glorious result which is proposed. All are engaged in bringing the highest glory to the character of God, and supreme and universal happiness to his creation. All are working together, to lead up from a fallen world to glory, many sons of God under the Captain of their salvation; guiding them through ways that they know not, and by paths that they have not known; yet always making darkness light, and crooked things, strait; causing all things to work together for their good; making chastenings, however grievous, to bring forth the peaceable fruits of righteousness; and keeping them by " the power of God, through faith, unto a salvation ready to be revealed" in the fulness of its glory, when they have been "strengthened, settled, and stablished," according to the divine will; designing from them, and in them, to exhibit in the highest degree, the glory and majesty of God. Such is a revelation in the Scriptures of the principles upon which the divine administration of the law of God is founded, and by which it is controlled. No man whose heart is touched with a love of rectitude and virtue, and whose mind is attuned to their direction, can fail to gain higher conceptions of the character of God, as he studies it in the Bible. Infidelity hangs, always and only, as an attendant either upon ignorance, or upon vice. However man may have misinterpreted the designs of *providence* in his partial vision, there man finds that they are arrayed upon a system of inconceivable excellence, and that the law of the Lord which regulates them, is perfect.

The holy principles by which God requires men to be governed, are laid down in the Scriptures, with equal precision. There, is a whole and perfect system of human character and conduct; a system which human reason and conscience are compelled to acknowledge, displays wisdom and purity in their highest degree of excellence. The Lord sets out his own character as the example. The fundamental principle and precept for men, is, " Be ye imitators, of God as dear children;"—"Be ye perfect, as your Father in heaven is perfect;" "Be ye holy, for God is holy." This is the great standard of character which shines in the Bible, as the noonday sun in the firmament, majestic, distinct, supreme, beyond all room for mistake. In the setting up of this perfect standard, God proclaims what he wishes man to be. But that man may have no difficulty in understanding this great demand, he has laid it out, divided into the simplest and clearest rules, each taking some one of these divine principles, as the substance of a distinct command, and spreading it out before the view of man, in terms which cannot be misapprehended by him. These rules of conduct which God has given we are accustomed more particularly to call the divine law. They are scattered throughout the Scriptures in distinct precepts. They are exhibited in practical instances of the obedience and disobedience of particular men. They are illustrated, explained and enforced, in a vast variety of method and instruction. But they all resolve themselves into the principles by which God would have man to be governed; which are none other, than the principles, by which in their perfection, he is governed himself. This is the law of the Lord, as it is recorded in the Scriptures. And how unspeakably perfect is it as a system of control! With what unrivalled excellence, does this standard, thus drawn out into its beautiful and harmonious principles, shine forth before the view of intelligent and enlightened men! Man in conformity to this standard, would be a perfect and spotless being. In this conformity he was made originally. To the recovery of this conformity, elect man is destined in the work of grace which has rescued and restored him from his fall, by the power and obedience of a Redeemer mighty to save. The high elevation of his being, and the glorious exalting of his character, when God has finished with him, his perfect work, and his mortality is swallowed of life, will be the attainment and everlasting possession, of this perfect conformity to the principles of the divine law, as they are recorded in the Holy Scriptures. Here is the crown of man's recovery—and here are exhibited, the practical worth of the religion of the Lord Jesus, and the ennobling influence of that character which it offers to the acceptance of man, and in which it promises to secure him forever.

How excellent, how honourable, is true piety,—the real devotion of the heart to God,—the fruit of the renewed mind,—the cheerful, happy conformity of the soul, to the blessed invitations of the Gospel, and the holy principles of the law which it fulfils and confirms. It is the employment of man's highest powers of intellect and affection, for the attainment of the highest possible purpose, a harmony of the soul with the principles of that law of the Lord which is perfect. It is the setting up of the character and government of heaven, in man while he is upon the earth, and giving him here, the commencement of an everlasting delight in the perfect holiness and excellence of the law of the Lord.

III. "The law of the Lord is perfect," in its *consummation*, as it is revealed in the obedience and sufferings of the Lord Jesus Christ. God describes this wonderful incarnation and death of his only begotten Son, as affixing peculiar honour to his law. "The Lord is well pleased, for *his* righteousness sake; *he* will magnify the law and make it honorable." The whole work of the Divine Redeemer had reference to the claims and character of this perfect law; and it is to be understood and estimated only as we comprehend the nature and extent of these claims upon man. It was to redeem man from the power of the law which he had violated, and under the necessary curse and condemnation of which he was held in bondage; and to bring in an everlasting righteousness for him, that he might be justified freely by the grace of God consistently with the honour and faithfulness of this perfect law,

THE DIVINE LAW.

that God sent forth his Son to be made of a woman, and made under the law. And by this one subjection and offering of himself, the Saviour hath fulfilled the law, merited its rewards, and perfected forever them that are sanctified in him. In every aspect of the law of God as it is related to man, the Lord Jesus is its consummation and fulfilment. And it appears yet more perfect and glorious, as it is beheld completed and honored by him.

Jesus is the consummation of the law as it is viewed in its active operation in the divine providence,—as the rule of the divine government. This work of the Lord Jesus is declared to be the great end, to which all previous divine arrangements tended, and in subservience to which they were made. The continued history of the world, and of God's government over it from the hour of its creation, has exhibited but the preparation which God has been pleased to make, for the attainment of this great result in the fulness of the appointed time. This final work, the interposition of the Son of God for man, the Apostle affirms to be the key to the whole previous mystery of the divine will. "Having made known unto us the mystery of his will, according to his good pleasure who he hath purposed in himself, that in the dispensation of the fulness of times he might gather together in one, all things in Christ." Here is the concentrating point of all the divine dispensations. Every thing in the providence of God, whether in the affairs of a world, or of individual men who are subjects of the Gospel, meets and is explained at the cross of the Lord Jesus Christ. The Apostle carries us also, far beyond the past offering of Jesus, to shew that the future consummation of the Gospel dispensation in its final and glorious result, will be the issue, in which the whole train of previous appointments shall be found to have gained their fulfilment, and their explanation. "Then cometh the end, when he shall have delivered up the kingdom to God, even the Father, when he shall have put down all rule, and all authority and power; for he must reign till he hath put all enemies under his feet." And will not this glorious result, which explains the whole mystery of divine government, and shews the great and glorious end of God's appointment, towards which all its arrangements have tended for ages and generations, magnify this law and make it honorable? Will not the will and appointments of God, seem in the highest degree, wise and benevolent, and faithful, as their results are beheld, in the everlasting joys of those ransomed multitudes, whom God hath thus delivered from condemnation and made partakers of his glory? Surely, when we there know as we are known; when we witness this wonderful issue of divine providence; when we behold thus displayed, the final and everlasting triumphs of the Son of God, we shall be ready to exclaim in this view of the consummation of the law of God's gracious providence in the Lord Jesus Christ, " the law of the Lord is perfect." How exalted will appear the plan which has led to such a result, and the result which has followed upon such a plan! Heaven inhabited, the earth redeemed, the whole family of God perfected in holiness, God, the Father, the Son, and the Holy Ghost forever glorified and honored,—as the great point to which all divine dispensations have been directed in every age,—and which in perfect glory and with perfect success, they have been sufficient to accomplish. And what honour will be given to the law, when it shall be seen, not only that it has been the chosen rule of God's own guidance,—but that it has guided too to the attainment of such wonderful results!

But the Lord Jesus Christ is also the consummation of the law, as it is viewed in its principles, as recorded in the Scriptures. In the wonderful scheme of grace which is revealed in the Gospel, and of which the Saviour is the great centre and sun, all the demands and claims of this holy, just, and good law, are perfectly answered and honored, and no exhibition of the law could so display its perfection, and unfold its beauty, to a mind intelligent upon this subject, as do the character and work of that glorious Mediator, who was made the end of the law for righteousness to his people. He has presented the highest possible pattern and example of obedience to its precepts. The holiness of his character was without a stain or defect. His conformity to divine commands was perfect and undefiled. This obedience on his part was entirely voluntary, and accomplished for the covenanted purpose of justifying many, by its offering in their behalf. It thus presented a righteousness for them, infinite in its worth, from the infinite excellence and dignity of his own nature, and infinitely glorious to the law, to which it was rendered, and to the government, to which it thus acknowledged subjection. Here was the highest possible honour given to the holiness of the law,—when "God over all, blessed forever," became himself subjected to it, and in this voluntary subjection, completely fulfilled it. Beyond this obedience, even the law to which he was voluntarily subjected, had no claims upon him. But he still farther became its consummation, by assuming upon himself, as the substitute and ransom for man, the penalty of his condemnation, and dying an accursed death, under the guilt of man assumed by him, and the curse which man deserved. He thus gave also the highest honour to the majesty of the law, by condescending himself to become the unresisting victim of its power, and by acknowledging in his own sufferings and death, the justice of its claims, and the rightfulness of its authority. He thus fulfilled it, in every possible aspect of its claims,—offering an obedience which must eternally magnify its purity, and a suffering which must honour its power forever. When we view this fulfilment of the law of God, as exhibited in the obedience and death of the divine Redeemer, we are able to say in the highest sense of the expression, and in the highest perception of its truth, "the law of the Lord is perfect." It was perfect before as the rule of the divine government, and in the principles and precepts which it recorded for man. But it had never been perfected by man's obedience, nor could it be thus honored by the obedience of fallen man for himself. But now that God's own Son has taken upon him our nature, that he might be the "end," literally, "the perfection of the law, for righteousness to those who believe,"—we are able to say in the sense of man's obedience, as well as in reference to all the preceding particulars which we have considered, "the law of the Lord is perfect." All that the providence of God in the revelations of his government designed, has been effected in the glorious exhibition of Jesus, in his work. Many sons are brought to glory through the power and merits of the captain of their salvation, who has been perfected in sufferings. And all that the commands of God required of men, has been accomplished by him who thus became a man for them, so that in Christ Jesus as their representative and righteousness, men sinful in themselves, are presented unto God, "faultless before the presence of his glory, with exceeding joy." And redeemed sinners, clothed with his obedience, and triumphant in his death, may sing with joy unspeakable and full of glory throughout eternity, in every possible sense of the expression, "the law of the Lord is perfect."

IV. I cannot imagine a theme more replete with joy and encouragement to a Christian heart, or more gratifying and improving to a sanctified mind, than the extensive one which we have now considered. How delightful is it to be, and to know that we are, under the uniform direction of the highest perfection of wisdom, faithfulness and love; to have the evidence and the promise that we are, and shall be, partakers of a scheme of grace, whose benefits are sure and everlasting, in whose provisions, every claim is satisfied, and every want is supplied. How transporting is it, to take this clear view of the divine excellency, to contemplate the reality and extent of all these perfections; and then to feel sure that we have an abiding interest in a Being whose glories are so unsearchable. "This God is our God;" "God even our own God shall give us his blessing." This is the blessed privilege which this subject presents to our view, exciting us to the highest efforts of obedience; leading us to the cultivation and maintenance of a spiritual mind; enabling us to follow after that holiness without which no man shall see the Lord; giving us that pure and happy spirit of love for the will and character of God, in which the psalmist so emphatically says, "O, how I love thy law, it is better to me than thousands of gold and silver; how sweet are thy words unto my taste, yea sweeter than honey to my mouth!" What can there be in the study and investigation of such a subject, which is not attractive and transforming in its influence, when the heart is attuned again to love the purity which it here sees in God,—and the soul is able to rejoice in the perfect removal of all its fears and dangers under the judgment of this holiness, by the all-sufficient mediation of the anointed Saviour? O, that we may be taught, to estimate this divine knowledge according to its worth; to contemplate the revelations of God which it makes, with delight; and to seek to be ourselves transformed into the same image, from glory to glory, by the Spirit of the Lord!

And while this subject is thus animating to the Christian heart, how inviting and encouraging is it to those who have hitherto neglected God! Though the holiness of the law condemns, and the more its excellence is understood, the more its condemning power is felt, yet the merits of the law-fulfiller, the great surety for the sinner, are seen to be all-sufficient. In him God the Father is well pleased, and equally well pleased with all who are in him, seeking their shelter by faith in his merits, and resting upon his righteousness and power. In him is life; life for all who come to him. But in what way can your guilt be pardoned, your natures be sanctified, your souls be accepted with God, and your condition be made secure with him, but by casting in your lot, with thankful faith and humble penitence, with that Blessed Lord who has fulfilled all righteousness for you, and offers himself with every attendant blessing freely and everlastingly to your acceptance ? How miserable is the sinner's condition who perishes in the midst of such offered mercies; shipwrecked at noonday, off the very haven that offered him security and rest, by his own headstrong confidence in his own wisdom, and his perverse rejection of an adequate and offered guide ! Let not this be your condition. Means of light and knowledge are every where around you. God the Saviour fulfilling all righteousness, stands ready to save and bless you. The perfect law accomplished and honoured in him, directs you to his pardoning and justifying grace, and thus becomes his instrument for converting the soul. The Spirit of God with it as his sword, dividing asunder, and discerning the thoughts and intents of the heart, wounds indeed but only that he may heal, and cuts off on every side, but only that he may cast away that which is unprofitable and vain. With all these privileges, in your possession, what can increase the kindness and confidence with which you are invited to cast in your lot with the people of God, and to partake of the security which is provided for them ? Improve these advantages while you may, and seek and find, and enjoy, a free access unto him, who hath said, " whosoever cometh to me, I will in no wise cast out."

LECTURES ON THE GOSPEL.

LECTURE I.

THE OBJECT OF THE GOSPEL.

The Son of Man is come to seek and to save that which was lost.—
St. Luke, xix. 10.

The Son of Man is the Lord Jesus Christ. By this appellation, he is described in his voluntary humiliation for man's redemption. In his own eternal nature, he was " the Son of God," " the only begotten of the Father," " the brightness of the Father's glory, and the express image of his person." But though " in the form of God," " equal with God," " the fellow of the Lord of Hosts," he " took upon himself, the likeness of man," and " the form of a servant ;" " God was manifest in the flesh," and thus became " the Son of Man," " made of a woman, made under the law, that he might redeem them that are under the law, that we might receive the adoption of sons."

When this wonderful event, the incarnation of the Son of God, was accomplished, he *came*, in the expression of the text before us, from God to man, from heaven to earth, from the most exalted personal glory, to the deepest personal humiliation and distress,—from the possession of perfect bliss, to lay down his life a sacrifice for sin,—to give himself, the just for the unjust, a ransom for his own rebellious creatures. The Father spared not his own Son, but freely delivered him up for guilty man. The Son came in a body which was prepared for him, content to do the Father's will. The Holy Ghost formed him in his human nature, his tabernacle of flesh;—and he thus became a man, a man of sorrows and acquainted with grief; and as the Captain of Salvation to the sons of God, he was made perfect through sufferings.

This coming of the Son of God to be the Son of Man, that he might effectually seek and save that which was lost, is the whole subject of the Gospel. The Sacred Scriptures of God announce glad tidings of good things to perishing men, because they fully proclaim and exhibit this one great fact, that "Christ Jesus came into the world to save sinners,"—that the Son of God hath come, to put away sin by the sacrifice of himself. The word Gospel means glad tidings. The glad tidings are; that there has been provided an all-sufficient and glorious Redeemer for guilty man, upon whom God hath laid the iniquity of us all; who has become a propitiation for the sins of the whole world, that whosoever believeth in him, should not perish, but have everlasting life.

This is the glorious intelligence of the Gospel. The Son of Man has come. He has borne the sinner's burden. He has made an end of sin for those who believe in him. He has brought in an everlasting righteousness as the gift of God to all who will receive it. Having done this, the Gospel which he commands his ministers to preach, is simply the intelligence of this grand fact. The sum and substance of all that we announce to man in the name of our Lord Jesus Christ, is that God " hath made him sin for us, when he knew no sin, that we might be made the righteousness of God in him." Being thus reconciled to us, and in this one offering for sin, displaying this reconciliation, he calls upon us in the annunciation of the fact, to be reconciled to him, and not to receive the grace of God in vain.

The text before us displays in simple terms, *the object and purpose of the Gospel*, the design for which the Son of God came into the world, and to accomplish which he consented to be numbered with transgressors. "The Son of Man is come to seek and to save that which is lost." The mission of the Son of God, constitutes the subject of the Gospel, and the design of that mission is to save the lost. In discussing the important subject which is thus presented, we may consider,

I. The condition in which the Gospel finds mankind.
II. The means which it proclaims, for their deliverance.

I. Consider the *condition in which the Gospel finds the whole race of men.* It is here displayed by a single word. They are "*lost.*" And its single object with them, is " to seek and to save" them. I shall not stay to demonstrate the fact, that man is lost,—that he is neither in the condition, nor having the character, in which he was at first created. God made man upright. Sin against God is man's own invention. I must consider the fact of man's fallen state established in itself, and would labour to impress upon your minds, a clear understanding and conviction of its extent. A thorough perception of your need as guilty creatures, lies at the very root of all attempts to understand and gain the remedy which God has mercifully provided. To acquire this, must be our present purpose. Man will never accept the offers of the Gospel, until he is clearly and thoroughly convinced of his guilt and ruin.

1. The Gospel finds you lost *under a burden of inconceivable guilt.* Every precept of the divine law testifies against you. There is not a duty required of you, which has not been left undone. There is not a transgression prohibited, with which in the sinful thoughts and purposes of your hearts, if not in outward act and deed, you have not been stained. You were born in sin; and from your birth you have gone astray. One transgression would have exposed you to everlasting banishment from God; and your iniquities have been multiplied as the sand of the sea shore. Every hour of your life, because spent in rebellion against God, is a record of con-

demnation against you; nor has there been a single hour which, if you were tried by it, would not sink you into unutterable despair. Your guilt in the sight of God, is therefore inconceivable by you. Until you have written down every sinful purpose and feeling of your lives,—and taken the amount of condemnation which the aggregate of these sinful purposes has necessarily brought upon you, you can have attained no just measure of your guilt. It is high as heaven; what can you know? It is deep as hell; what can you do? It is utterly beyond the compass of your minds, to calculate, or comprehend, the extent of actual guilt which lies upon every soul to whom the Gospel brings its intelligence and offer of mercy. It is a load, which the arm of omnipotence alone, can heave off from any sinner; and the Gospel as the power of God unto salvation, announcing that this guilt has been borne by one mighty to save, comes to seek and to save, those who are lost beneath its weight.

2. The Gospel finds you lost in *a state of extreme personal corruption and unholiness.* The depravity of your fallen nature is exceeding great, and its influence extends to every power of your minds, and to every affection of your hearts. It is vain to dispute about the words *total depravity,* which are so often used to express this aspect of man's natural state. The assertion simply is, that there is nothing in you by nature, which is not sinful, "the heart of the sons of men is full of evil." Their understandings are darkened; their will is perverse; their affections are earthly and sensual; their conscience is partial; their memory will not retain heavenly truths; their bodies are under the influence of a depraved mind; and every member, instead of being an instrument of holiness, is a willing servant to sin. From the head to the foot, there is no soundness or spiritual health in the unrenewed or natural man. In your whole character, and through your whole lives, in this condition there is no good thing. If

your everlasting salvation were made contingent upon the simple condition of your finding one thought or desire in the whole compass of your past days, which was not stained with sin, you would be forever shut out from hope. There is none of you who hath done good,—no, not one. That there may be depravity beyond yours in degree, none will attempt to deny. But that there is anything in your fallen nature which is not depraved, the word of God denies most solemnly and repeatedly. And the Gospel finds you lost in this extreme state of personal unholiness, when it comes to seek and to save you.

3. The Gospel finds you lost in *a state of enmity to God.* The natural mind of every man is enmity against God, and will not be subject to his will. In some persons, it may break forth into more open acts of hostility than in others. But it is not less really enmity to God, when it is cloaked with a fair exterior, or shut up and concealed under false professions of frienship. There is a direct and positive hostility and opposition between the mind of God,—and the mind of every unconverted sinner. They pursue opposite, and wholly inconsistent ends. While the one is gathering, the other is labouring to scatter abroad. Many persons may be wholly unconscious of any distinct purposes of opposition to the will of God, and they may deny that they have such. The simple reason is, they do not stop to consider what the will of God is; or they have formed such erroneous views of his character, that they have no hostility to a being whom they have made altogether such an one as themselves. To a God of perfect holiness, a God who cannot abide transgression,— a God who will by no means clear the guilty,—there is not an unrenewed man upon earth, who is not an enemy. Your whole course of character and conduct, in an unconverted state, is operating to thwart the divine purposes in the redemption of the world; to cause iniquity to abound, when he would

make an end of sin;—and to withhold from the Lord Jesus the heart which he would bring home to the dominion of God, reconciled and subdued. By these wicked works, you prove yourselves the enemies of God, and in this lost condition, the Gospel comes to seek and to save you.

4. The Gospel finds you lost in *a state of utter inability to return to God, or to restore to yourselves, the divine image or favour.* So far are you from being able to recommend yourselves to God, that every imagination of the thoughts of your heart is only evil continually. The Spirit of God alone can enable you to will, or to do, any thing that is good. You have not a wish to be reconciled to God, until he imparts it. Your dispositions and affections are so entirely averted from him, and you love darkness and sin, so much better than you love light and holiness, that you find in yourselves no native desire to be brought either to a full knowledge of yourselves, or to a knowledge of God. This aversion of your minds from God forms an utter incapacity in yourselves, to return to him. And were there no other power to operate for the conversion of your souls, but the determining power of your own wills, Ezekiel might prophesy to the dry bones, with as much hope, as we should preach the Gospel unto you. It is even more entirely beyond your power, to restore to yourselves the divine image and favour which have been lost by your sin. This is a path which no human wisdom hath ever trodden, and which no mortal eye can ever discern. And except as the result of God's unsearchable riches of grace, all possibility of reconciliation to him would cease forever. So far as it regards a way to render God merciful to the sinner's soul, or to render this soul inclined to God, though the wisdom of all created beings should be united, to decide upon the method which would be successful, the Gospel finds you wholly lost, and must seek you, and save you, as beings whom no other power can restore.

This is the condition in which the Gospel finds you. In your fallen nature, you are *lost*, under a load of intolerable guilt,—in an extreme degree of personal unholiness,—in the enmity of your hearts to God,—and in an utter inability to restore yourselves to the divine favour,—or to restore the image of God to your own souls. I have no wish to overstate this subject. But a discernment of this condition by yourselves, is indispensable. Until you become acquainted through the convincing power of the Holy Spirit, with your own necessities,—it is vain to direct your notice to the gracious provisions which God has revealed in the Gospel for your rescue and relief. Your natural condition as sinners against God, may be adequately illustrated, by a comparison of it with the actual condition of fallen angels. They have contracted guilt, and are unable to remove it. They have lost the divine image in which they were created, and are unable to recover it. Having no provision of grace made for them, they are left in endless and irremediable misery. The simple difference between them and you in this respect, is the difference which sovereign grace has made;—grace which has interposed in your behalf, and not in theirs, because " God hath had mercy upon whom he would have mercy." The Son of God, took not upon him the nature of angels, nor the guilt of angels,—but he took upon him, the seed of Abraham, and made himself an offering for their sin. But to persuade you to this view of personal guilt, is the great difficulty in preaching the Gospel. The pride of man sternly rebels against it. But until you do thus perceive and acknowledge yourselves to be wholly lost, and forever lost, so far as any other power than this amazing grace of God is considered, we can never hope to lead you to Christ, nor will you be persuaded to hear of a Saviour with thankfulness, or to embrace with gladness, the salvation which he has provided for you.

II. Consider the *means for this salvation which the Gospel* proclaims. The Saviour's object is a single one. "The Son of man has come to seek, and to save that which is lost." Every other purpose which the Gospel accomplishes in reference to man,—and every other aspect under which the Saviour is presented in regard to man, is subordinate to this. As a teacher of morals, a revealer of wisdom, a guide in life, an example of holiness, the character of the Lord Jesus is comforting and honourable. But all these offices and characteristics are merged in that one glorious, indispensable character, a Saviour for the chief of sinners. And this is the character which the text presents.

The first object of the Lord Jesus, was to *seek* a world that was lost; a world that had started forth as it were, from its proper orbit of submission to God, and had wandered off, unknowing and unknown, in regions of everlasting darkness and despair. Like the shepherd, whose ninety and nine sheep had remained under his protection, while one only had gone astray, the Saviour left the innumerable hosts of beings, who still owned his just dominion, and came to look for this one poor race of creatures; that in the wonderful method which he had devised, he might save them from destruction, and bring them back to acknowledge and delight in the holy government of their Creator.

Having visited and *found* this alienated world, his next object was to *save* it; to put an instant stop to the course of condemnation and ruin; to arrest the proceedings, and to satisfy the claims of violated justice; and to subdue the purpose of rebellion, which actuated the heart of man. In the accomplishment of this purpose, he has rendered the forgiveness of man consistent with the character and government of God, and has provided means to reconcile the alienated heart of man, to God, from whom in this rebellion, it had been averted. In the pursuit of this great object of salvation, the Gospel has made every provision, which the lost condition of the soul of man demands. It offers to man's acceptance, a salvation in every respect honourable to God, and adapted to his utmost wants.

1. For the *inconceivable guilt* which presses down your souls to death, the Gospel proclaims a sufficient *substitute* and *surety* in the person of God's own dear Son, a divinely appointed Redeemer. This gracious Saviour gave himself a ransom for all. As the Son of man, he came to stand in the sinner's place. He was divinely formed, as the virgin's son, that he might partake of the nature of man, without the inheritance of his unholiness and condemnation. He was the subject of all the sinless infirmities of our imperfect nature, but he was free from its corruption and guilt. He was a victim without blemish and without spot. Having no sins in himself to demand atonement, he was able to make himself an offering for the sins of others. Being infinite in majesty and power, the offering which he made, was adequate to the need which required it. In his sacred person, were united both God and man, and having humbled himself unto death, even the death of the cross, the Father laid upon him, the iniquities of us all. For you he suffered as a sacrifice. For you he endured the curse, and the penalty of the law,—which, if required of you, would have consigned you to eternal woe. For you, he obeyed its holy precepts, to work out a righteousness which should be imputed unto all, and put upon all, who believe. He thus became perfectly a ransom in the stead of you,—voluntarily bearing your guilt,—enduring its condemnation and curse, and accomplishing your title unto life eternal. When you with thankfulness, personally accept his righteousness, to be put upon you, this work of the Son of man for each of you will be accomplished. Your sins shall be remembered against you no more forever,—and your souls shall find eternal peace with God. This great offering of the Son of man has completely restored the relation of peace between

you and God,—so far as the purposes and mind of God are concerned. It has rendered God's purposes of love to you, perfectly consistent with the holiness, justice, and faithfulness of his own character. It has met the denunciations of the offended law. It has satisfied the utmost claims of the Divine majesty. It has done every thing which was necessary, to save you from your lost and ruined state. And having opened a perfect and sufficient way of rescue for you, from the everlasting punishment of sin, and a full and glorious entrance into the kingdom of God, it offers to all of you, its abundant means of spiritual cleansing and healing. You are complete in him.

2. For the *unholiness and depravity* of your souls,—your hostility to God, and your inability to return to him, the Gospel proclaims an adequate relief, in the influence and power of the *Holy Spirit*, the third person of the blessed Trinity, whom the Saviour sends to dwell in every heart that will receive him, as an everlasting comforter and guide. It is his work to bring back your affections to God, and to restore to you the image of divine holiness. He delivers you from your native enmity to God, by taking away from you, the evil heart of unbelief, and giving to you a cheerful and grateful submission to the will, and the plans of God. He supplies the defects of your entire incapacity to do good, by renewing you through his own power, and leading you both to will and to do, according to his good pleasure. He reveals the Saviour's excellence and attractions to your mind, and makes you to love, and to desire, the things of Christ.

Your personal inability to turn to God and live, though it be the direct result of sin, and no original weakness of your unfallen nature, is an entire inability. You are wholly destitute of a desire or power to prepare yourselves by good works for a return to God. You are dead in your sins. In this state the Spirit of Christ comes to you, to bring the knowledge of his salvation. He quickens you by his divine power—that power which raised Christ himself from the grave. He shews you the extent of your wants and dangers. He humbles you under a consciousness of them. He stirs you up to cry after God. He gives you a godly sorrow for sin. He reveals the fulness of a Saviour's power, and the glory of his finished work, to your view. He enables you to exercise faith in him, and to receive him in your heart, as your hope of glory, with joyful confidence, in all the offices which he sustains for you. He fills you with love to Christ, and constrains you to devote yourselves to him. He gives you ability to mortify the indwelling power of sin, and to honour the Lord whom you now serve, in a holy conversation. He transforms you more and more entirely after the image of Christ, and renders you meet to become partakers of the inheritance of the saints in light. The Holy Spirit is thus the divine agent in applying personally to your souls, the perfect and all-sufficient redemption which the Son of God has wrought out for you; and thus under the gracious provisions of the Gospel, you have access through Jesus Christ, by one Spirit unto the Father.

In the means of deliverance which the Gospel thus provides for you, it accomplishes its one grand object, "to seek and to save, that which is lost." The outward difficulties in the way of your salvation, the Gospel removes, in the proclamation of God the Son, as a sacrifice and righteousness for you. The inward difficulties, arising in yourselves, it equally removes, by the offer of God the Spirit, as a sanctifier and new creator of your souls. When you were all without strength, Christ died for the ungodly, and thus came to seek and to save, a world which was lost. While you are individually dead in sins, the Holy Spirit comes as the gift of Christ to apply to your souls, the work which he has finished, and to seek and to save you personally, from your lost estate. These are the means of deliverance which the Gospel provides for sinners who are lost. They are perfectly sufficient for the end designed. They supply every possible want. They meet every possible difficulty. They come up to the utmost extent of the sinner's need. And whosoever is willing to receive them, finds in them, a full and everlasting salvation. The Gospel thus attains its great and all-important object. It proclaims the perfect righteousness of the Lord Jesus, reconciling God to you. It offers the all-powerful influence of the Holy Ghost to reconcile you to God. It announces God to be already reconciled in his Son. It intreats you to be reconciled to him, by the Spirit. It is thus effectual for the purpose of the Son of man "to seek, and to save that which was lost."

III. In concluding my remarks upon this important subject, I must ask you to examine with the utmost fidelity, how far this object has been attained among you.

"The Son of man has come to seek and to save," this whole congregation of sinners, pressing forward to the judgment seat of God. Had the gospel produced its proper effect, there would not be in this assembly one transgressor still alienated from God through the blindness of his mind. But alas, how far are we from this result! What mean the number of slaves to the world, of captives to Satan, to whom the solemn voice of the Almighty God this day comes in the warnings of his word? What mean the giddy children of folly and mirth, for whom hell has opened her mouth, and still enlarges herself without measure? Whence the swarm of infidel hearts that yet lift up themselves in rebellion against the Creator of heaven and earth? O, how very partially has the great object of the gospel been attained among you! Could I go from soul to soul before me, and see the mark of God's infallible determination of character rise upon your foreheads as I approached each; upon what numbers should I read that solemn word, LOST, LOST! in many cases, perhaps, beyond the reach of recovery! And what would be the probable result—but, that the greater portion of this assembly of immortal beings would be proclaimed, to be still under the wrath of God, and without hope in the world? This fact is awful; is it a fact? Am I now addressing hundreds who are denying the Lord that bought them, and bringing upon their souls a swift destruction? And are you careless and unconcerned under such views of your character and condition? Do you feel nothing? Have you *no* desire to be brought back to the fold of Jesus? Have you no wish to be saved in the day of his power? Will you choose as your portion, the darkness and despair in which unpardoned sin will inevitably involve you? I would ask you honestly and affectionately, will you determine to drive the Son of God from your souls, and lie down in the unbeliever's everlasting portion?

I would speak to you, as a poor sinful creature, with humility and tenderness; but I would speak to you also, as the minister of God to you for good, with authority and much assurance; I warn the multitude of dying and yet unconverted sinners to whom I speak, that they cannot escape the just judgment of God. I call upon you in the name of the glorious Redeemer, who desires not your death, to awake from the ruinous delusion which you are playing upon your own hearts. Lay up no more sorrow for the last days. Be no longer infatuated with the false promises of the destroyer. The Son of man has sought you, O shall he not be allowed to save you and bless you with peace? Every thing is waiting the result of your own determination; heaven and hell are often suspended upon a moment's choice: and this night you either go back with the shepherd to the fold, or you bind yourself the more irrevocably to the power of the destroyer.

Poor deluded sinner, *lost!* O, how much is meant by that one word *lost.* The man has wandered from his home, the shadows of the evening are stretched out, the coming darkness hurries on despair. Alone in a wilderness, wearied with anxiety and fatigue, with no track to lead him to his home, no prospect of repose but on the bosom of the desert, no shelter for the night but the chill atmosphere of his solitude, with what feverish delirium he throws himself upon the earth. Home, children, friends, comforts and joys, all crowd into his bewildered mind. But these are gone. He shall see them no more. He is *lost*, and many a heart is swelling with anguish at the fear that he is lost forever. No sound arrests his ear but the desert's blast, or the wild beast's roar; and hope, and peace, and reason too, have taken their flight from his disordered mind.

But see, a messenger of kindness comes to this lost man to tell him of a path to his home, and to lead him back to its secure repose. He wakes him from his dream, intreats him to arise and go with him, assures him that he will lead him in safety to his own abode, and with a thousand words of sympathy and love intercedes with him for his own deliverance. But reason and feeling and recollection have gone, and though he is lost, he refuses to hearken to his guide. He will listen for a moment to his kind offer, and then lie down in the madness of despair, finally to perish, and turn a deaf ear to every intreaty and remonstrance. You pity the image which fancy has created, but you are *lost*, and will not pity the actual miseries of your own ruined, deserted souls, nor allow the Son of man, this messenger of mercy, to bring you back to his Father's house in peace.

LECTURE II.

THE GOSPEL WAY OF SALVATION.

By grace ye are saved through faith, and that not of yourselves: it is the gift of God.—EPHESIANS, II. 8.

THE great object of the Gospel is the eternal salvation of man. To accomplish this object, has been the design of the Son of God, in all that he has done, and suffered, and taught. The accomplishment of this great purpose, is all that man requires. Let the sinner be *saved*, and he may be happy in the possession of this salvation, though he be poor, and heavily burdened with the sorrows of the present life. Let him live and die without the attainment of this salvation, and all the wealth and indulgences of the world, cannot purchase for him, the comfort which he needs. The few years of his existence here, are but of small importance; whether they pass away in sorrow or in joy, they will soon pass, and their pains and pleasures be alike forgotten. So far as this life is concerned, therefore, it would be reasonable in you, to dismiss anxiety and care. But you have to die;—and after death, the judgment; and after the judgment, eternity is before you. These claim, and must have your faithful consideration, and intense concern. Seventy years of life, even if you are sure of their possession, we will allow you to despise. But the countless ages of a future state cannot be thus lightly treated. For them, the great question is to be settled, and to be settled *here*, shall you be SAVED or LOST?

The object of the Gospel of the Lord Jesus, is to settle this important question for you, and to save you with an everlasting salvation. It teaches you how you shall attain this everlasting salvation, how you shall escape the just judgment of God, and come before his spotless throne, in perfect and eternal peace. This is the subject of instruction which I desire to bring before you, in the present discourse, in which I would speak, of *the Gospel way of salvation.*

By nature, you are in a state of utter ruin and condemnation. You have no peace with God, and when awakened by the Holy Spirit to see your real condition, no comfort or hope in yourselves. Eternity appears before you filled with the blackness of darkness forever. You have no foundation for hope when God takes away your soul. God, in his righteous indignation against you, appears a consuming fire, and you feel that it is a fearful thing to fall into the hands of the Living God. But how you shall escape this anger, or be delivered from the proper consequences of your own transgressions, it is utterly beyond your power to determine. This is a mystery which would have remained hidden in God forever, had it not pleased him, in the riches of his grace, to reveal it to you, in the Gospel of his Son. To the simple decision of this point, the text before us, comes with the revelation of the wisdom of God, while it answers, as from the very throne of the Most High, to every question and every doubt, " By grace are ye saved, through faith ; and that not of yourselves, it is the gift of God."

In considering this subject, the text presents three natural divisions, in the three assertions which it makes :

I. " By *grace* ye are saved," as the *cause* and the *instrument.*

II. "Through *faith,*" as the *method.*

III. " It is the *gift* of God," as the *origin.*

I. " *By grace ye are saved.*" When we are first awakened

and convinced of sin, by the Holy Spirit, we ask, like the jailor at Philippi, "what shall we *do* to be saved?" Probably in all cases, the first idea which occurs to the mind, is, that we must *do* something, in order that we may in some way merit or earn the salvation which we want. The self-righteous spirit is instinct in man, and immediately rises, to propose its own method of relief. The performance of some particular duty, the hearing of some preacher, the reading of some book, the new obedience of life to come, or our grief and sorrow for life past, all severally occur to the mind, as a price for the blessing we need, or as a reason and method for future hope. It is often long, before we are willing to trust ourselves wholly to the free and sovereign grace of God, and the entirely finished salvation of Christ, as the foundation of all our confidence and joy. But the salvation which the Gospel provides, is wholly of grace, both as flowing from the original unmerited favour and mercy of God the Father, and as applied by the divine and special power of the Holy Ghost. The Father hath sent the Son to be the Saviour of the world. The Holy Spirit takes of the things of Christ, and shews them unto men; and by his new creating power, enables them to receive him and to believe in him, unto life everlasting. The first aspect of the text declares salvation as the gift of grace, to the entire exclusion of human *merit*. The second proclaims the application of this gift, by the power of grace, to the equal exclusion of the *power* of man. These two points we shall distinctly consider.

1. "By grace are ye saved," in the free exercise of *divine mercy*, shutting out every thought of human works or deservings. Indeed the idea of merit in a fallen and imperfect being is in itself entirely absurd. Consider the condition of our first parents, after their disobedience to God. What could *they* do, to recommend themselves to the favour of the God against whom they had offended? I will not ask, what they could do

to merit the gift of God's dear Son,—and the influences of his Holy Spirit upon their hearts,—for it is obvious that no thought of the possibility of such a method of restoration, could by any means have entered into their minds. But what single personal act, or service could they render to God, for which he should be induced to pardon their disobedience and restore them to his favour? Or, what can the fallen angels now do, to restore the image and favour of God to themselves? They are surely as capable of earning their salvation, if a sinful being may ever earn it, as is any unconverted sinner on earth. But if it should be said, that though man could not originally earn salvation for himself, yet since God has mercifully bestowed a Saviour upon man, we must be expected to do something to deserve his favour, or by some service, to repay him for his kindness; I ask, what can we do? "What have we, that we have not received?" "Without him, we can do nothing." And if the bestowal of his grace, must precede every good act in us, it is evident, that we can do nothing to deserve it. We are wholly dependant upon God's sovereign pleasure, for the ability both to will and to do. The first gift of a Saviour sprang from God's unmerited love, and so must our salvation by him in all its parts. We have nothing to offer him. All our sufficiency is of God; and whatever we render him, we only give him that which is his own.

The Gospel opens to us therefore, a salvation perfectly free. It has provided every thing which our souls can want. And having made such abundant provisions, it asks us to receive them all without money and without price. They are provisions of grace, which are clogged with no conditions. You are to accept the whole, as the gift of God to those who are perishing, and thus they become your own forever. Neither the depth of previous guilt nor the extreme weakness and corruption of your nature, forms any difficulty. Salvation is as freely offered to the pirate in his dungeon, as to the man who is in the morality of his conduct, not far from the kingdom of God. Whosoever will, may take a blessing, which is offered to all who hunger and thirst after righteousness, and to which man can add nothing, and for which man has nothing to give. In making this free offer of mercy, the Gospel does not ask what you have been, or what you have done. It addresses you as the chief of sinners, as crimsoned with the stains of guilt; and presents the full glories of its finished and perfect salvation, as freely to one, as to another, asking nothing but an humble and thankful acceptance of the gift. The whole work of merit has been finished; and the whole offer of it is free and simple.

2. But how shall you obtain this gift? How shall it be applied personally to your souls? The text answers you with equal distinctness, *"by grace ye are saved."* The Holy Ghost must come upon you, and the power of the Highest must overshadow you, that you may be created anew, and led in entire self-renunciation, to embrace the offers which are thus freely made. The Spirit of God, gives a real conviction of sin; a godly sorrow for sin; a true repentance from sin; and leads you to the Saviour who is revealed as your atonement, and righteousness, for forgiveness and peace. He bestows upon you that new heart and new nature, which are promised in the covenant which God has made and proclaimed in the Gospel. His power is all-sufficient; and every step which is taken, in the way of life, is the working of his mighty power. When you are dead in sins, he awakens you to spiritual life. While you are infirm and feeble, he strengthens and sustains you, with new communications of strength. He refreshes you with the living water that flows from Christ the fountain; and feeds you with the living bread, which is Christ the gift of God. From the first hour, to the last, of your spiritual life, by the grace of God, you are what you are. There is no dependance placed in human power. Your own wisdom, strength, or

determination, are not the instruments of your safety. The Gospel demands nothing of you, which it does not first impart to you, and work within you, that from the divine fulness, you may receive grace upon grace. When it requires you to repent, or believe, or walk in new obedience, it offers to you as gifts, the very qualities which it commands you to exercise. Nor is there a single Christian attribute which can flow from any other source, than this amazing sufficiency which is thus laid open.

Th s view of salvation as wholly of grace, is most important to you, and cannot be too deeply impressed upon your minds. The Saviour asks nothing from you, but what he at the same time offers to give you. There is not a grace in the renewed heart which proceeds not from his own gift. The very same Spirit upholds and sanctifies the steadfast believer, which first awakened the careless guilty, and consoled and transformed the penitent transgressor. The Gospel sets up no one with an independant stock of religious character or influence. Your manna must fall every morning, and be gathered before the sun is hot. Your barrel and your cruse shall never fail, but they shall never be filled. As your day is, so, and only so, shall your strength be. And you might as reasonably close the shutters of your house at noonday, to retain for future use, the light of the sun, which you have already received, as think of retaining grace and strength, when separated from immediate and uninterrupted communication with the great source of both. You can live only while Christ lives in you. From the first to the last, the work of your sanctification is all divine, and the glory belongs entirely to God.

Thus the Gospel salvation is in these two distinct aspects, a salvation by grace, to the entire exclusion, both of human merit, and of human power. The provisions which God has made, it asks men to accept with confidence and gratitude; and then promises, and gives them the power to accept them.

The full foundation for your hope was laid, when the Prince of life rose from the dead, after having offered himself upon the cross, as a sacrifice for sins. Upon this foundation, you are able to build securely, and happily, when the Spirit of God is permitted, to lead you back, from your love and pursuit of sin, to acknowledge and to receive Christ the Saviour, as your righteousness and peace.

II. The text states the method in which you become interested in this salvation, " by grace are ye saved, *through faith.*"

Every gracious provision of the Gospel is made for us, by the mercy of God, entirely independant of ourselves; and the work of our salvation is accomplished, when by the Divine Spirit we are finally interested in these abundant provisions which God freely offers us in his own Son. When we are thus united to Christ, we are partakers of his abundant merit, and of the Father's mercy in him; our sins are pardoned through his atonement; our souls are justified through his obedience; his divine power is covenanted for us; and because he lives, we shall live also. All these provisions of grace, are beyond ourselves, and independent of our works; and it is by faith in the power and truth of him who offers them, that we are interested in them. The foundation is laid; it is perfect; it is sufficient. Whether we believe or not, it remains the same. God cannot deny himself. Would you become partakers of this offered grace, you must believe the record which God hath given you concerning his Son; and look in confidence to him, for the communication of these benefits to yourselves. You must rest your hopes, and your affections, upon that unmerited love of God which has offered salvation; and trust in that all-powerful influence of his Spirit, which may apply this salvation to you. There is no other method, by which you may obtain an interest, in the mercies which God has treasured up in Jesus Christ. Your simple confidence in the power and promises of Christ, is the way, which the Scripture uniformly teaches, by which his fulness of grace, and his finished work of righteousness is to become yours. If I have treasured up in my house, abundant provisions for the destitute, which I offer freely to their use, if they will receive them, how can they obtain the blessing which is provided, but by believing that it is there; and that it will be indeed bestowed; and then by asking in this confidence of faith for its bestowal? God's treasures of grace are laid up for you in Christ. They are not now to be provided or made; or to be increased in any degree by any thing that you can do. Believe that they are there; believe that they are all-sufficient; believe that they will indeed be given; and then ask for them with the sense of their need, and the desire to obtain them, which faith produces; and you shall not be sent empty away. It is the character of his people, that they "have known, and believed, the love, which God hath to them." This perfect love casts out all fear, and gives them new and simple confidence and hope.

It is true, you are required to repent of sin; and to obey the commands of God, in a new life of holiness. But these are the attendants and results of a sincere faith. You can have no repentance unto salvation, without believing in him whom you have pierced, who is exalted to bestow it. You cannot obey a single command, but by his power dwelling within you. All these gracious dispositions and habits are fruits of his Holy Spirit; and are so far from being any preceding qualification by which you obtain salvation, that they are themselves a part, and a most important part, of that very salvation, which is offered you freely in the Lord Jesus Christ, as the purchase of his obedience and death. "He that hath the Son, hath life;" and all the traits, and attributes, and acts of life, flow out from it.

Do you ask for a godly sorrow for sin? for a subjection of

your unholy affections? for the dominion of holiness and love within your hearts? May not the Lord Jesus reply to all this, "believest thou that I am able to do this?" And will not his bestowal of these, and of all other things accompanying salvation, depend upon the answer which your conscience must render, to a question like this? "Only believe," we may still say to you, in reply to every difficulty, and these and all other mercies will be certainly bestowed. The treasury of God's mercy and love, in which attributes, he is "rich," is freely opened to you. Everything which you want, is there. Your coming thither in faith, will bring you to such provisions of grace, as pass man's understanding. You can purchase nothing. You have nothing to offer. You can render no return. When you are vitally interested in Christ, you will need nothing more. By faith you are thus engrafted in him. There you will find no deficiency for your own power to supply. When he dwells within you by faith, as your hope of glory, every holy trait, every lovely disposition, every spiritual habit, every heavenly desire, shall spring and rise, and flourish, and spread abroad in your heart and character, from Christ who dwelleth in you, by the power of the Spirit with which he sanctifieth you. But until by faith, you put on Christ, and yield yourselves to him, you are dead in your sins. "He that hath not the Son of God, hath not life." And a dead man might as justly be expected, to rise up, and offer a price for that life, the possession of which is implied in this very rising, as you expect to offer anything, from a depraved and dead soul, upon the worth of which Christ may shew the further power of his grace. You are to be saved wholly by grace; that grace is applied to you through a faith which is of the operation of God. So that even here, to take away, all pride and glorying from yourselves, the grace, and faith, and every mercy, are declared to spring from other power than yours. They are all "the gift of God," a gift to those who are poor, and destitute, and perishing in sin.

III. "That not of yourselves, it is *the gift of God.*" This last assertion does not refer merely to the faith which has been just declared, as the method of salvation, but to the whole salvation by grace, of which the text speaks. Every part of man's salvation, is equally the free gift of God. The original purpose to save, the glorious sacrifice which has been made, the offer of the benefits of that sacrifice to you, the acceptance of it by your own hearts, and the peace and holiness which this acceptance gives, are all equally the result of a principle of love in God, which looks to no merit, or strength, or recompense, in the creatures, to whom the gift is made. The same determinate counsel and purpose of divine mercy, which delivered up a Saviour to be crucified for you, and elected you as the objects of this amazing gift, will in the last day, finish your salvation by crowning you with him. Your last breath will be as much dependant upon him as your first; and eternity will be spent, not in personal congratulations upon your own strength, or wisdom, or perseverance, but in raptured hallelujahs of thanksgiving, to him who has loved you, and given himself for you, and washed you from your sins in his own blood, and redeemed you from every kindred and tongue, and people and nation, to make you kings and priests unto God for ever.

These precious truths have been controverted in every age, and there have been multitudes of men who have opposed this casting down of human merit, and this ascription of all praise and glory, to the grace of God. Still the Bible teaches the same thing; and the plain and simple way of salvation which it first laid open to sinners, it lays open now. And it seems to me that nothing can be more plain and evident, and intelligible, than is this way of salvation which the gospel offers. On the one side there is a poor, wretched creature, wanting every thing and having nothing to give; and on the other, there is a bountiful Sovereign and Lord, who offers every thing freely, and asks no price from the subject of his grace.

The gospel is provided in all its operations as a remedy for existing evil, and as such it is in every part exclusively "the gift of God." If you come back to consider the actual state of a fallen being, the actual condition of your own souls by nature, you will find yourselves to be entirely in a guilty, polluted and helpless condition. In this state of spiritual ruin, God has provided for you a *remedy;* and he both inclines and enables you to accept and apply that remedy. For your guilt he applies to you the atoning blood of Christ; for your pollution and weakness, he sends the Holy Spirit to bring you to Christ, and to begin and carry on a work of grace within your hearts. By looking to Christ you may obtain peace with God and in your own conscience; and by yielding yourselves to the influences of God's Holy Spirit, you may become renewed and sanctified in all your powers. Your renovated health will begin immediately to appear. You will be enabled to mortify all your former corruptions, and to walk holily, justly and unblamably before God and man, and will become transformed into the divine image in righteousness and true holiness. But to what then shall be ascribed the change which has taken place within you? Will it not be altogether owing to the remedy which God has prescribed and enabled you to apply? To your latest hour you will continue to apply the same remedy; for through the whole of this life you will be only convalescent and not perfectly recovered. And when in the full establishment of your spiritual health, in the heavenly inheritance, you tell the history of your restoration, it will be to the sole honour of that Almighty Physician who visited you in your lost estate, and brought a balm which was adequate to your need. Now is not this perfectly plain and simple? Is it not exactly *the* gift which every sinner wants for the peace of his mind, and for the sanctification and salvation of his soul? Yet in this representation, all is of grace. Both the Saviour himself, and unmerited salvation through him, are the free gift of God; and not according to works of righteousness which we have done, but according to his mercy we are saved by the washing of regeneration and the renewing of the Holy Ghost.

I have thus endeavoured to set before you *the gospel way of salvation.* You find it a way perfectly adapted to your condition and to your necessities. It calls for your sincere thankfulness to God, who has been willing to provide it, and for your cordial acceptance of the gift, while it is so freely presented. But all will be of no avail to you unless you embrace with rejoicing, the remedy which is thus presented. Let not the subject, therefore, be allowed to rest in your understandings unfruitful and barren. Seek to have your hearts interested in it; hear the voice of the Spirit, which says to you, "This is the way, walk ye in it;" and turn not to the right hand or to the left. Let me beseech you to seek a deep acquaintance with your real state before God, and the application to yourselves of the gracious remedy which is offered you in the gospel.

Had you but a due preparation of heart for the reception of this gospel,—were you truly convinced of your unworthiness and danger, the glad tidings of salvation would distil as the dew upon your souls, as the showers that water the mown grass. Did you feel that the sorrows of death compassed you about, and the pains of hell had got hold upon you, in the deep and piercing sense of your own guilt, the sound of salvation purchased by our incarnate God would transport your souls, as it did the angels, when they sung, "Glory to God in the highest; and on earth, peace; good will towards men." Unspeakable joy would spring up in your hearts from the thought of an indwelling God, undertaking your cause and working effectually upon your souls. The great and universal reason why you hear the gracious invitations and promises of the gospel so inattentively, and with so little effect upon your characters, is, that you are not convinced of your danger. You do not feel and mourn over your lost condition. "They that are whole need not a physician." Because so many of you believe yourselves to be whole, the remedy is heedlessly rejected, and your souls are left to perish. O that God would tear off from your hearts, the veil which Satan and the world are uniting to weave over you, and make you to see the pollutions which are there open to his view! Why are you so anxious to deceive yourselves in this matter? There is a day before you when hell shall be naked, and destruction shall have no covering; when every false excuse shall fail, and every extenuating plea shall become utterly useless; and when, though discovery shall be perfect, it shall be too late to be beneficial. If you *are* insolvent and ruined, why attempt to delude yourselves with the contrary belief? But *are* you not? Do you not feel so? Then Jesus is no Saviour to you. You may as profitably own Mahomet or Brahma for your Lord, as Jesus. He will not, he cannot save you till you feel yourselves to be *lost*. I pray you look at your characters in the mirror of God's infallible word; and while he proclaims that you have altogether gone out of the way, acknowledge the truth of his representation, and be willing that he should bring you back to himself in peace.

Upon this deep acquaintance with your own character and state alone, can be built a proper acceptance of the gospel. However your understandings may be enlightened with a knowledge of the gospel way of salvation, it will profit you nothing while this knowledge is merely speculative. Though the patient in the hospital should deliver a lecture upon his own disease, and the adaptation of the remedy to his want, it would avail but little should he still refuse to apply the remedy to himself. If you neglect the gracious remedy of the gospel, or substitute any other in its stead, you do so to your eternal ruin. I beseech you to look to Christ by his Holy Spirit, for the justification, and the sanctification of your souls. In no other conceivable method can you find salvation from the condemnation of the law, the bondage of sin, and the everlasting punishment of hell. There is no other name given for salvation, but the name of Jesus, and that name is worse than useless to you, unless it be permitted to dwell in your heart, as your hope and comfort. Yield yourselves to his power. Be willing to be saved by grace through faith; and so receive the unspeakable gift of God, that his power may operate within you, to bring you home to that fold of ransomed sinners, which is under one shepherd, Jesus Christ, the Great Bishop and Shepherd of souls.

LECTURE III.

THE HISTORY OF THE GOSPEL.

Blessed be the Lord God of Israel, for he hath visited and redeemed his people.

As he spake by the mouth of his holy prophets, which have been since the world began."—St. Luke, I. 68—70.

In one previous discourse, we have considered the great *object* which the gospel designs to accomplish; " to seek and to save that which is lost." In another, I have spoken of the *way* which the gospel lays open for the attainment of this object, which is " by grace through faith, as the gift of God."

Before I proceed to consider several distinct attributes and characteristics of the gospel, I wish in my present discourse to set before you the *history of the gospel.* By this expression, I do not mean the narrative of facts which the writings of the Evangelists contain, but the history of the gospel itself, as a dispensation to man, showing its origin and its progress, in the clear manifestations of its grace to those for whom it was designed, since the fall of man.

As an appropriate introduction to this subject, I have selected this text from the sacred hymn which Zacharias uttered at the circumcision of his son. This hymn was spoken by the immediate inspiration of God, for it is said, " that Zacharias was filled with the Holy Ghost, and prophesied" in the divine language which is here contained. Every assertion therefore which this hymn makes, must be infallible and eternal truth.

The son of Zacharias was the forerunner of the Lord Jesus Christ, the Saviour of the world; and on the occasion of his public dedication to God, his father prophesied of the character and work of that Saviour before whom he was to be sent.

The Redeemer was not yet born in the lowly nature which he had assumed. But the faith of Zacharias was led forward to him, when it is more than probable that none of his auditors, beside his own wife, understood the allusions which he made. "Blessed," he says, "be the Lord God of Israel, for *he* hath visited and redeemed his people, and hath raised up a horn of salvation for us in the house of his servant David." In the figurative language of the Israelites, a horn implies great strength, and in the text, "a horn of salvation," is a strong salvation; an all-sufficient salvation; a salvation to the uttermost; or, as in our prayer-book "a mighty salvation;" because accomplished by the mighty God of Israel, although he stooped to be a babe in the family of his servant David. The reference of this high title, "THE LORD GOD OF ISRAEL," to the child who was to be born of Mary, becomes evident in the succeeding verses of the hymn, in which Zacharias addresses himself to his own child, whom he now held up in dedication unto God, "And thou, child, shalt be called the prophet of the Highest, for thou shalt go before the face of the Lord to prepare his ways." And this perfectly corresponds with the statement of the angel before the birth of John, "He shall be filled with the Holy Ghost, even from his mother's womb; and many of the children of Israel shall he turn to the Lord their God, and he shall go before *him*, (the Lord God of Israel,) in the Spirit of Elias, to turn the hearts of the fathers to the children, and the disobedient to the wisdom of the just, to make ready a people prepared for the Lord."

The great event for which Zacharias thus praises God, was the incarnation of the Lord God of Israel; the whole sum and substance of the gospel. This raising up of a mighty salvation in the family of David, in the birth of him who was to be the Saviour of the world, Zacharias says was a fulfilment of all the divine promises of salvation to the people of Israel. "Blessed be the Lord God of Israel, for he hath visited and redeemed his people, as he spake by the mouth of his holy prophets, which have been since the world began." The incarnation and suffering of the Son of God, is the subject of the gospel. This gospel has been proclaimed by the inspired prophets of God, from the beginning of the world. The interesting subject which I now propose to you, the history of the gospel, will lead me,

I. *First*, cursorily to trace these different publications of the gospel to men, from the earliest ages of the world, in order to show that the great truth upon which we rest our hope, the incarnation of a mighty Saviour, was from the beginning of the world spoken to our fathers by the holy prophets whom God inspired.

From the day of man's fall from God, one great plan has comprehended the whole arrangement of divine providence and divine mercy. This one plan is the redemption of the world, by our Lord Jesus Christ. For this the earth and men have been suffered to exist. For this the mighty revolutions of the sons of men have been overruled. For this the least event in the life of each individual subject of redemption is made to operate. And all things work together for this unspeakable good to those who love God, who are called according to this purpose.

The scriptures teach us that all the various parts of man's

salvation have been devised from the foundation of the world. The great covenant of redemption between the persons of the Deity, in which the Father, the Son, and the Holy Spirit united to bring back the captives of Satan, was made before the world was created. The great sacrifice which the law demanded, and which this covenant of redemption provided, was then appointed, and Jesus is called the Lamb, slain from the foundation of the world. The book of life was then prepared, and the saints are said to be those who are written in the Lamb's book from the foundation of the world. The everlasting home for the saints was then provided; for thus says Jesus of the redeemed, "Then shall the king say to them on his right hand, come ye blessed of my father, receive the kingdom prepared for you from the foundation of the world." The view which is thus presented of the great salvation of the gospel, is high and comforting. For the everlasting good of the feeblest Christian, the power of Almighty God has been exerted from the beginning of the world; and the gospel, which in its rich and attractive invitations is preached to us, is the simple, but glorious intelligence of that which occupied the wisdom and the love of heaven, before this world was formed.

The redeeming visit of the Lord God of Israel, of which Zacharias speaks, was planned and determined before the creation, and has been announced as the object of faith to the people of God, in every age since the world began. This I will proceed to exhibit to you, and may your hearts unite with the father of the Baptist in blessing the Lord God of Israel for this work of grace.

1. We will first speak of that period of history between the fall of man and the covenant with Abraham, and shew how, in all this interval of time, God was proclaiming the glad tidings of the gospel to men.

As soon as Adam fell, the Son of God immediately entered

upon the office and work of a mediator. This work he had undertaken before the world began; for he thus says of himself, " I was set up from everlasting, from the beginning, or ever the earth was." Now the appointed time had come, and in the moment of man's transgression, he immediately presented himself as the daysman between a holy, infinite, offended majesty, and offending mankind. His mediation was at once accepted, and wrath was prevented from going forth to execute the amazing curse which had been denounced against transgression. It is manifest that Christ began his work of mediation instantly upon the fall, because God immediately exercised mercy, and did not cut off man at once as he did the angels who had sinned. But no mercy could be extended to fallen man, but through a mediator. The exercise of divine forbearance and mercy shows the commencement of the work of the gospel, and when the Saviour came to comfort our first parents, on the day of their transgression, in the garden of Eden, he came to seek and to save that which was lost, as much as when he came afterwards to take upon himself the nature of man of the virgin Mary.

From that day Christ took upon himself the care of his church in all his offices. He undertook to *teach* his people as their great *prophet;* to *intercede* for them as their *priest*, and to *govern* them as their *king*. He was then set up as the captain of the Lord's host; as the captain of salvation to his church, to defend them against all their foes, and from that hour God acted solely through a mediator, in teaching, governing, and blessing the children of men.

While on the day of the fall the Son of God commenced the attainment of the great object of his mediation, on the same day intelligence of this was also proclaimed to man, and the gospel was first preached upon the earth. God said unto the serpent, " I will put enmity between thy seed and her seed: it shall bruise thy head and thou shalt bruise his heel." Here was the first revelation of the covenant of grace; the first dawning of the gospel upon the earth. By the transgression of man, the light of God's favour had been shrouded in darkness, which neither men nor angels could scatter; and when, on that day of sin, God called man to account, his heart was filled with shame and terror. These words of God were the first dawning of a returning light. Before they were uttered there was not one glimpse of mercy; not one beam of comfort, nor a single source of hope to the sinner. Here was a certain intimation of a merciful design to be accomplished by "the seed of the woman," which was like the first glimmering of morning in the eastern sky. This gracious promise was given before the sentence was pronounced upon either Adam or Eve, from tenderness to them, lest they should be overborne with a sentence of condemnation, without having any thing held out whence they could gather hope of deliverance.

In the institution of sacrifices, with the skins of which Adam and Eve were clothed, the gospel was again revealed to man, and a permanent type set up of the sacrifice of Christ, by which the power of Satan was to be subdued. The ordinance of sacrifices was instituted immediately after the revelation by the promise of the covenant of grace. Thus the first stone in the great edifice of man's redemption was laid in prophecy of Christ, and the next in this standing type of his one sacrifice for sin.

Not long after the gospel was thus first proclaimed upon the earth, and the way of salvation through a mediator was laid open, God began the work of actually saving the souls of men. It is probable that the first fruits of the redemption of Christ were Adam and Eve. It is probable, I say, from God's manner of treating them, in comforting them by a promise, under their awakenings and terrors; for while they stood trembling and astonished before their Judge, without any expedient from which they could gather hope, then God offered them an encouragement, and told them of his designs of mercy through a Saviour before he passed the sentence against them.

But it is certain that in their children, the great Captain of Salvation manifested his power to save to the uttermost. In the instance of righteous Abel, we hear of the first ransomed sinner who entered the inheritance of glory through Christ's redemption. In him the gospel thus wrought its perfect work. In him the angels first acted as ministering spirits to bring a lost soul to glory. And in him the holy inhabitants of heaven had the first opportunity to behold one of this fallen, ruined race, brought to the enjoyment of the heavenly rest. Thus, while *they* saw the first effect of the full operation of the gospel, and could sing " worthy is the Lamb that was slain to receive honour, and glory, and blessing," *he* first experienced this operation of redeeming love, and first raised in heaven that song of experience " to him who had loved him, and given himself for him, and redeemed him" from misery and death, and had made him a king and priest unto God for ever. By faith Abel had accepted the promises which God had given unto man; and offering, in this faith, a sacrifice which was indeed excellent and acceptable, he obtained witness that he was righteous; and by this instance of a living and sufficient faith, " he being dead, yet speaketh."

By Enoch, God was pleased again with great clearness to testify the coming of the Lord to establish the kingdom which was committed to him upon the earth. " The Lord cometh with ten thousand of his saints to execute judgment upon all." This may refer to any particular coming of Christ, and it cannot reasonably be confined to any one. But it speaks generally of his coming in the power and glory of his kingdom, and is fulfilled, both in his first coming to purchase a people for himself, and his second coming to finish the salvation of this people, and the destruction of his enemies, and to set up his glorious kingdom on the earth. The *coming* of the Lord God of Israel to visit and redeem his people, and to place his enemies under his feet, forms the whole matter of the Gospel. To this the faith of Enoch was directed; and while he prophesied of it to the men of his generation, he embraced it as the hope and comfort of his own soul. By faith in this appointed Mediator, he was translated that he should not see death; and was not, for God took him.

Noah also became a preacher of righteousness, and by the Spirit of Christ, preached to those whose souls were in captivity and bondage to the power of sin. The righteousness which he preached, and of which he became an heir, was the righteousness of faith, or the righteousness of the Mediator not yet finished, embraced by faith. With him God renewed his covenant of grace, and gave him a promise of peculiar blessings in the posterity of Shem. God accepted the sacrifice which he offered, and established with him and his seed after him, that everlasting covenant in all things well ordered and sure.

By faith in this one Mediator, who was to be peculiarly the seed of the woman, by whose sacrifice a real satisfaction would be made for sin, and by whose obedience a perfect righteousness would be provided as an object of faith, all, from Adam downwards, who were saved at all, obtained redemption. To them, in every generation, the Gospel was preached; and the great fact, which forms the Gospel, the incarnation and sufferings of the Son of God, was held out to them as the one grand object of their faith. By *this* faith all the elders or patriarchs who were redeemed, have obtained a good report, and transmitted a name to posterity which is honourable to God, and honourable to themselves. This faith in the divine promise of a Saviour, was to them the substance of every thing they hoped for, and the sufficient evidence of their truth, although they were things not seen. Since the world began, God hath spoken to men by his holy prophets of the coming of the Redeemer, who is all our joy and all our salvation.

2. After we have thus traced the publication of the gospel from Adam down to Abraham, there will be no difficulty in understanding and acknowledging its clear and full revelation to him. The Apostle Paul says, that God preached the Gospel unto Abraham, in that gracious promise, "In thee shall all nations of the earth be blessed." The single object for which Abraham was called, and for which his family were separated from all others was, that the promised Saviour might be made a more particular object of faith, as coming from him. To him, in a new and more specific manner, the covenant of grace was revealed; and the rite of circumcision was instituted as the outward sign of that covenant established with his family. To former patriarchs God had preached the Gospel in proclaiming a Saviour who was to come as the sinner's only hope. To Abraham he preached the same Gospel yet more clearly, in promising a Saviour to come particularly from his posterity. The glad tidings of a sufficient Mediator were clearly made known to him; and his faith in the promises of the Gospel was so established and entire, that our Saviour says of him, "he saw my day, and was glad." By faith in a coming Redeemer he was justified and saved. And the faith which he had in Christ, the sure confidence with which he relied upon his mediation and offering, are repeatedly adduced in the New Testament, as illustrating the faith with which we are required to embrace a Saviour who has finished the work which was given him to do, and has gone to the glory which he had before the world was.

To Isaac the covenant of God's mercy was renewed, and the promised Saviour foretold, as coming from his posterity; and to Jacob, still more clearly, was the Gospel preached, while Esau and his family were rejected. In the ladder which was presented to Jacob, as connecting together earth and heaven by the ministration of angels, an incarnate Saviour was offered to his faith. An open way of salvation was thus exhibited to him in vision, while in the very time of the exhibition, God renewed that gracious promise of a Redeemer from his seed, upon which the faith of his fathers had rested.

Another most remarkable proclamation of the manifestation of God in the flesh for man's salvation, was given to Jacob, in his wrestling with God and prevailing in the contest, after his return from Padan Aram. Here was a representation to his faith of the whole scene of Christ's humiliation; God was shown to him as dwelling indeed upon the earth, and subjecting himself to the power of his creatures; and the all-important fact, that there was a way in which man might prevail with God and obtain a blessing, was established in his mind. So frequently had the covenant of promise been renewed and confirmed with Jacob, that his faith rested upon a Saviour with remarkable distinctness and comfort. And when upon his bed of death, he left his last blessing to his sons, the most precious and desirable of all blessings, a Saviour from sin, he bequeathed to them also. One of the clearest predictions of the time, and of the success, of the publication of the Gospel, which the Old Testament contains, is in the last blessing of Jacob to his son Judah.

To Adam, the promise of a Saviour was given in the general expression, "the seed of the woman." To Noah it was annexed to the descendants of Shem. To Abraham it was limited to his posterity by Isaac. To Isaac it was confined again to Jacob; and when by Jacob it was transmitted to his children, the descendants of Judah were selected as those from whom the Christ should come. Judah was to be the ruler of Israel in the person of David and his successors on the throne. And "the sceptre shall not depart from Judah," said the dying Jacob, " nor a lawgiver from between his feet, until Shiloh come, and to him shall the gathering of the people be." Thus the light of the Gospel shone more brightly in every succeeding age, as the time drew nearer in which all its promises were to be fulfilled, and its covenanted Mediator was to be manifested among men.

3. After this period it is hardly necessary to trace the history of the publication of the Gospel. From the time of Moses the whole Scriptures are full of the revelations of Gospel mercy. Every sacrifice in the tabernacle or temple; every type of the Jewish institutions; every prophecy and promise of succeeding generations preached Christ to the faith of men. The wonderful visit for the purpose of redemption, which the Lord God of Israel was to make to the earth, in the fulness of his appointed time, was unceasingly proclaimed. The tide of prophecy swells from age to age, until in the time of Isaiah, it has grown into an unlimited flood; and the Gospel is hardly preached with more clearness and power by St. Paul than by him. From the beginning of the world Jesus was made the one great object of faith; and the predictions of his character and office are multiplied until his time and place of birth, his miracles and instructions, his sufferings and the manner of his death, his resurrection and subsequent ascension to glory, are spoken of so particularly and so minutely, that the language of the later prophets, appears to be rather a history of what is past, than a prophecy of what is yet to come.

From this history of the gospel, you see that the sinner's ground of hope has been the same from the beginning of the world. The same Jesus who is preached to you for your acceptance, was preached to men from Adam down to Moses, and from Moses to the day in which we live. No child of man has ever passed into the heavens but through his redemption. His offering was equally availing and prevalent for Adam and Abel and ourselves. By his own obedience no man has ever found acceptance before God. But the same Almighty grace which has rescued the believing sinners in this congregation, brought the first ransomed sinner to glory, and every other one since his time. We offer no new commandment unto you, but that commandment which has been from the beginning, that you should believe on him who has been set up from everlasting, as the one Mediator between God and man, in whose blood alone there is redemption for your souls, even the forgiveness of your sins.

II. How elevated is the view which this subject presents of the character of our Saviour Christ! His love how wonderful, that interposed for man in the moment of his transgression, when there was no arm that could save, and there seemed no possibility of finding any expedient by which the apparently inevitable punishment of sin could be turned aside. How great the power which has been exercised to accomplish this work of redemption in every age. Angels who have witnessed from the beginning his labours of love, know how worthy he is to receive blessing, and honour and glory for what he has done, and they gladly unite to praise him for all his goodness, and all his mercy. Unnumbered multitudes of ransomed saints in the enjoyment of the glory which he has purchased, ascribe all the praise for their redemption unto him. He is the head of all things in heaven and on earth, and all living beings live through him. To the once crucified and now exalted Jesus, the universe, which is upheld by the word of his power, unites to render its thankful homage.

How unspeakable is the privilege which this subject presents to the true believer in Jesus Christ! The least in the kingdom of heaven is united by an everlasting bond to the glorious assembly who have been redeemed through the blood of the Son of God. The Redeemer has but one church. Angels, and living saints, and dead, but one communion make. The innumerable company of angels are subjected unto him. The ransomed believers in his power, from righteous Abel down to this day, are partakers of his glory; and to this holy and heavenly assembly, the weakest believer on earth is eternally united. The poorest Christian in the world is the constant subject of angelic protection and care. And though men may despise him, the hosts of heaven delight to watch over him, to minister to his wants, to console his sorrows, to defend him from dangers, and to bring him to the salvation of which he is made an heir. How delightful is the thought that we are never alone! In all our afflictions we have a great High Priest whom angels worship; who can be touched with the feeling of our infirmities, and remembers whereof we are made. In our seasons of bodily suffering or family distress, in our periods of earthly adversity and want, he will be a present and all-sufficient help. When the shades of death are gathering around us, he will stand by us to alleviate our distress and to elevate our hope. He will pass with us through the dark valley that we may be in perfect peace. In the great day of judgment he will own us amidst assembled worlds, as the satisfying travail of his soul. He will proclaim to the universe that we are the jewels whom he has purchased for himself, and over whom he will rejoice for ever. He will accept us, poor and worthless as we are, freely through the value of his own blood, and crown us with everlasting glory in heaven. How unspeakable is the privilege of being united to the whole company of the redeemed, through the precious and all-sufficient offering which is published to us in the gospel; and that privilege belongs to every one who has sought for refuge in the precious blood of a divine and mighty Saviour.

How amazing is the conduct of those who persevere in rejecting the mercies which this gospel presents to universal acceptance! With what unutterable joy Adam must have heard of a hope of returning peace! With what transport

Abel must have taken possession of that home of glory to which he was carried so suddenly from the trials of the world! And why should any of you, who need a Saviour as much as they, and to whom the blessings of redemption are as freely offered as they were to them, take upon yourselves the voluntary and persevering rejection of all that Christ has done in your behalf. How much you will desire to see one of the days of the Son of man when the wish will be entirely vain! It is a fact with the unconverted sinner,—despise the assertion of it as he will,—that the hour will come, when, trembling and astonished, he will crouch before the Son of man, and beg and cry for the mercy which he has so often cast heedlessly away How amazing is it that the man who knows that death, and judgment and eternity are spread before him, should be willing to throw away a hope, the sufficiency of which he acknowledges, while he has nothing to supply its place upon which he dare trust himself. And yet this is the conduct of every unconverted soul before me. There is not a man here, destitute of spiritual religion, with a heart unrenewed by the Holy Spirit, but is rejecting what he knows to be a sufficient hope, while the rejection of this hope leaves his soul utterly without comfort and peace. How amazing in the sight of angels must be this course. They wondered when mercy was proposed to man. They must wonder still more when this mercy is again offered, after it has been rejected. They must wonder most of all, if sinners still persevere in this rejection, and finally determine to choose darkness rather than light.

LECTURE IV.

THE WISDOM OF THE GOSPEL.

We speak the wisdom of God in a mystery, even the hidden wisdom which God ordained before the world unto our glory.—1 CORINTHIANS II. 7.

THE *object* which the gospel is to attain, the *way* in which it is to attain it, and the *history* of its attainment of this object in past ages, have occupied our attention in three former discourses. I wish now to speak of the several characteristics of the gospel itself, as a dispensation of divine grace and mercy to man; to show its unsearchable *wisdom*, as an expedient for man's salvation; its almighty *power* as an instrument for the accomplishment of this end; the *grace* and *love* which are displayed in the gift which it offers unto man, and its *excellency* and *glory*, as a revelation of the character and purposes of God in his relation to fallen man.

My present subject is the *unsearchable wisdom of God, as displayed in the gospel, as an expedient or plan for man's salvation.*

The text which I have selected contains St. Paul's description of this wisdom, as proclaimed by him and his fellow apostles. When he carried the gospel of Jesus to the enlightened and philosophical inhabitants of Corinth, he was aware that they sought after wisdom, and expected him to develope to them some new scheme of philosophy which should furnish matter for their own speculations. In opposition to this desire of theirs, he professes to them the single determination with which he came to them, which was to make known to perishing transgressors, Jesus Christ and him crucified, as the only foundation for hope or acceptance before God.

This preaching rejected all the enticing words of man's wisdom; all the false and delusive words of persuasion with which other teachers were accustomed to come to them, and depended for its whole success, upon the demonstration of the Divine Spirit and the power of God. He did not attempt to flatter them upon their own powers of understanding, nor to submit to the decisions of their natural and darkened reasons, the truths which he was sent to teach. He told them of their sins and dangers, and he held out to them freely the remedy which divine grace had provided for their wants. Such preaching, which dealt only with men as poor and depraved creatures, which addressed them from an eminence of authority, as those who were lost, was regarded by them as foolishness, and their proud hearts despised him for the bold assertions which he made of the necessity of man, and of the abundant mercy of God.

But though he has often adopted their own scornful expression, and called the preaching of the cross of Jesus foolishness, he denies that such was really the character of his preaching. "We speak wisdom," he says, "among them that are perfect," or able to understand us, "yet, not the wisdom of this world;" no wisdom of man's discovery. "But we speak the wisdom of God in a mystery; the wisdom which has been hidden, but which God ordained before the world to our glory."

The apostle here, as in many other places, calls the gospel the "wisdom of God." He describes it as wisdom which reveals such things as eye hath not seen, nor ear heard, nor the heart of man conceived; as wisdom which is revealed to man solely by the Spirit of God; the Spirit which searcheth all things, even the deep things of God, and which the natural or unrenewed man cannot discern or understand.

"We speak," he says, in preaching the gospel, "the wisdom of God."

This display of Divine Wisdom, which the gospel makes, has before been "hidden in a mystery." It was not clearly ravealed until the preaching of Jesus brought life and immortality to light. It was concealed in the types of the Jewish religion, and in the predictions of the Jewish prophets; and so hidden in the mysterious representations of the Old Testament, that none of the princes or wise men of this world knew it, but in their ignorance of it, crucified the Lord of glory.

But although the wisdom displayed in the gospel was hidden in a mystery, before its full and perfect revelation, in the coming and sacrifice of the Lord Jesus, it was wisdom ordained before the foundation of the world. The whole plan of bringing from among men many sons to glory, through the sufferings of the Captain of their salvation, was devised and determined before the creation of man; and the gospel which Paul preached, and which we preach, is but the intelligence of that plan of mercy which God ordained then, for man, as a manifestation of the unfathomable depths of his own wisdom.

From this declaration of the apostle I derive my present subject of discourse.

The gospel displays the unsearchable wisdom of God, which ordained a plan of salvation and glory for sinners, before the foundation of the world, and concealed it in the mysteries of the Old Testament until *he* came, in whom all these mysteries were to be fulfilled and made plain.

I. The gospel displays the wisdom of God, in a consideration of the *peculiar difficulties which it was required to meet.*

In this view it may well be called the "wisdom of God in a mystery," for the extent of wisdom displayed is deeply mysterious.

In the fall and disobedience of man, so many difficulties, and apparently such insurmountable difficulties were created, that all hope of his restoration would seem impossible. A holy being had become a polluted and guilty one. How should he be restored? The holy and unbending law of God had been violated. How should the breach be made up? The majesty and faithfulness of an all-powerful God had been offended. How should it be appeased? It will be remembered that these questions were now agitated for the first time. All these difficulties had occurred in the case of the angels who had sinned; but there was no purpose to save them, and therefore there was no necessity to ask, in their case, how the difficulties should be overcome; with them sin had its perfect work, and the wages of sin was death.

In the case of man's transgression there was a previous determination to save them from the ruin in which they were involved, and the demand for wisdom was to solve the way in which it should be done.

We will suppose for a moment that it had been left to man to devise a way for his own restoration to the Divine favour; or that every created mind had been consulted by him for that end; and can you conceive that any way would have entered into the thoughts of any finite being, but an immediate and absolute pardon, by a single sovereign act of mercy? We may see many difficulties attending such an exercise of mercy; and whether it would have been at all consistent with the honour of God's character, it is utterly impossible for us to say. None but God can know what it is within the power of God to do. But we may safely say, even if we suppose such an act of mercy, under existing circumstances, *possible*, it was not the way which would the most highly honour the character of God, nor was it the way which was *most* suited to the wants of the occasion, and therefore it was not the way which a God of infinite wisdom thought best to adopt. Indeed, while I say we may see many difficulties attending an exercise of absolute mercy, under the circumstances of man, it appears to me entirely proper to say, that such an act of mercy would have been impossible. God, who delights in mercy, would surely have spared the sufferings of an innocent and holy Saviour, had the salvation of man been possible without their endurance.

How great was the difficulty which was here presented! and what wisdom was demanded to meet the necessities of the case! Every thing in the case was new. Every path to be trodden was hitherto untried. The breach which sin had made was infinitely wide. It was an ocean over which no created intelligence could travel; and the redemption of a single soul was so important and precious, that so far as men or angels were concerned, it must have ceased forever.

To meet this infinite demand; to make up all the difficulties which the case involved, and to bring God and man together across this unmeasured alienation, was required in the gospel; and here the wisdom of the plan by which it proposes to accomplish the purpose is gloriously displayed. When all created minds acknowledged that the case was hopeless, God brought forward to the view of his creatures the hidden wisdom which he had ordained before the world. He thus exhibited new views of his manifold wisdom. He made the fall of man an occasion of manifesting more clearly his own glorious perfections. This was his purpose and design,—and the difficulty in removing man's guilt, and restoring a ruined world to his favour, and at the same time bringing eternal glory to the character of God, was met and answered in the abundant provisions of the gospel. There is not a question to be asked in reference to man's salvation, which the gospel does not answer. It abundantly saves the sinner, and brings the highest glory to God.

The wisdom of the gospel provisions supplies all your wants. It makes a guilty being a pardoned and justified one. It converts a polluted and defiled creature into a holy and perfect one. It satisfies all the demands and denunciations of the law. It perfectly compensates the offended faithfulness and majesty of the Creator, and restores man to God, and reconciles God to man. The difficulty which existed in the case of the first transgressor remains in the case of every other sinner to be converted unto God; and the wisdom of the gospel as an expedient of salvation, is displayed in meeting and supplying this amazing difficulty whenever a sinner is brought home to God.

II. The wisdom of the gospel is displayed *in the manner in which it glorifies all the divine attributes.* While it manifests abundant mercy on the part of the Great Creator, in his dealings with his creatures, it does not in the least degree compromise any other of his perfections in the exercise of mercy. If you will conceive of the relation in which man, as a sinful being, stood towards God, you will see how all the attributes of the divine character were at war with him. God had given him a law in the hour of his creation, and had bound that law upon him in the most solemn manner. He had voluntarily and unnecessarily broken that law, and now, in the presence of all beings, the Creator and his creature were at variance,—as it were, in an awful contest, whether the Creator should be true to his word, in the punishment and destruction of the creature, or the creature should triumph in his rebellion over the instability of his God. Angels stopped to witness the result. Fallen spirits watched the progress of this conflict; and there seemed to depend upon the issue the one momentous question, shall God be the ruler of his creatures or no?

The holiness of God was called to express its abhorrence of sin, as it had done before. The justice of God was called to execute immediate vengeance on those who had committed sin, as it had done upon Lucifer and his host. The truth of God was called to fulfil the threatenings which had been denounced against sin; and yet, amidst all these difficulties, God so loved the world that he had determined the whole of men should not perish, but some of them should have everlasting life.

If the transgressor should receive an immediate and unconditional pardon, how should the holiness of God be displayed, or his justice honoured, or his truth preserved inviolate? Shall all these glorious attributes be despised and passed over utterly unheeded? The character of God is glorious, and must be glorified in the salvation of man; but how it should be so glorified, the wisdom of men and angels could never determine. No means had been provided for the restoration of fallen angels, and no angel could tell what means should be provided for the restoration of fallen man.

The attributes of God evidently required the punishment of sin. If the idea of a substitute had entered into any created mind, the difficulty was at once seen, how can an innocent being be punished for the guilty? Can God accept a substitute? Can it be imagined that he would inflict, with his own hand, sufferings belonging to the guilty upon one without sin?

Here the gospel displays its wisdom. It announces a substitute for the sinner. It exhibits the whole system under which this substitute was offered and accepted.

But if only the fact that a substitute would be accepted had been suggested, all creatures might ask, where shall one be found who can bear the punishment deserved by the millions of mankind? Were all the angels in heaven able to render such a service to a single man? Could any one less than the living God himself undertake such a work? Could it be conceived possible, that God should be willing to do this for creatures who had trampled upon his laws? And if he were willing, how could it be done? How shall God endure sufferings for man? How shall any thing which he thus does be put to man's account? And if God were willing to become man, and to put himself in the place of man, and to do and suffer what man was bound to do and suffer, how could it consist with the holiness and justice of God, to let the innocent suffer and the guilty go free? yea, to let the innocent suffer, that the guilty might go free?

The more we enter into the consideration of these things, and contemplate all the difficulties, which the holy attributes of God inevitably threw in the way of man's recovery, and the impossibility that any created wisdom should devise a way in which they could be reconciled, we see the wisdom of the gospel the more wonderfully displayed. Here divine wisdom interposes; here the wisdom ordained in the councils of the Eternal Trinity, before the world began, is exhibited; and the intelligence of God's own determination unravels every obscurity and doubt, and throws new and infinite honour upon his own character.

Behold this glorious plan. God's co-equal, co-eternal Son, shall undertake for us. A body shall be given him. In the fulness of the time before appointed, he shall be born as man. As the substitute and surety for our souls, he shall bear our burden of sins in his own sacred body upon the cross. By his own obedience unto death, he shall work out an everlasting righteousness, commensurate with the utmost claims of the law for all who believe. Thus every attribute of God shall be honoured, and God shall be just, and the justifier of him that believeth in Christ Jesus.

Contemplate this "wisdom of God in a mystery." A mediator! That mediator, God; that God, man! That

Deity incarnate, suffering! Those sufferings borne in the stead of man! His whole obedience, too, accepted for sinful man, and imputed unto him! Sinners by this rescued and reconciled to God! Sinners so reconciled, restored to the divine image, approved of God, justified before the assembled universe, exalted to thrones of endless glory! and all this in perfect consistency with the honour of God; yea, glorifying in the highest degree, the divine perfections! This is God's plan for the salvation of a ruined world. This is the intelligence which the gospel brings. Surely in the contemplation of it we can only exclaim with the apostle, " O the depth of the riches of the wisdom and knowledge of God; how unsearchable are his judgments, and his ways past finding out!" And with him also, we may declare in reference to all who are ignorant of this wisdom, " Eye hath not seen, nor ear heard; neither have entered into the heart of man the things which God hath prepared for them that love him." Would to God we could all say also with him, " God hath revealed them unto us by his Spirit, that we might know the things which are freely given to us of God."

III. The wisdom of the gospel is displayed *in its perfect adaptation to the accomplishment of the great purpose which it designs*. The mark of true wisdom is in the best arrangement of means to obtain a desired end. The great object of the gospel is to seek and to save that which is lost, to convert sinners unto God, to make a time of restitution throughout the world, in which God shall return to bless his creatures, and men shall return to submit themselves to God. It operates upon a lost and ruined world; and from it, it wishes to bring many sons unto glory. Its wisdom is manifested in its being perfectly adapted to accomplish this whole end.

The provisions of the gospel are the evidence and fruit of God's reconciliation to man. The one great offering for sin which it presents has made up every breach, has taken away every obstacle, has opened to the sinner a path of glory and blessedness. God is able to forgive and save every transgressor on earth, in consistence with his own honour; and therefore as our last head showed, so far as *he* is concerned, the wisdom of the gospel is proclaimed, in his acknowledgment that it is sufficient, and that he is willing that all should be saved and come to the knowledge of the truth.

But man is yet alienated, and must be brought home to God; and the gospel shows the wisdom of its plan in its perfect adaptation to the great end of converting and renewing him. The great fact of the gospel, the incarnation and sufferings of a glorious Saviour, is the one great instrument of good to the rebel sinner; and the continued exhibition of this one great fact is the means, and the only means, of bringing back to God the hearts of his creatures.

Take the instance of the individual sinner converted unto God, and what has produced the effect upon him which is so manifest?

He was dead in his sins; cold, heartless and unconcerned. The one object, then, was to rouse him to reflection, and to produce a true sorrow for sin in his heart. But what could do it? No remonstrance of moral precepts, no appeal to the dominion of reason, no arguments founded upon his own ability to rise. No. Had these been all the instruments employed, he would have remained eternally, as multitudes do under such instruments, a dead and ruined sinner. But he heard of a crucified Jesus. He was made to look upon him whom he had pierced. He saw an agony and bloody sweat drawn out by his transgression. His conscience felt and owned the guilt. A crucified Jesus! This planted thorns in his pillow; this made him water his couch with his tears; this agitated his breast with grief and anxiety. The preaching of the gospel, the exhibition of the great fact of the gospel, convicted him of sin. Ingratitude to a Saviour, contempt of his blood, neglect of a soul for which *he* died, filled him with anguish, and compelled him to ask forgiveness from him who had borne his sins and carried his iniquities. In this effect the wisdom of the gospel was displayed. It awakened and convinced a sinner who could resist every thing but this one instrument of God. It brought down into the dust of humiliation, a rebel who could harden himself against every other instrument and power, who could mock at all other solicitations as the horse mocketh at the battle.

When this rebel was awakened, convinced and made to cry out in the bitterness of his anguish, the next object was to elevate his affections to God, to bind him eternally to a Saviour, and to save him from going back to the captivity of Satan; but no instrument could do it save the same gospel. The same great fact which had aroused him, gave him peace. It was not the moral or natural perfections of the Deity; it was not the beauty of his service nor the holiness of his habitation, that bound his heart to heaven, and led him to seek the inheritance of the saints in light. It was a bleeding Lamb, a suffering Emmanuel, a Redeemer crowned with thorns, that took away the anguish of conviction, gave him peace in believing, and filled his soul with love to God. He was made alive by receiving Christ to live in him. He was brought to glorify God in his body and spirit, which were his, by feeling that he was bought with a price, and that Jesus had died for him. The life he now lives is sustained by the gospel alone; and being made one with Christ, through a cordial acceptance of his salvation, he brings forth fruit of holiness unto God.

This has been the one course of proceeding from the beginning; and millions of rebellious beings have been awakened, convicted, created anew, and bound in an everlasting covenant to God, by the operation of this single instrument of good. Here the gospel has displayed its wisdom, and God has been infinitely honoured in the operation of this plan.

This is not the wisdom of this world. It appears to be foolishness in the carnal eye. Unconverted men can see no beauty in Jesus, no reason in the simple preaching of what he has done, no connexion between this and any change to be accomplished in the human character. In their proud language it is unphilosophical and absurd. But in spite of all their objections, and contentions, and pride, it still produces the effect desired when nothing else can do it; and thus shows itself to be the wisdom of God, though from the men of this world it is hidden in a mystery.

The apostles went out to tell the simple fact of the crucifixion and exaltation of the Son of God for the salvation of sinners; and though all the wise men derided them, their preaching made multitudes cry out together, "Men and brethren, what shall we do?" and added multitudes to the church, who should be saved. They feared no repetition; they expected no weariness; they provided for no love of change; they ceased not to teach and to preach Jesus Christ, and God confirmed his word every where by its glorious results. We have the same gospel, and it still produces the same effect. Though disputers of this world still deride, the more exclusively and entirely we preach Jesus Christ, the more abundant are the effects upon the hearts and characters of men. When we are willing to trust God's wisdom, and to throw ourselves altogether upon the great fact of the gospel, to preach, not ourselves, but Jesus Christ the Lord, we are blessed; sinners are awakened and converted, and God is honoured in spite of all the exclamations of proud and captious men, "How can these things be?"

The gospel is the only possible instrument for this end. There is no sinner converted but by its power; and the wisdom of God is thus unceasingly displayed. Every song in heaven, and every true prayer and thanksgiving upon earth, unites to utter the same truth; we are washed and made white in the blood of the Lamb; and mysterious as this wisdom is to the princes of this world, it is wisdom ordained before the world to our glory.

These three views display the wisdom of the gospel as an expedient for man's salvation; in the difficulty which it meets, in the glory which it brings to God, and in its adaptation to produce the end which it designs; "We speak the wisdom of God in a mystery, even the hidden wisdom, which God ordained before the world to our glory."

IV. How vain are the objections which men make to this system of grace and salvation! This is God's plan. It is marked with the wisdom of his character. It has glorified him, in an amazing degree, in the effect which it has produced throughout the world. Though many of you may see no reason in this system, and may persuade yourselves to believe that there is something in it which is contrary to your reason, rest assured, if you will throw yourselves with faith upon it, you will find it to be the power of God unto salvation to your souls. You have not a want which it will not supply. It will meet your whole necessities. It will abundantly answer your prayers.

This is the true and proper test of the fitness and wisdom of the gospel; the test of experience. Try this system. Taste and see that the Lord is gracious. To this point would I lead your affections and plans. I cannot stop to argue about the externals of this plan before the tribunal of man's wisdom. You may be speculatively believers, while you are practically unbelievers. You can know nothing of the wisdom or the fitness of the gospel, unless you are willing to receive it and try it under the shape in which it comes to you, as a remedy for your diseased and ruined souls. If you are willing to be convinced of your necessities; if you are ready to acknowledge that you have deep and fatal spiritual wants, and are willing to lay yourselves down as a free offering before the feet of a crucified Saviour, this gospel will tell you all you can desire to know, and give you all you can need to possess.

Your blinded reasons may urge a thousand questions which God has not answered, and which man cannot answer, about this heavenly system; and you may be persuaded to say, I cannot accept it because I cannot understand it. This is no fair or accurate test of any remedy for evil. Go with a deep conviction that you are guilty, and deserve condemnation; that you are ruined, and have no help. Go with a penitent and sorrowful spirit, in remembrance of your sin, looking upon the load you have heaped upon a dying friend. Go with the language of unfeigned humiliation, with a sincere desire to obtain pardon and peace in the relation between your soul and God. Go thus to the feet of Jesus, and ask for the remedy which he bestows. If, then, you are sent back empty, if you find that the gospel can do nothing for you, that your load of guilt is unremoved, and your souls have no peace with God, then may you, with much greater show of reason, pronounce upon the unfitness of the gospel to answer your necessity. But until you have tried and found the trial vain, you cannot with the least propriety, urge a single objection to the terms and operation of the gospel.

Are you willing to make this trial? Are you ready to test, by experience, the sufficiency of Christ? He invites you; he advises you; he warns you; he encourages you; he intreats you all, to submit your wills, your desires, your characters, to him; and by his Spirit he will enable you to know and understand the things which are freely given you of God; and this acceptance of the gospel shall furnish you a salvation that can be obtained by no other instrument or method.

LECTURE V.

THE POWER OF THE GOSPEL TO SAVE.

I am not ashamed of the gospel of Christ, for it is the power of God unto salvation, to every one that believeth.—ROMANS, I. 16.

ATTEMPTS to discredit and oppose the preaching and influence of the gospel of Christ have attended its progress in every age. When inspired apostles proclaimed its saving truths, they were in no degree more acceptable to sinful men than they are now. To the self-righteous Jews, the gospel was a stumbling block, because it conceded nothing to the merit of human works. By the conceited Greek it was accounted foolishness, because it paid no deference to the arrogant claims of human reason. It was inconceivable to those who confided entirely in their own wisdom and strength to do good, that the change of the whole character, and the salvation of the soul of man, should be effected by means apparently so unsuited to the end. Accordingly they opposed and derided the preaching of the gospel, as the tale of babblers, and the fancy of an uneducated sect.

But what then? Because wicked men deride, shall apostles shrink and be silent? St. Paul avows a purpose far from this. In the face of all opposition and of all reproach, he declares himself not ashamed of the gospel of Christ, because it would prove to be, as it was designed to be, the appointed and successful instrument of the power of God, for the salvation of mankind. Infidelity might scorn its influence. But faith would reap the glorious benefits which it conferred.

"The gospel of Christ" is the intelligence of what God, the Father, the Son, and the Holy Ghost, has done for the salvation of man. It is the history of the advent, incarnation and death of God's dear Son as a Saviour for sinners, and the offer to them of all the blessed results of his work of merit and grace. It announces God as reconciled to man in the death of his Son,—and by the influence of this intelligence, it persuades men by the power of the Spirit, to be reconciled to God. This is God's appointed instrument, and the power of God, for the salvation of those who believe.

This is the subject to which I would call your attention in this discourse; *the gospel of Christ the manifestation of divine power in the salvation of mankind.* It is a subject so glorious, that we may well unite with the apostle as we consider it, in the assertion, "I am not ashamed of the gospel of Christ." We may regard this manifestation of divine power, under the two aspects, of the work which God has accomplished *for* us, by the meritorious obedience and death of the Lord Jesus Christ,—and the work which he accomplishes *in* us by the renewing operations of the Holy Spirit.

I. The Gospel manifests the power of God, in the revelation which it makes of *what God has done for us by the obedience and death of his dear Son.*

As transgressors against God, the law held us in bondage, kept us under condemnation, and bound us over to endure the wages of sin in everlasting death. We were wholly without hope, because we were without power to satisfy the law, and break the bondage wherein we were held. But this bondage, God has broken by the gift of his own Son. He has been set forth in the suffering nature of man, as the propitiation for our sins. He has thus released us from condemnation, and provided a sacrifice and offering which meets every penalty of the law, and gives a new and glorious hope, to all who are ready to come unto God through him. In the obedience which the Lord Jesus has thus rendered to the law, and the satisfaction, which he has made to its demands, he has silenced all its denunciations, and opened a new and certain way of life to the guilty; and the gospel, in proclaiming this wonderful provision of divine mercy, becomes the power of God unto salvation to those who believe. But release from condemnation is not all we need. We must have also a title to glory, a right to enter into the kingdom of God. And this can only be the result of a perfect and unspotted obedience of divine commands. Here also, the power of God interposes, and the gospel proclaims the work. In the obedience which the Saviour has rendered to those commands which are holy, just, and good, and which cannot be annulled, He has brought in an everlasting righteousness for all who believe in him. By his obedience, the law is magnified, and many whom it condemned, are made righteous. In this perfect offering of obedience God displays his power to save. He can justly exercise loving kindness to those who were condemned to death, and can raise the prisoner from the dungeon to set him upon the throne; and in the very act of his release can honour the law which held him in condemnation.

Again, as fallen beings, Satan held us in captivity—we were under the power of the god of this world, and he exercised over the hearts and habits of all, a ruinous dominion. But from this power the Lord Jesus Christ has rescued us. He has overcome him that had the power of death. When he hung bleeding upon the cross, and was, to the view of the ignorant, himself subdued and destroyed, he triumphed over Satan, spoiled principalities and powers of darkness, and made a show of his conquest openly. And by the proclamation of this one great fact, that Christ Jesus died upon the cross for sinners, the gospel has been the instrument of overthrowing the kingdom of Satan in every age, and setting up the empire of the Son of God upon the earth.

w*

Thus the power of God is manifested by the gospel in its revelation of what God hath done *for* us by his Son. The influence of this work is displayed in heaven, in the acceptance there, of this sufficiency of the Lord Jesus Christ in his offering for sinners; in his prevailing intercession as our great High Priest; and in the continual crowning of the subjects of his redemption for his sake. It is exhibited on earth, in the increasing testimony which is borne to the glorious redemption that has thus been finished; in the providence which causes all things to work together for the salvation of those whom it has purchased; in the continual progress of the truth, in its conquest over darkness and error; in the converting and justifying of multitudes of sinners, and giving their guilty consciences peace with God; in the glorious triumphs which it accomplishes for them over death, and the abundant entrance which it gives them to an eternal glory. It is manifested in hell, in the restraint which has been put upon the power of Satan; in the limits which it affixes to his designs of malice; in the subjection which it compels him to acknowledge to the Lord Jesus Christ as head over all; and in the triumphs which it is daily attaining on earth, by the ransom of men from the grasp of his power. Throughout the universe, the gospel thus proclaims the power of God, as manifested in the salvation of men. It opens a satisfaction and righteousness sufficient for the whole world. It provides a new and living way to God, for every sinner who will receive it. It thus restores a lost world to God, against whom they had rebelled. And declares the whole work of merit in their behalf, as complete in the obedience unto death, of the Great Captain of their salvation.

II. The gospel manifests the power of God, in *its exhibition of the work which God accomplishes within us, by the Holy Spirit.*

1. Take a view of this exhibition of divine power, as it has

been given, upon the immense scale, which *the past history of the Church of Christ presents.* Reflect upon the whole progress of the gospel in the world, and upon the innumerable multitudes of souls who have been actually rescued by its operation, from the bondage of sin, through the power of the Holy Ghost. How wonderful is the display which is thus made of the divine power! Who has caused this "little stone cut out of the mountain without hands" to grow into a mighty mountain, and establish itself in all the kingdoms of the earth? Who has constrained such millions of sinful men to submit their hearts to a doctrine every where spoken against, upon the testimony of a few poor and despised persons; to a doctrine wholly opposed and offensive to the propensities of their own nature; to a doctrine involving unceasing self-denial, and the assumption of a severe and painful cross? Who has induced men thus to submit themselves to one whom they have never seen, and in whom if they had seen him, they would have beheld no beauty that they should desire him? Who has persuaded them to endure all griefs and sufferings, in hope of a reward, long deferred, and offering no ground of assurance that it should ever be bestowed, but faith in his power who had promised it, and requiring on the way to its attainment, a perpetual contest with persecution, suffering, and death?

In all these effects, which men have seen, and do not, and cannot deny, how elevated is the view which is presented of the power of the gospel, as a divine instrument! Call up before you, the uncounted souls who have been rescued from the power of Satan, and brought into subjection to the King of Saints. By what means have they been delivered from their bondage? How have they broken their chains? Has the power of human eloquence, the excellency of human speech or wisdom, the influence of argument or moral suasion accomplished this effect? No, not in a single instance. Nothing but the gospel, with the power of the Holy Spirit, has ever emancipated a single soul, or conferred upon one, the enjoyment of lasting peace. But this has been in every age quick and powerful, and sharper than a two-edged sword, as God's appointed means for turning thousands from darkness to light, and from the power of Satan unto God. Multitudes in every age have been living witnesses of its power; and by its enlightening, comforting, sanctifying energy, have been created anew, and filled with all joy and peace in believing.

This extensive exhibition the world still beholds. It still wonders at these effects, and is unable to account for them. They are seen, wherever the gospel is faithfully ministered. The simple preaching of a crucified Christ, is still the hammer which breaks the rock in pieces, and the mould which forms after the divine image, the subjects of its power. Wherever you look abroad upon the Christian Church, you see this invariable connexion between divine truth, and divine power. Thus myriads are every year converted unto Christ. Angels behold with joy the power of the Lord. The name and work of Jesus are constantly glorified. And extensive revivals of religion under the preaching of his truth, show the presence and power of God in his Church, and his blessing upon the truth which he has revealed. With false systems of doctrine, all the eloquence and talent of men convert no sinner's soul. But the lifting up of a crucified Saviour, however feebly done as it regards the talent of the preacher, draws all unto him. Under other preaching, religion dies, and hardly the form of godliness remains. Under the simple preaching of the cross of Christ, grace, mercy and peace are multiplied among men, and God confirms his word with the demonstration of his own Spirit, and with divine power continually attending.

2. Take a view of this exhibition of divine power, upon the narrower, but not less interesting scale, which *the restoration of the individual sinner to God and holiness displays.*

See here, what God is doing for man, under the gospel, by his Holy Spirit.

Who *awakens and converts the careless sinner*, and turns his mind from the power of Satan unto God? His natural mind refuses all subjection to the will of God. The strong man armed keeps his palace, and his goods are in peace. Without any concern for himself, and in a determined contest with his Creator, he sets himself to oppose the grace of the Lord Jesus. And never, until he is subdued by a power stronger than himself, is his soul spoiled of its rebellion, and renovated in love. What but the gospel of Christ, is thus mighty through God, to the pulling down of his strong holds, and of every imagination which exalteth itself against God? When Jesus stilled the tempest with the two words, "peace, be still," men wondered at the exhibition of his power, and said, "What manner of man is this, that even the winds and the sea obey him?" But the conversion of a sinful heart is a far greater work than the stilling of the ocean. The sea will sometimes be calm of itself. But the wicked are always, "like the troubled sea when it *cannot* rest, whose waters cast up mire and dirt." To still *this* raging sea, is a divine work alone. How remarkably God contrasts these two, by the prophet Jeremiah! "I have placed the sand for the bound of the sea, by a perpetual decree, that it cannot pass it; and though the waves thereof toss themselves, yet they cannot prevail; though they roar, yet can they not pass over it. But this people hath a revolting and rebellious heart. They are revolted and gone." What subdues this revolting and rebellious heart, but the power of God in the Gospel? What stills it into the calmness and beauty of a spiritual life, but the word of God by his Spirit? This is the chosen instrument of divine power, and is made the savour of life unto life, in the new creation of the sinner, not by the will of the flesh, nor by the will of man, but by the power of God. How elevated and wonderful is this display of divine power! The minister of Jesus speaks in the ears of a dead man, whom no thunder could have awakened, and he rises up to give glory to God. The Saviour calls upon men through him, to deny themselves, to part with their chosen sins; sins which they have esteemed their ornament and subsistence; to reject with contempt, the allurements and opposition of the world; to rejoice if they are counted worthy to suffer shame for Christ's sake; and they obey him instantly, without conferring with flesh and blood. Their earth-bound affections are lifted up to heaven. Their boastful spirit of rebellion is humbled to the meekness of the lamb. The very heart which *yesterday* proudly said, "Who is the Lord, that I should serve him? I will not have this man to reign over me," *to-day* asks in humble dependance at the feet of Jesus, "Lord, what wouldst thou have me to do." I ask what power has accomplished this change of heart and character; what power can accomplish it, but the gospel?

Who *justifies the penitent believer*, and gives him perfect peace and acceptance with God? It is the gospel which the Holy Spirit brings. This comes to the mourning transgressor, as a ministration of righteousness, as a word of reconciliation and peace to his anxious soul. This opens the prison doors, and sets the captive free. The power of the law was great, and the mighty thunderings with which it was given, represented it. But it was a power for destruction only. It could only hold down a man who was dead before. It could never give him life again. How much greater is that power of God in the gospel which gives him new life; raises him up to a new and everlasting being,—passes by his transgressions, and gives him liberty and boldness in the presence of the King of Saints! This the gospel by the Holy Spirit is made to do. It takes away the burden of guilt from the sinner's soul; it silences every accuser; it fills him with the confidence of hope; it forbids every weapon which is formed against him to prosper; it condemns every tongue, that rises in judgment against him. The justification which it gives, is a perfect and entire one. The sins of a life, however accumulated, however aggravated, are blotted out in one moment, and that forever. A new and perfect righteousness is bestowed upon him; and he stands before God, not only without a stain of guilt, but with a character as perfect, and a title to an inheritance of glory, as entire, as if he had been perfectly obedient, and without transgression. In this total change of the sinner's relation to God, the gospel makes every thing sure forever. It turns aside the edge of judgment; and rejoices in a victory over condemnation; and asks in triumph, " Who shall lay any thing to the charge of God's elect ? It is God that justifieth ; who is he that condemneth? It is Christ that died, yea rather, that is risen again ; who is ever at the right hand of God ;" and thus relieving the believer's soul from fear, from danger, and from death, it shows itself the power of God unto salvation.

Who *carries on in increasing holiness*, the work of grace which has been thus commenced, for the converted and justified sinner? The application of the same Gospel by the same Spirit, is the only instrument for renewing the souls of men in holiness. They are sanctified through the truth; according to the Redeemer's prayer, " Sanctify them through thy truth ; thy word is truth." They are thus daily led to be more conformed to the image of God. The heavenly teaching of the Spirit forms Christ more perfectly in their souls, —writes the divine law upon their hearts; and makes it their delight to do his will. This is a continual exhibition of the power of the Gospel. The impression upon adamant from the touch of a seal, would not be more wonderful, than this transformation of an earthly and degraded soul into the perfect image of Christ, by the preaching of the word of his truth. Yet men beholding in the Gospel, as in a glass, the glory of the Lord, are changed into the same image, from glory to glory, by the Spirit of the Lord. They are thus made partakers of a divine nature. Christ is made their sanctification. They are made holy, because they are made one with him, and receive from his fulness, grace upon grace. The application of the great truths of the Gospel to their hearts, by the power of the Spirit, destroys the temptations of sense,—overcomes the allurements of the world; bruises Satan under their feet; makes them in the likeness of the Lord Jesus, holy, harmless, undefiled, and separate from sinners. What other instrument produces this effect? Surely none. And in this, there is a constant display of the power of God in the Gospel, for the salvation of those who believe.

Who *upholds, and preserves unto final salvation,* those who are thus brought to a knowledge of the truth? The Gospel is the great instrument of the Spirit, for keeping every child of God through faith unto salvation. By the divine power attending its ministrations, it is able to keep him from falling, and to present him before the throne of God with exceeding joy. It is an incorruptible, abiding seed within him; a tree of life which brings forth permanent and increasing fruit. Every branch engrafted into Christ which beareth fruit, is purged, that it may bring forth more fruit. From him, the believing soul receives life more and more abundantly. How glorious is this exhibition of divine power in feeble, fallible man! It is like keeping a spark alive in the midst of an ocean; a sustaining of hope against hope. The subject of a Saviour's grace is encompassed with innumerable difficulties. Many and heavy loads unite their weight upon him. He bears the burden of a wounded spirit; the anguish of indwelling sin; the weight of a suffering body; the scorn and reproach of Satan and the world. But amidst all these, Jesus gives him, by his Spirit in the Gospel, "beauty for ashes, the oil of joy for mourning, the garment of praise for the spirit of heaviness." When fearfulness and trembling come upon him, and his steps are almost gone, this is his comfort in his affliction, that the word of God hath quickened him, and that God will perfect that which he hath wrought for his servant. He leans, under the teaching of the Gospel, upon no created strength; he looks not for the help of man. He trusts to the word of divine promise in the Gospel, and stays upon his God as there revealed. He casts his whole care upon him who hath begun a good work in him, confident that he will carry it on unto the day of the Lord Jesus. In this trust, he is never forsaken, nor is the Spirit of God taken from his soul. This divinely preserving power of the Gospel is often displayed through a long course of years, and in circumstances of great trial and distress. "Eighty and six years," said Polycarp upon the day of his martyrdom, "have I served Jesus of Nazareth, and he has never forsaken me." What can be a more delightful testimony to the worth and power of the Gospel, than the reflection of an old man who has passed through all the sorrows of life, and gained the period when all the charms of earth have lost their power, "I have been young, and now am old, and yet saw I never, the righteous forsaken;" "to me, Jesus is still precious?" But this testimony is given every day, and God is thus honoured in the power which he exhibits in the Gospel, to sustain and preserve all who have trusted themselves to him.

Who *finally crowns* the subjects of grace in eternal glory? There is the consummation of this display of divine power. For every child of God on earth, this work of grace shall be assuredly perfected. As the ransomed of the Lord, they shall return to Zion, with songs and everlasting joy upon their heads. They shall obtain joy and gladness, and sorrow and sighing shall flee away. Then how wonderful will be the display of power in that work which God has accomplished for man through his Spirit by the Gospel! How amazing the grace which has brought so many children of wrath and sin, to be heirs of everlasting glory! The sufferings of Jesus will have received their full reward. He shall be glorified in his saints, and admired in those who believe. He shall rejoice forever over the vast multitudes whom he has redeemed, and washed from their sins in his own blood, and brought home to God. Countless armies shall assemble before him with his mark upon their foreheads; all, the fruits of his redemption; plucked from the jaws of the lion; begotten again by his Spirit to the enjoyment of this lively hope; secured in an everlasting possession of the glory of God, and of the presence of the Lamb. But who hath done all this? What instrument of amazing power has been here displayed? Every soul will answer, "God, through the offering of his Son, and by the power of his Spirit, in the Gospel." The work in every instance has been the same. A vessel of wrath, fitted to destruction, has been brought as a vessel afore prepared for glory, to the everlasting habitation of God, for the Master's honour and use. Unnumbered millions, who were by nature, poor, and miserable, and blind, and naked;—for whom when they were without strength, Christ died; will be seen gathered in the Father's house, rescued by the power of the Spirit through the Gospel, and made to shine as the brightness of the firmament, and as the stars forever and ever.

III. In this wonderful exhibition of divine power in the Gospel, we are taught the *proper ground for human hope.*

It is the power of God as promised and exercised in the gospel of Jesus. If you look upon your own characters, you find yourselves utterly weak and unworthy. All reflections upon yourselves will inevitably be of the most humiliating and painful character; and if you were compelled to receive the wages which you have earned by your own conduct, you could not sustain the load. You have nothing which you can offer unto God. There is no part of your lives which could furnish you a sufficient hope of acceptance before him, and if he should call you into judgment, it must be to condemn and destroy you. But while you are thus entirely deficient in yourselves, there is offered to you in the gospel of Jesus, a sufficient and abiding hope. There the divine power presents itself to your acceptance, as all-sufficient for your wants, and invites you to lean upon it, as a staff which can never be broken.

Will you then be persuaded to cast out all idea of trusting in yourselves; to renounce all dependance upon your own character and conduct, and to seek a righteousness beyond yourselves, in the perfect and spotless obedience of the Son of God? You are simply invited to *accept* the provisions of the gospel; and as Noah, believing God's word, sought refuge and protection in the ark, and as the persecuted Israelite, trusting the divine command, found a shelter in the city of refuge, so to flee to the work which the Lord Jesus has finished, and venture yourselves upon that without fear, and plead nothing but that for your acceptance before God. If you are convinced of your wants, and of your total inability to save yourself, and are ready to be freely justified, and freely saved by the power of Christ, every thing is ready for you. The sacrifice and obedience of Jesus have been accepted in your behalf. God is well pleased in him, and well pleased to save you, for his sake; and nothing is wanting, but that you, with a penitent and humble spirit, should receive the blessings which are so freely offered you in Christ Jesus. The gospel presents you all with a foundation upon which you may securely build. Without fear or doubting you may embrace this glorious hope; and when you do embrace it in your hearts, all your guilt shall be removed, all your dangers shall pass away, and everlasting light and glory shall rest upon your souls.

Do not trust yourselves before a heart-searching God with any other ground of hope; for plead what you will, you will be inevitably condemned. When God riseth up in judgment you cannot answer him, or stand before him, save in the all-sufficient and prevailing merits of an incarnate and suffering Saviour, which have been thankfully embraced and dwelt upon by you.

2. You see to whom all the *praise* is to be given for the work of salvation. In this work man is nothing. He brings to it no strength, no merit, no claim of any kind. You are to ascribe the whole glory to that mighty Saviour who loved you, when you were dead in trespasses and sins, and interposed his power and his worthiness for you, when you were perishing, without strength and without hope. To him let your thanksgivings be every day addressed, as you are led on from strength to strength. In him let all your confidence be placed, for what he has promised to do for you, while you are passing the wilderness of life; and when you are brought to rest, in the presence of his glory, to him will you find yourselves constrained to offer all the honour and praise for what he has been pleased to undertake and finish in your behalf. He is the great object of universal praise; all the angels of God worship him; all the spirits of just men made perfect, ascribe honour unto him; and from our hearts he asks the same tribute of thanksgiving and honour. Give him glory before your feet stumble upon the dark mountains, and he turn the light which you look for, into the shadow of death. Be wise in making him your friend while his mercies are offered you in his word, and let the power of the gospel be for you a power to save.

For reflect, I pray you, in conclusion, that the same power which the gospel has to save, it has to *destroy*. It increases the condemnation and misery of those who reject it, and it were far better, never to have heard its gracious invitations, than having heard them, to cast them voluntarily away. To this destroying power of the gospel for those who reject it,

Jesus refers when he says, "Whosoever shall fall on this stone shall be broken, but on whomsoever it shall fall, it will grind him to powder." It has an irresistible energy. It comes with an overwhelming force upon those who have despised its mercies, and makes it better for such persons if they had never been born. This gospel must appear in the great day, as a witness for, or against every child of man. It will bear testimony for all who have accepted its invitations, that justice is satisfied, and all condemnation must pass away; that the lamb is worthy, and for his sake, infinite honour and glory must be bestowed on them. It must witness against all who have refused its mercies, that they are without hope; the law must take its course, while their condemnation and ruin have been awfully increased, by choosing death rather than life. With a destructive weight it falls upon such, to grind them to powder, to consign them over to everlasting ruin, and to bind them in chains of eternal darkness and death.

Happy will it be, for all before me, to have this powerful gospel, a witness of approbation and not of condemnation, in that solemn day.

LECTURE VI.

THE POWER OF THE GOSPEL TO CONDEMN.

Whosoever shall fall on this stone shall be broken; but on whomsoever it shall fall, it will grind him to powder.—St. Matthew, xxi. 44.

It is an abiding promise of the Most High, " My word shall not return unto me void; it shall accomplish that which I please, and prosper in the thing whereto I sent it." Not one of the divine purposes can fail; nor though men do not believe, can the truth of God ever be made of no effect. But such a promise has a special application to that word of reconciliation which is revealed in our Lord Jesus Christ; to those glad tidings of mercy which this divine Saviour has proclaimed to mankind. The preaching of the gospel, as the solemn and authoritative publication of the will of God, can never be made a matter of indifference to men. God's glorious designs will in no degree come short of their ultimate accomplishment, whether men will hear, or whether they will forbear. "We are unto God, a sweet savour of Christ, in them that are saved, and in them that perish;" the instruments at all times of manifesting his power, and showing forth his glory. But it remains to be determined by men's acceptance, or rejection of the gospel which we preach, whether we shall be to them "a savour of life unto life, or a savour of death unto death." The gospel of Christ comes with all the weight of infinite authority, to a world at enmity with God. And while for some, it effects its grand object, in their conversion unto God, as the power of God unto salvation; to others, it becomes the occasion of increased guilt and condemnation. In comparison with their new amount of transgression thus accumulated, it may be justly said, that had not its blessings come upon them, " they had not had sin, but now they have no cloak for their sin." " This is their condemnation, that light has come into the world, and they have loved darkness, rather than light, because their deeds are evil." The gospel is in every case a manifestation of divine power among men. To those who refuse its offers of mercy, it is still the power of God, though they pervert its influence, by their own rebellion, to their increased condemnation and more aggravated ruin.

This latter exhibition of the divine power in the gospel, our Lord describes in our text. He reminds the Jews of the testimony which the Scriptures had given unto him, as the chosen corner stone, which, though rejected by those whose duty it was to build upon it, was nevertheless exalted to be the head of the corner, in man's salvation; and which in this exaltation in defiance of the opposition of men, manifested the Lord's work, marvellous in human eyes. He warns them, that while their rejection of this chosen foundation of human hope, would not overturn his purposes, it would inevitably injure, perhaps finally destroy themselves. " Whosoever shall fall on this stone, shall be broken; but on whomsoever it shall fall, it will grind him to powder."

My design with this text, is to consider the *power of God as exhibited in the gospel, upon those who reject its offers of salvation.* It describes this exercise of power, under a twofold aspect.

I. Its *present operation*, in some respects beneficial to those upon whom it is exercised.

II. Its *future operation* wholly condemnatory and destructive.

The fact that men do thus reject the offers of the Gospel cannot be denied. Comparatively few to whom the truths which it reveals, are uttered, receive them with love, and are begotten again by their renovating influence, to that lively and glorious hope which the Gospel sets before them. Multitudes under the most faithful preaching of the Gospel, continue to harden themselves against the word, and remain impenitent for sin, and without a hope of the glory of God. The same divine testimony which is made to pluck some from eternal ruin, only furnishes arguments to others, by which they may resist its influence. The fire which melts the wax, is equally powerful and sure in its operation to harden the clay. The experience of numbers will testify, that the preaching of the Gospel has far less power over their minds now, than it had in some previous period of their life; and the difficulty in shaking off the serious impressions which it makes upon them, is continually growing less. But has this preaching of the truth therefore produced *no* effect upon them? Alas, far enough from this. The responsibility which they have assumed, is momentous. The consequences which must flow from their neglect of so great salvation, eternity can alone adequately reveal. The Son of man came not to destroy men's lives, but to save them. And yet it would be good for some, to whom he has come, if they had not been born. The main object of the Gospel, is to declare a free and finished salvation to guilty man, through the blood of God's dear Son; and to open thus to perishing sinners, a way of escape from the wrath to come. But when the attainment of this object is arrested by man's perversion, and sinful men count themselves unworthy of eternal life, the almighty power of the Redeemer is still displayed; and every knee is compelled to bow to him, and every tongue to confess his greatness, and his glory. Men may wickedly set their faces against the truth, they may even raise the cruel arm of persecution to arrest its progress, and to cast down its dominion. But the darkness of a cloud might as well attempt to extinguish the lustre of the celestial bodies, or the violence of a tempest, to disturb the order of their motions. There is a power attending the progress of the Gospel, which shall certainly prevail over the gates of hell; and a wisdom, which no adversary shall be able to gainsay or to resist.

I. The Gospel manifests this power of God over those who reject its offers, in a *present operation, in some respects beneficial to those who suffer it.* "Whosoever shall fall on this stone, shall be broken."

1. It *impresses convictions*, often very deep and solemn convictions, upon their minds. One of the peculiar offices of the Holy Ghost, is to awaken and convince the consciences of men, by the instrumentality of the word of God. With some, this conviction is the preparation for a thorough and spiritual conversion. He leads them from the consciousness of their misery and danger in an unpardoned state, to count the message of the Gospel worthy of all acceptation; to adore the grace which offers them reconciliation with God; and to accept with thankfulness, as their garment of salvation, the perfect righteousness of the Lord Jesus Christ. But there is often a conviction of the truth fastened upon the minds of others, which is allowed by them, to produce no saving change of character or state. It is a conviction which drives them from their strong hold of opposition, makes their own hearts secretly condemn them, and constrains them to acknowledge the truth which they do not love. Thus the Saviour proclaimed his truth to the Jews, with such a convincing power, that "no man was able to answer him a word." Thus the persecutors of Stephen were not "able to resist the Spirit with which he spake," though they gnashed their teeth

upon him, in their fury, and conspired and accomplished his death.

This is the universal operation of the word of God. It shuts up under the deeper consciousness of sin, all who will not fall down before it, and give glory in their conversion, to the Lord God. It so surrounds men with its powerful annunciations, and hedges in their way with invitations and warnings, that there is no avenue left them for escape. God calls upon men themselves, to decide upon the justice of his demands, and the truth of his representations. "O my people testify against me, what have I done unto thee? Wherein have I wearied thee? How shall I pardon thee for this? Are not my ways equal? I will judge you every one after his own ways." He thus elicits their condemnation from their own mouth; and in an undeniable demonstration of their personal ingratitude, seals upon them, their own conviction and acknowledgment of their guilt. While in the solemn declarations of the Scripture, we affirm that "the unrighteous shall not inherit the kingdom of God," that "God hath concluded all under sin," the consciences of many, who will not submit to the warnings of the Most High, are compelled to acknowledge to these descriptions of the sinner's state and danger, "such also are some of us." Their vain ideas of security are overthrown. Though they profess themselves free from guilt, they do not feel so. Their delusive hopes are swept away. Their refuges of deceit all fail them. They stumble at the word being disobedient. They will not acknowledge, or build upon the appointed corner stone. But they find it ever in their way, and falling upon it, they are broken, in unavoidable convictions of their guilt and danger.

2. The gospel *excites fears*, often awakening and alarming fears, in the consciences of the unconverted. Fear is an uniform attendant upon conscious guilt. When the conscience of a guilty man is aroused, he trembles at the shaking of a

leaf. The shades of solitude have a darkness for him, which the pious and believing do not find. The truth of God seems to wring from him, the despairing exclamation of Ahab, " Hast thou found me, O mine enemy ?" The Scripture gives many solemn and instructive illustrations, of this arresting influence of the divine message upon the minds of the worldly and rebellious. See the prisoner in chains pronouncing sentence upon his judge, and the proud man who fills the throne of power, trembling under the justice of the condemnation. Hear the wicked Ahab say of Michaiah the prophet, " I hate him, because he doth not prophesy good concerning me, but always evil;" and yet he quails and trembles, while the fettered prophet exclaims, in the majesty of conscious truth, " if thou return at all in peace, the Lord hath not spoken by me." See Felix quivering under the power of the truth, when the man who was bound with a chain for the hope of Israel, " reasoned before him, of righteousness, temperance, and judgment to come." Thus numbers have trembled under the solemn preaching of the word of God, who have notwithstanding perversely rejected the warnings which it proclaimed. Perhaps it will be said that every unconverted man is not thus alarmed under the preaching of the divine word. But the reason for this, is not to be found, in the inefficiency of the word, or in the greater stoutness of their rebellious hearts, but in the ignorance which fills the minds of some, and the seared obduracy which has been allowed to encase the consciences of others. But even here, when the convincing power of the Spirit attends the dispensation of the word, and rouses from their slumber, the legion who have taken possession of the sinner's soul,—he will see its truth, and believe and tremble under its influence, though seven other spirits of sin, worse than the first, afterwards enter into him, and he is finally left to perish in his transgressions. Such fears will excite men to solemn determinations of amendment, and vehement desires for salvation, though they endure only for a season. Often will the strong and exceeding bitter cry of Esau, "Hast thou not another blessing? Bless me, even me, O my father," be heard in death, from men who have thus sold their birthright, and trodden under foot the Son of God. They water their couch with unavailing tears. They find their peace of mind to be banished forever. And yet they will not relinquish their habits of sin, the guilt of which gives them such uneasiness, and often distress. Thus the gospel displays its power, even over those who reject its offers of grace. They fall upon this stone, and are broken.

3. The gospel *lays powerful and important restraints* upon the unconverted. It often almost persuades them to submit to its influence, and follow Christ in newness of life. We cannot look upon the present state of the world, without being convinced, that corrupted as it now is, the mighty hand of God is notwithstanding remarkably laid upon it, for the restraint of its iniquity. Sin rarely produces its perfect work. The tide of its determinations is arrested. The divine assurance "hitherto mayest thou come, but no further," stays the accomplishment of its plans. Unconverted men do not, and cannot, push to the extreme point, the tendency of their corrupted principles. They are held back in courses which they fondly love, and forced into external compliances, which they have no inward principles to sustain. The preaching of the gospel exercises a power, to bind them down to comparative moderation in their transgressions, and to compel them to desist from their headstrong course of degradation and ruin, even though like the chained tiger, they may fret themselves into rage, under the imposition of its restraints. This restraining power of the gospel is habitually seen, exercised over many who will not submit to its converting power. Herod would do "many things" under the persuasion of John, though he would not part with Herodias, even for him.

Agrippa was "almost persuaded to be a Christian," after the preaching of St. Paul, yet he could not enter into his bonds. Even Ahab, reeking with the blood of an innocent subject, humbled himself in sackcloth, under the warnings of Elijah. The native tendency of the human heart is to entire alienation from God. This tendency under the preaching of the gospel, God habitually restrains. Like an invisible power which should hold a mass of rock floating in the air, does the secret energy of the truth retard the tendency to ruin, of the unconverted soul,—a tendency as inherent as the gravitation of the stone,—and compel the carnal mind to stop and question with itself, whether it shall serve God or Mammon.

The Gospel thus shews itself to be the power of God, even over those who willingly reject its offered blessings, and remain without an interest in its promises, by convincing, alarming, and restraining them, even though they may remain finally unconverted. They fall upon this chosen and exalted corner-stone, in their refusal to employ it according to the divine command, as the foundation of their hope, and they are broken. They feel and acknowledge its power, notwithstanding they affect to despise it. They are kept back by its influence from their full courses of rebellion. They are not able to do all their will. And although they are finally condemned, for thus loving darkness rather than light, the restraints under which the gospel places them here, are a beneficial operation. God displays towards them, in all this course of authority over them, remarkable long-suffering and mercy, enduring with them, as vessels of wrath fitted to destruction, and giving them space to repent of their evil deeds, before they are finally called into judgment before him.

II. The gospel manifests its power over the unconverted, in a *future operation which is wholly condemnatory and destructive.* "On whomsoever it shall fall it will grind him to powder." What words could more emphatically and solemnly display the utter final destruction of ungodly men? A sinner falls on this stone in his own rejection of it. It becomes to him a stumbling stone, and a rock of offence. But he is arrested and held back by its power, in his progress of wickedness to destruction, even though he perishes in this rejection at the last. It falls again upon the sinner, in its final influence for condemnation,—ripening him for judgment, and increasing his condemnation,—so that his final condition becomes far worse, from the precious privileges which he has so ineffectually enjoyed. "That servant which knew his Lord's will and prepared not himself, neither did according to his will, shall be beaten with many stripes: but he that knew not, and did commit things worthy of stripes, shall be beaten with few stripes; for unto whomsoever much is given, of him shall be much required." "He that despised Moses' law, died without mercy, under two or three witnesses: of how much sorer punishment, suppose ye, shall be thought worthy, who hath trodden under foot the Son of God, and hath counted the blood of the covenant, wherewith he was sanctified, an unholy thing, and hath done despite unto the Spirit of grace?"

1. The gospel produces this effect of condemnation upon those who reject it, by the *increased hostility and opposition* against itself, which it excites among them. It thus displays its power often in a very remarkable way, and wicked men exhibit a consciousness of this power equally remarkable. When a man cautiously buckles on his armour, and stands with much determination upon his defence, and enters into a contest watchful and guarded, he shews himself expecting an antagonist of great comparative power. It is fighting not as one that beateth the air. How often do sinful men with such a spirit and determination as this, meet the preaching and the power of the truth of God. They fill their mouths with arguments; and in manifest fear of the influence of the word of God, they fix themselves, in prepared and steadfast opposition to its power. Let the secret places of their wickedness be

untouched, and the prophets cry peace, peace to them in their sins, and they will move on quietly and softly. Great external decorum in their relations to the ordinances and services of religion, will often conceal the real bitterness of their unsubdued hearts. But let the word of God be brought into direct opposition to their plans and habits of unbelief and sin, and they are driven from their assumed tranquillity, the philosophic dignity of their demeanour, to the extremes of anger and violence. Like the river which flows easily and silently in an unobstructed channel, but foams, and chafes, and rages, when its progress is arrested or impeded by intervening rocks. Sin cannot bear to be disquieted ;—far less, to be encompassed and shut in, by the solemn and unbending warnings of God. And the gospel becomes thus a remarkable test of the character of men ; as the manner in which the avowed preaching of it is received, becomes generally, an equally striking test of the measure of fidelity in its ministration. If the trumpet of the watchman give an uncertain sound, the most worldly and unsubdued hearer, will be willing to endure, perhaps to listen. But if the messenger of Christ come forth, with simple, solemn, and unequivocal words of warning ; if he make the sins of men to find them out, in his pointed appeals from God to their consciences and hearts ; then the gospel shews its power, in the extreme hostility which it excites. And as the hunted lion will turn at last in despair, upon his pursuers, and spend his utmost strength in a last defence, so do the raging passions of the unconverted soul, unite themselves in the vain determination to cast down the power of this gospel, and to sustain by efforts of violence, the dominion of sin. This hostility of the finally unconverted against the truth and will of God, is thus increased by the preaching of the gospel, in proportion to the fidelity of its ministration. And the rejected gospel thus matures them for a judgment which lingereth not, and a damnation which slumbereth not. The despised corner-stone is thus rolling back upon them in an alarming return for their contempt. And the sad final result, the text describes. "It will grind them to powder."

2. The gospel shows this power over the unconverted, in *the aggravation which it adds to their condemnation and punishment.* Every neglected privilege is a swift witness against the soul to judgment. The unspeakable mercies of the gospel, abused and trampled on, constitute that amount of guilt, for which the infallible word of God has denounced a far sorer punishment than death without mercy. "If I had not come and spoken to them," said the Saviour of the unbelieving Jews, "they had not had sin; but now they have no cloak for their sin. If I had not done among them, the works which no other man did, they had not had sin; but now they have both seen and hated, both me and my Father." The violations of the precepts of God's holy law, do not form the only, nor the chief provocation, for which the wrath of God breaks out upon the unconverted to the uttermost, at the last. For all these, pardon was freely offered; and for the condemnation which they have deserved, a ransom was freely provided. Sins like crimson and scarlet could have been washed away, in that blood of Jesus Christ which cleanseth from all sin. But the continued rejection of the mercies of the gospel, the refusal of this ransom and forgiveness, the rejection of the anointed Son of God by whom they were offered, constitute a transgression, for which there remaineth no more sacrifice, and the guilt and ingratitude of which make all other sins of no comparative account. This burden, the rolling back of a rejected gospel brings upon the unconverted man forever. The wicked of all lands, and all generations, will rise up in the judgment against him, and condemn him. His portion is the wrath of the Lamb, the just vengeance of a despised Redeemer, from which he will vainly seek a refuge beneath the rocks and the mountains. Every year's continuance in the

unprofitable enjoyment of the means of salvation, renders this condemnation the more certain and inevitable. In the degree in which advantages are great, will judgment be the more speedy, as well as the more dreadful. Just as the sun ripens the more hastily, the fruit which is trained against the wall, does the faithful preaching of the gospel mature with the greater rapidity the measure of their guilt, who have unavailingly received its great and peculiar bounties. Forbearance may be long and patiently extended, towards those who have never known this more excellent way. But a swift destruction must attend the ingratitude and hardness of their hearts, who despise the free and clear offers of that life, which is laid up for guilty man, in God's dear Son. The stone must fall on them, and grind them to powder. Long neglected grace will call down a swifter and heavier judgment. And the gospel will shew the power which attends it, in a resistless and everlasting condemnation, of those who have thus loved darkness rather than light.

III. How serious and important are the considerations which are presented in this testimony from the word of God! How fearful is their condition, who are living without God in the world, amidst the abounding mercies which he hath offered in his Son, and converting the unspeakably gracious blessing of a Saviour for the perishing, into an increased condemnation, and more aggravated curse! And yet there are no truths connected with the redemption of man, more undeniably certain, than those which have been here considered. The responsibility which is thus made to rest upon man amidst these privileges, cannot be avoided, or laid aside. If the careless sinner refuse to hear the preaching which only aggravates his condemnation, and heap to himself teachers more suited to his itching ears, he does not alter in any degree, the condition or prospects of his soul. The same responsibility arises, and the same condemnation accrues, from a refusal to listen to what the Lord God hath spoken. The glad tidings of a Saviour are proclaimed, and it is the duty of sinful men to hear with thankfulness, obedience and joy, the heavenly message which is delivered to them. Jehovah hath spoken to us in his Son; and every soul which will not hear this last great messenger from God, shall be cut off from among his people. The only way to escape condemnation, is freely and thankfully to submit yourselves to God; to kiss the Son, before he be angry, or his wrath be kindled but a little; and thus to accomplish that determination, which the Spirit of the Lord would lead your hearts to make, to seek him while he may be found, and to call upon him while he is near. You must embrace the truth with a thankful and contrite heart, receive Christ within you, as a hope of glory, and thus become new creatures in him. The longer this full conversion unto God is deferred, the greater becomes your danger and your guilt; and the more rapid the progress, and the more irreversible the certainty, of that everlasting destruction which you will bring upon yourselves. Here only is there salvation. If you are ever plucked from ruin, it can only be, by finding by the experience of your own hearts, in the Lord Jesus Christ, as offered in the Gospel, the power of God unto salvation. To lead you to this, all the invitations and influences of the gospel are continually combined; goodness and mercy are thus following you all your days. God is waiting to be gracious to you, and even after so long a time, he urges you still to hear his voice, and harden not your hearts. And if, amidst all these amazing mercies, you refuse to hear his gracious intreaties, and count yourselves unworthy of eternal life,—how manifest it must become to yourselves, and to all others, that your damnation is just.

LECTURE VII.

THE GRACE OF THE GOSPEL AS A DIVINE GIFT.

The unsearchable riches of Christ.—EPHESIANS, III. 8.

We understand these, as the unsearchable provisions of grace, which are contained in the gospel of Christ. These provisions the Apostle Paul was sent to offer to the gentiles; and in the whole of his ministrations, he shows us the remarkable difference which there is between that view of the gospel which is the result of speculative examination merely, and that view of it which has been formed from an experience of its life-giving power. The man who examines the gospel upon its exterior, sees much in it to admire, for its beauty of moral precepts, its attractive examples of personal character, and its peculiar revelations of the existence and character of God; and upon this ground he may advocate and enforce the system of religion which he conceives the New Testament to contain.

The man who has experienced the power of the gospel to convert and sanctify, forgets these peculiar reasons for valuing its revelations, in his wondering admiration of it, as a system of unsearchable grace for the chief of sinners. Our minds will naturally dwell upon that aspect of this system, with the most constancy and delight, which we feel to be most suited to our individual wants; and if we have felt ourselves to be ruined sinners, and have sought in the gospel a remedy for our necessities, we shall pass over every minor characteristic, and adore the exceeding riches of grace which Almighty God has been pleased here to exhibit.

This view of the gospel occupied the thoughts and affections of the apostle Paul. He seldom speaks of Jesus or his dispensation, except under the idea of a scheme of glorious salvation; of which, in infinite mercy, he had been made a subject, though he was before a persecutor, a blasphemer, and injurious. Paul's knowledge of the truth was the result of an experience of its power; and to the same experience, he desired to bring all to whom he addressed himself, as an ambassador of Christ. He had found a home, a resting place for his soul, dwelling in Christ; and Christ had found an equally permanent abode in his soul, dwelling in him.

No view of the gospel is so honourable to God, or so comforting and suitable to ourselves, as this to which your attention is now to be directed: *the riches of its grace as a divine gift to man.* The apostle states to the Ephesians, that God especially designed, in the salvation which he had provided in the gospel, "to show in the ages to come the exceeding riches of his grace in Christ Jesus;" and to further and promote this design, had commissioned him, though less than the least of all saints, to preach among the Gentiles " the unsearchable riches of Christ."

I have selected these words of the apostle as a text, because they show the fact, which it is my design to exhibit in this discourse, that the provisions of grace offered to sinners in the gospel, are truly unsearchable. They are adequate to supply every want; they are adapted to every circumstance and relation of man; they are sufficient for the necessities of the whole race of men.

I. The unsearchable grace of the gospel is displayed in the *freeness* with which it offers every blessing to man. It requires nothing to be done by us in order to merit its blessings. It never puts us upon earning an interest in the mercies which it has provided. To the utmost meaning of the terms, every blessing of the gospel is a free gift of God to man. They are as much so as the manna which was rained from heaven upon the Israelites, or the water which followed them from the rock in their wanderings through the wilderness. Under this character, as free and unmerited gifts, the privileges of the gospel are presented through the whole inspired volume. The first promise of a Saviour is a remarkable illustration of this fact. That promise was not given in answer to any solicitations on the part of our first parents. They could hardly be supposed able to conceive of the possibility of such a promise. Indeed it was not literally given to them at all. It was included in the threatening which was denounced by God against the serpent who had deceived them, and not personally addressed either to Adam or Eve; "I will put enmity between thee and the woman, and between thy seed and her seed; it shall bruise thy head, and thou shalt bruise his heel." The Saviour was thus a free gift of God, a gift unthought of by man; and every blessing which the Saviour brings, is as entirely a free gift as himself. "The wages of sin is death, but the gift of God is eternal life through Jesus Christ our Lord." The whole amount of mercies and privileges which the gospel bestows, are unclogged with any conditions. The gracious invitations which it addresses to men, are entirely unlimited in their application. "Ho! every one that thirsteth," it says upon the high places of the earth, "and he that hath no money, come buy and eat; yea, buy wine and milk without money and without price." And again, in the conclusion of its book of grace, it says again, "The Spirit and the bride say come, and let him that heareth say come, and let him that is athirst come, and whosoever will, let him take of the waters of life freely."

Now here is exhibited the unsearchable riches of the gospel. It comes to creatures who can do nothing to deserve its blessings, or to acquire an interest in its glorious promises, and presents itself as perfectly suitable to their wants, by offering freely and unconditionally to their acceptance, all the mercies they can desire. Fallen creatures can do nothing to restore themselves. The angels who are confined in chains of darkness can do nothing to obtain salvation from their ruin. They are utterly incapable of meriting God's favour, and we are equally so. No salvation would avail us any thing which required us to do any thing previously, to deserve its bestowal upon us.

The whole Scripture unites to caution us against the thought of earning grace: " Say not in thine heart, who shall ascend into heaven ? that is to bring Christ down from above; or who shall descend into the deep? that is, to bring up Christ again from the dead. But what saith it? The word is nigh thee, even in thy mouth, and in thy heart; that is, the word of faith which we preach; that if thou shalt confess with thy mouth the Lord Jesus, and believe in thy heart that God hath raised him from the dead, thou shalt be saved. For with the heart man believeth unto righteousness, and with the mouth confession is made unto salvation."

Yes, *we* do preach, as the Holy Ghost preaches throughout the whole Bible, that to receive every divine blessing by faith, freely, as it is freely offered, is the only office assigned to any child of man. After we have embraced the invitations of the gospel, we have much to do to honour and adorn it in all holy conversation and godliness; yet our first reception of its blessings must be altogether free, and we must stand indebted for them solely to the sovereign grace of God.

But while I merely say the gospel shows its riches of grace in offering every blessing freely, I say too little. St. Paul expresses the greatest jealousy upon this subject. He declares that if we attempt to do any thing, however good in itself, expecting by it, either in whole or in part, to *merit* our salvation, we make void the whole gospel. " Behold I, Paul, say unto you, that if ye be circumcised, Christ shall profit you nothing." Salvation must be wholly of works, or wholly of grace. If salvation were of works, in ever so small a degree, there would be room for boasting; for we should have done something for ourselves. Whereas, under the gospel, boasting must be utterly excluded ; and salvation from first to last, must be received as a free gift of God for Christ's sake.

What unsearchable grace is this! and still more so, if you consider to whom such offers are freely made. The invitations of the gospel are presented and pressed upon the attention of beings universally depraved; beings who perversely reject all that has been done for them, who stand out to resist its gracious influence, and to fight against God, until they are subdued and led captive by a power stronger than themselves. These gracious invitations of God follow these creatures, through all the wanderings of their sinful lives, still pressing upon their attention the solemn call, " Turn ye, for why will ye die." The gospel of Jesus, in the tenderness of its compassion, literally persecutes the sinner with its entreaties that he would be saved. It will not give him up. It is like a rich and noble prince, who should follow a mendicant up and down, beseeching him to accept the assistance which he offers; and thus freely offering, and perseveringly offering, unsearchable riches to sinners who could deserve nothing, who despise and reject the mercies which are presented, and weary the patience of the Most High with their perverseness, the gospel displays its unspeakable grace as a gift of God to those who are really perishing in their sins.

II. The unsearchable grace of the gospel as a divine gift, is displayed in the *full* and *perfect* manner in which it communicates its blessings to man. There is not a want in the sinner which it does not abundantly supply. Are we by nature wretched and miserable, and poor, and blind, and naked? It gives us, without money or price, gold tried in the fire, that we may be rich; and white raiment to cover us, that the shame of our nakedness may not appear; and it anoints our eyes with eye-salve, that we may see. It fills the hungry with good things, and exalts those of low degree. How beautifully, and in what lively colours, is this fulness of gospel provisions exhibited by the Spirit of God, speaking through the prophet Isaiah in that passage which our blessed Lord applied to himself in the first public discourse which he ever delivered: " The Spirit of the Lord is upon me, because the Lord hath anointed me to preach good tidings unto the meek; he hath sent me to bind up the broken-hearted, to proclaim liberty to the captives, and the opening of the prison to them that are bound; to proclaim the acceptable year of the Lord, and the day of vengeance of our God; to comfort all that mourn; to appoint unto them that mourn in Zion, to give unto them beauty for ashes, the oil of joy for mourning, the garment of praise for the spirit of heaviness, that they might be called trees of righteousness, the planting of the Lord, that he might be glorified." This passage precisely illustrates the aspect of gospel grace, which is before your minds, the fulness with which it supplies every want of man; because it takes a view of mankind in a vast variety of conditions, in every stage of sorrow and distress, and represents the gospel as adapting itself to every different state, and as supplying every want under which men are suffering.

Look then upon the fulness of these provisions; conceive of miserable man in every condition in which he can be imagined; bowed down with a sense of guilt, or harassed with the temptations of Satan, or sinking under persecutions from men, or under the hidings of God's favour, or in the prospect of immediate dissolution; and in every condition the gospel presents him with all that he can want: pardon for all sin, strength against every temptation, support under every trial, comfort under every affliction, and life everlasting, by the simple exercise of faith in Jesus, as life was given to the dying Israelite by looking upon the brazen serpent. If there were a possible situation for which the gospel would not yield a supply, if there were a single thing which it required us to furnish from our own store, it would display no *unsearchable* riches of grace, nor would it be adapted to our necessities.

When the Israelites wandered in the wilderness, if they had been provided with bread and water, but had been left to their own guidance, or no miracle had been wrought to preserve their clothes, or to keep their feet from the effect of long and wearisome toil, how evident is it that the want of any one blessing would have rendered all the others nugatory and useless. God must supply *all* their wants, for they had no ability to supply one themselves. Just so is it with us. Should the gospel leave a single necessity unsatisfied, all its other provisions, however rich and abundant, would be in vain. Go, for instance, to the bedside of a dying sinner, and say, "You must render such and such services to the Lord before you can be accepted by him," what hope or comfort would such tidings inspire? How cruelly would such a message mock the anguish of a man who feels that he can do nothing; who is conscious that he is sinking into perdition, and must be plucked by some powerful arm from the gulf which stretches beneath his soul! But tell him, or any other sinner, that "Christ died for the chief of sinners; that those who come to him he will in no wise cast out; that sins like scarlet may be made as white as snow; that there is a fountain which cleanseth from all sin;" and you offer hope and comfort which are entirely and immediately abundant; you present a foundation upon which the soul may build without fear, and may see a sinner made a precious jewel in the Redeemer's crown for ever.

Thanks be to God! there is not a desirable blessing for man which the gospel does not impart to us in our hour of need. Pardon, peace, holiness and joy, are all offered freely, and bestowed abundantly for the Redeemer's sake. We find all fulness to dwell in Jesus Christ. He is made our wisdom and righteousness, and sanctification and redemption; and receiving from him grace upon grace, we stand complete in him. When our hearts have embraced his sufficiency, we are rich, we are full; we drink of a fountain which destroys all thirst for every other one, and have no disposition to go from him to draw elsewhere. Jesus is all in all, an answer to every accusation, a remedy for every evil, a supply for every necessity, an eternal antidote to despair. In him we have life abundantly, and feel assured, in the hope of treasures passing man's understanding, which he has laid up for us.

In this wonderful fulness of supply, the gospel displays riches of grace truly unsearchable; for ages have past, and no want has ever been found which it could not answer; and the Christian must still exclaim, at the close of the longest experience of its power, "O the length and breadth, and height and depth of the love of Christ, which passeth knowledge! How unsearchable! how past finding out!"

III. The unsearchable grace of the gospel is exhibited in the perfect *security* with which it bestows its mercies upon the sinner. The cordial embracing of the invitations of the gospel finally secures to every believer, the everlasting possession of its inestimable blessings. The gospel offers us salvation with all its attendant benefits, as the matter of an everlasting covenant, in all things well ordered and sure, confirmed to those who truly believe in the Lord Jesus Christ. It represents that covenant as confirmed by God himself with an oath, in order that by two immutable things (that is, the certain faithfulness of the divine promise, and the additional solemnity of a divine oath,) in which it is impossible for God to lie, we may have strong consolation, who have fled for refuge, to lay hold of the hope set before us. It represents the Lord Jesus Christ as the mediator of that covenant, and all its blessings as treasured up in him for our everlasting benefit. It states these blessings to be treasured up in him, that they may be made finally secure; because if they were entrusted to the mutability and perverseness of our wills, they would be inevitably lost.

The statements of the Scripture upon this treasuring up of a believer's hopes in Christ, and their infallible security as laid up in him, are remarkably strong and expressive. The Lord Jesus Christ is said to live in the believer, and the believer to have died with him. "I am crucified with Christ, nevertheless I live; yet not I, but Christ liveth in me." If this be our character, and Christ lives by his spiritual presence and influence in our hearts, while Christ lives we shall live also. But the apostle speaks in yet stronger language in another place, addressing himself to the Colossian Christians, "Ye are dead;" *i. e.* to the world and the flesh, to selfish hopes, "and your life is hid with Christ in God; when Christ, who is our life, shall appear, then shall ye also appear with him in glory." Here Christ is not only called *our life*, but our life is said to be "hid with Christ in God;" and because it is so, we may hope that when he shall appear, we shall also appear with him in glory.

Let us examine, for a moment, the real meaning of these words.

When God first made man, he committed the life of the whole family to Adam as their head and representative, that they might stand or fall in him; but, notwithstanding Adam was made perfect, and had but a single restraint imposed upon him as a test of his fidelity, he fell; and by this one apostacy brought death and ruin upon his whole posterity. Now, in restoring men to his favour under the gracious system of the gospel, God says, "I will not commit your eternal interests into your own hands; if I do, so weak are you, so encompassed with temptations, so prone to disobedience, what can I hope but that you will cast them all away and perish. I will give you another covenant representative and head, even my beloved Son, in whom I am well pleased, and commit all your interests to him. *He* shall be your hope. *He* shall be your life. Your life shall be hid with Christ in God; then shall I be sure that no enemy shall prevail against you, for he is mighty to save, and none can pluck you out of his hands."

But this full and final security of a believer's hopes does not depend upon any single passage of the Scriptures. I consider it the statement of the whole Scriptures, and inseparably connected with the gospel as a system of unsearchable grace. Every truly believing soul is given into the hands of the Redeemer, that he may keep it by his own power, "through faith unto salvation." In his intercession with the Father, recorded in the 17th of John, he affirms, that of those who had been given to him, he had lost none; that they had kept his word, and he had bestowed eternal life upon them, according to the divine covenant.

St. Paul, in addressing the Philippians, was confident that he who had begun a good work in them would carry it on unto the day of the Lord Jesus. He knew that the same Lord would be the finisher, who had been the author of every true faith; and from this confidence he pressed upon every believing soul the assurance that the Lord would never leave or forsake them, so that they might boldly say, "The Lord is my helper, I will not fear what man can do unto me;" and all might trust that what God had promised he was able also to perform.

This security which the gospel offers to every sinner who flees to it for refuge, gloriously exhibits its unsearchable riches of grace. It gives us an inestimable hope. It assures us that if we are ready to commit ourselves to Jesus, " he is able to keep us from falling, and to present us before the throne of his glory with exceeding joy." It bids us be careful for nothing, but live the life we now live in the flesh, by faith in the Son of God, " who loved us and gave himself for us," to know and remember, in whom we have believed, and to be assured, that he is able to keep that which we have committed to him unto that day, and to preserve us blameless unto his heavenly kingdom.

Thus are the unsearchable riches of gospel grace displayed. It offers with the utmost freedom to every sinner, all the privileges and mercies which the Lord Jesus Christ hath purchased. If he is willing freely to accept them, it bestows upon him fully and perfectly a covenant title to salvation, and all things which accompany salvation; it communicates every holy habit and grace, and enables him to walk worthy of the Lord unto all pleasing; makes him humble, and watchful, and persevering; and to show its ability to save unto the uttermost, it secures to him finally and unalterably, the blessings which it has freely promised, and for the enjoyment of which it has fully prepared him.

IV. These unsearchable riches of grace I desire with my whole heart and strength to press upon your acceptance. I would have you experience in your souls, the worth, the unspeakable worth of the gospel of Jesus, and be able to comprehend with all saints, that love of Christ, which passeth knowledge, that your souls may be filled with the fulness of God. These provisions of the gospel are sufficient for you all. They are perfectly sufficient for the *comfort,* the *holiness* and the *full salvation* of every soul who is ready to receive them.

They are sufficient for your *comfort*. If there be any of you brought by a view of their own sinfulness to the very borders of despair, what can they need more than to hear that God himself has undertaken their cause, has assumed their nature, and expiated their guilt by his own sufferings unto death? What could they wish to add to this? What can, by any possibility, be added to it? If this be not sufficient, what can be? Your sins, though they were more and more aggravated than those of any human being, are but finite still; they are many, but they may be numbered. The atonement which is offered for you, and the righteousness which is wrought out for you, are of infinite value. The blood of Jesus Christ will cleanse from *all* sin, and all who believe in him will be justified from all things, from which they could not be justified by the law of Moses. Let a man's sins be of never so deep a die, they cannot be more red than scarlet and crimson, and these can be made as white as snow. We can hardly conceive of greater guilt than David's, after all the mercies which he had received; and yet he prays, and prays with success, "Purge *me* with hyssop, and I shall be clean; wash *me*, and I shall be whiter than snow;" and then he acknowledges the abundant efficacy of the remedy, "Thou hast made the bones which thou hast broken to rejoice." What abundant instances the history of the church has given of the sufficiency of the gospel for the sinner's comfort. Behold three thousand Jews on the day of Pentecost, whose hands were yet stained with a Saviour's blood—scarcely one hour had they believed in this crucified Lord, before they "all ate their bread with gladness and singleness of heart, blessing and praising God." Behold the Ethiopian Eunuch, going on his way rejoicing; and Saul of Tarsus straitway preaching Christ whom he had laboured to destroy. Thus, wherever Christ is preached and received, true joy springs up in the heart. "Though we see him not, yet believing in him, we may rejoice with joy unspeakable and full of glory." This is, and is to be, the invariable effect of a proper acceptance of the gospel throughout the earth. "Sing, O ye heavens," says the prophet, in looking forward to this day, " for the Lord hath done it; shout, ye lower parts of the earth; break forth into singing ye mountains, O forest, and every tree therein, for the Lord hath redeemed Jacob, and glorified himself in Israel." Only let the gospel descend as the dew upon any place, or upon any soul, and " the wilderness will be glad, and the desert will rejoice and blossom as the rose;" for the Lord, by the ministrations of its unsearchable riches of grace, will comfort Sion ; he will comfort all her waste places; he will make her wilderness like Eden, and her desert like the garden of the Lord ; joy and gladness shall be found in every habitation; and in every soul which receives this gospel, thanksgiving and the voice of melody. There is not a human sorrow which it cannot console; and if you will accept its invitations and offers, it will be found an abundant source of comfort to you all.

These unsearchable provisions of grace are sufficient for the *holiness* of every sinner who believes in Jesus. Nothing can ever change the heart of man but the gospel of Jesus. Philosophy and moral precepts labour in vain to renew the character of the sinner. But where the gospel is truly preached, and truly received, the passions of men are subdued, their lusts are mortified, their habits are changed, their dispositions are made new, and they are turned from the power of Satan unto God. The gospel can make you all holy ; it reveals to you, and brings into union with you, a dying Saviour in all the wonders of his love, and thus will create in your souls a desire to love and serve him. It shows you that you are bought with a price, and then, for this reason, gives you a desire to glorify God in your bodies and spirits, which are his. To carry these new desires into effect, it brings down the

Holy Spirit into your souls, and thus strengthens you with might in your inner man, and works within you every good work; sanctifies you in soul, body and spirit, and renders you meet to become partakers of the inheritance of the saints in light. It will fill you with new principles, and impart to you new powers, and give you purposes and dispositions to which you have been entire strangers. Your characters may be entirely purified and cleansed, if you are willing to embrace these unsearchable riches of mercy which are offered you in the gospel of Jesus.

And finally, these provisions of grace are sufficient for your *full* and *complete salvation.* You cannot be placed in a situation in which they will not afford you strength equal to your day. They will make you conquerors, and more than conquerors. They will render your very troubles a source of joy, and your conflicts an occasion for more exalted triumphs.

Like Paul, you may glory in infirmities, while the power of Christ rests upon you. Like him you may rejoice in the prospect of death, when to depart is to be with Christ. Like him you may triumph in the inseparable love of Jesus, and the complete salvation which he affords, if you are ready to count every thing but loss for his sake; and with him the gospel shall so carry you through things temporal, that you shall in no wise lose the things eternal.

And now let me beseech you to receive these unsearchable riches of Christ. Here is bread from heaven for the famishing, and living waters for the weary and thirsting soul. Would to God you all felt your need of them, and would hunger and thirst for no other supplies than these! O let none despise this gracious supply. Whether you are old or young, learned or unlearned, rich or poor, Christ is alike needful for you, and will be alike sufficient for you. Do not persuade yourselves that he is unnecessary to you. Do not pour contempt upon him, as unsuitable. Do not attempt to add to him, as insufficient; but accept him, and live upon him as all your salvation and all your desire. Gather this bread of heaven as your daily portion, and refresh yourselves by this living fountain as your whole delight; and in the strength of this food, go on your way rejoicing. And as ye have received Jesus Christ the Lord, so walk ye in him; rooted and built up in him, and established in the faith as ye have been taught, abounding therein with all thanksgiving.

LECTURE VIII.

THE GLORY OF THE GOSPEL AS A REVELATION OF GOD.

And Moses said, I beseech thee show me thy glory. And he said, I will make all my goodness pass before thee, and I will proclaim the name of the Lord before thee.—Exodus, xxxiii, 18, 19.

The privileges granted to Moses in his communications with God were altogether peculiar. It is said the Lord spake unto Moses face to face, as a man speaketh unto his friend; and the testimony is added after his death, that there arose no other prophet in Israel like unto Moses, whom the Lord knew face to face, in all the signs and wonders which the Lord sent him to do in the sight of all Israel. God revealed his will to other prophets before and after the time of Moses. But no one had the same view of the divine character, and knowledge of the divine purposes, which was allowed to him. This difference in the method of his communications, God refers to in the controversy which arose from Aaron and Miriam against Moses. " And he said, hear now my words: If there be a prophet among you, I the Lord will make myself known unto him in a vision, and will speak unto him in a dream. My servant Moses is not so, who is faithfull in all mine house; with him will I speak mouth to mouth, even apparently, and not in dark speeches; and the similitude of the Lord shall he behold."

This " similitude of the Lord," or the apparent glory of the divine presence, Moses saw continually while he was receiving the law from God on the mount. The cloud into which he then entered, was the cloud of divine glory that overshadowed the mountain. The request of our text was made after his having been forty days in the mount. It was presented at the door of the tabernacle. Moses had pitched the tabernacle without the camp; and when he went forth to enter into the tabernacle, the cloudy pillar descended and stood at the door of the tabernacle; and the Lord talked with Moses, speaking to him face to face, or in the most free and intimate communication, as a man talketh with his friend. The conversation which was then held, includes the request of our text. "And Moses said unto the Lord, See, thou sayest unto me, Bring up this people, and thou hast not let me know whom thou wilt send with me, yet thou hast said, I know thee by name, and thou hast also found grace in my sight. Now therefore I pray thee, if I have found grace in thy sight, show me now thy way, that I may know thee, that I may find grace in thy sight, and consider that this nation is thy people. And he said, My presence shall go with thee, and I will give thee rest. And he said unto him, If thy presence go not with me, carry us not up hence. For wherein shall it be known here, that I and thy people have found grace in thy sight? Is it not in that thou goest with us? So shall we be separated, I and thy people, from all the people that are upon the face of the earth. And the Lord said unto Moses, I will do this thing also that thou hast spoken; for thou hast found grace in my sight, and I know thee by name. And he said, I beseech thee show me thy glory."

Moses' petition here, pointed to some more clear and significant exhibition of the divine character than he had yet received. What he had seen of God's purposes and government, in the revelations which had been made to him, impressed the conviction upon his mind, that there was to be a further manifestation of God to man than any which he had yet distinctly understood, and excited the desire in him to behold these peculiar exibitions of divine glory which should be made to God's people in subsequent ages. All that had been made known to him was in preparation for some future development of the glory of God; and that glory to which his institutions were thus an introduction, he longed to witness: " And he said, I *beseech* thee show *me* thy glory." In answer to this prayer God promised to give him the exhibition of his glory which he desired; and in complying with his promise, he revealed to him, as the highest possible manifestation of his glory, those purposes of grace and love which were to be made known and accomplished by the gospel of our Lord Jesus Christ.

These remarks naturally led me here to announce the particular subject which I design to consider, as connected with the prayer of Moses.

It is the glory of the gospel as an exhibition of the divine character.

I. That I do not here go aside from the real intention and meaning of the passage, it will be my object first to show.

Moses' desire was for some fuller exhibition of the character of God. In promising compliance with this desire, God does not direct him to the *works of creation;* although, from them the invisible things of him are clearly seen, even his eternal power and Godhead. He does not tell him to look upon the sun as it shined, and the moon walking in brightness, and there behold the glory of the Lord who hath created these things; who bringeth out their hosts by number; who calleth them all by their names, by the greatness of his might, for that he is strong in power, and not one faileth.

He does not tell him to look upon the awful thunders and earthquakes, and unearthly sounds with which the *law* had been given upon Mount Sinai, still trembling beneath the footsteps of a descending Deity; upon the solemn and awakening displays which were there made of the holiness of a God who cannot look upon iniquity; although here, as well as in the wenders of creation, it had been often declared that God had showed his glory to men.

Neither the glory of divine power displayed in the creation, nor the glory of divine holiness exhibited in the law, was that manifestation of the Deity, which God chose to style peculiarly his glory. And, passing by both these, were there no notice of what he did intend, we should be left to settle upon the gospel, as the only remaining manifestation of the divine character which has been made to man.

But the Lord describes his purpose and design most significantly. He says, "I will make *all my goodness* pass before thee." But where has *all* the goodness of the Lord been exhibited, but in that wonderful dispensation in which was manifested the love of God, in that he sent his Son to die for us? and how could *all* the goodness of the Lord pass before any mind, from which the riches of gospel grace were concealed? "And I will proclaim the name of the Lord before thee; and I will be gracious on whom I will be gracious; and I will show mercy on whom I will show mercy." But the name of the Lord, as bestowing sovereign grace and mercy, can be proclaimed only in that gospel which announces God manifest in the flesh for sinners, and the fulness of the Godhead dwelling bodily, in a man of sorrows and acquainted with grief. Under no other dispensation can God be gracious and merciful to sinners, for no other one makes atonement for sin.

Still more minutely describing his purpose, God assures Moses, that it would be impossible for any mortal to behold the full glory of his presence. "No man can see my face and live." He dwells in light inaccessible which no man can approach unto. No man hath seen God at any time; the only

AA

begotten Son that dwelleth in the bosom of the Father, he hath manifested him. And referring to this new and lasting way of intercourse between himself and sinful men, God says, "There is a place by me, and thou shalt stand upon a *rock*, and it shall come to pass, while my glory passeth by, I will put thee in the cleft of the rock, and will cover thee with my hand while I pass by." That rock was Christ, and here is presented the perfect security with which the glory of God is beheld under the gospel. The believer is hidden in a cleft of the rock; while even there, but partial displays are yet made to him of the divine glory. "I will take away my hand, and thou shalt see my back parts, but my face shall not be seen." We know not yet what we shall be, but we know that when he shall appear, we shall be like him, for we shall see him as he is; and even now, though we see him not, yet believing in him, we rejoice with unspeakable and glorified joy.

Thus in answer to the request of Moses, the Lord promised to make known to him the rich grace which he had prepared and designed to reveal to men, in the gospel of Jesus, as the peculiar glory of his character; and thus made known that all-important truth, which angels united to repeat on the eve of the incarnation, that the dispensation which brings peace on earth, and proclaims good will to men, brings "glory in the highest," to the character of God.

This was the promise to Moses. It was to be fulfilled on the ensuing day; and early in the morning Moses rose up, and went up unto Mount Sinai, as the Lord had commanded him. "And the Lord descended in the cloud, and stood with him there, and proclaimed the name of the Lord. And the Lord passed by before him and proclaimed, The Lord, the Lord God, merciful and gracious, long-suffering, and abundant in goodness and truth, keeping mercy for thousands, forgiving iniquity, and transgression, and sin, and that will by no means clear the guilty; visiting the iniquity of the fathers upon the children, and upon the children's children, unto the third and to the fourth generation. And Moses made haste, and bowed his head toward the earth, and worshipped."

Here the Lord proclaimed his name and his glory, and to do it he revealed his purposes of grace, which were to be accomplished in Christ Jesus, recording it forever, that in nothing is the glory of the Lord so wonderfully displayed, as in the grace which passes by transgressions and sins; according to that exclamation of the prophet, in looking forward to the gospel revelation, "Who is a God like unto thee that pardoneth iniquity, and passeth by the transgression of the remnant of his heritage? He retaineth not his anger forever, because he delighteth in mercy. He will turn again and have compassion on us; he will subdue our iniquities, and thou wilt cast all their sins into the depths of the sea."

II. If then God preached the gospel to Moses as the peculiar manifestation of his glory, which is thus apparent, I am warranted in speaking from this passage, of the glory of the gospel, as the clearest and most glorious exhibition of the Deity which has been made to man. The Old Testament is filled with predictions and types, all pointing to the same glory in the gospel of Jesus. The temple of the Lord is called a glorious rest; a glorious high throne; a house of glory, of beauty, of holiness; and it is said, that at the dedication of it, "the glory of the Lord filled the house of the Lord." This glory was the cloud which manifested the especial presence of the Lord. But yet the glory of the latter house was to be greater than the glory of the former house, because there the sun of righteousness was to arise, with healing in his wings, and the gospel was to be preached, with the Holy Ghost sent down from heaven. In the gospel of Jesus, the dispensation of grace and mercy which has been made through him to man, God has revealed his character and will to us, in a peculiar degree, and therefore it is styled, in the highest possible language of honour, " The glorious gospel of the blessed God."

In all the works of God there is glory, because they are his. David for this reason employs the terms *glory* and *handywork*, promiscuously for the same thing. " The heavens declare the glory of God, and the firmament showeth his handywork." Whatever he does is glorious from his own character. But the more he communicates of himself to any of his works, the more glorious they are; and therefore, in the very passage in which David celebrates the glory of creation, he shows the higher glory of the divine revelation and law. " The law of God is perfect, converting the soul; the statutes of the Lord are right, rejoicing the heart."

Men stand in higher rank than brutes, and the angels in heaven mount up in loftier grades than men, simply upon this principle, that the more of his own image God has bestowed upon any of his creatures, the higher in station and the more glorious in appearance they are. But, of all the manifestations of himself which the Deity has made, there is none in which he may be so fully known, communicated with, depended upon and praised, as the gospel of Jesus. This is a glass, in which the angels who surround his throne, see and admire the unsearchable riches of grace; and in which they behold, in his mercy to men, a revelation of his character, that they never elsewhere witnessed.

In creation and providence, God is seen clearly and wonderfully; but it is only as a God of power and wisdom, producing and upholding all things to promote the glorious end for which he has designed them. In the law, God is displayed solemnly and truly; but it is only as a God of vengeance and recompense; threatening and executing wrath upon those who offend against him. But in the gospel he is exhibited as a God of boundless compassion, as a God of love; and his power and his wisdom, and his faithfulness, all come in as subservient to his bounty and grace. Here we behold his glory, full of grace and truth. We see him humbling himself, that he might be merciful to his enemies; suffering in himself, that he might bear the punishment of their transgressions; and removing every obstacle to their forgiveness and acceptance, that he might not only offer them pardon, but beseech them to be pardoned, and reconciled to him again. In the creation, he is a God above us; in the law, he is a God against us; in the gospel alone, he is "Emmanuel;" God with us, God like us, God for us.

It is the gospel which reveals God to us as he is. He is invisible in himself; we cannot see him but in his Son. He is inaccessible in himself; we cannot approach him but through his Son. Would we therefore behold his glory, we must seek it in the acceptance and study of that dispensation which proclaims him to be " the Lord, the Lord God, merciful and gracious, long suffering, abundant in goodness and truth, keeping mercy for thousands, forgiving iniquity, transgression and sin!"

III. But while I make these general assertions of the gospel, as a revelation of the character of God, and proclaim its glory as a dispensation, on this account, it will be more satisfactory to look into its contents more minutely, and see how the gospel exhibits in their full glory the different perfections of the divine character.

The great object which God designed to secure by the gospel, was the salvation of men. To the attainment of this object, the attributes of God interposed serious obstacles. In the dispensation of the gospel, these obstacles have been removed, and the attributes of God displayed in consistent and glorious operation. Just in proportion in which there was difficulty in reconciling the divine perfections, does the gospel which has accomplished this reconciliation, display their glory and manifest its own excellency. By it the perfections of

God are far more gloriously exhibited, than they could be in any other method. For instance, suppose that man, with all his descendants, had been consigned to misery as the consequence of his sin. The justice of God would have appeared, and his truth would also have been seen; but it would not have been known that there existed in the Deity such an attribute as mercy; or that if it did exist in him, it could ever find a fit scope for exercise, since the exercise of it must necessarily involve in it, some remission of the rights of justice, and some encroachments upon the honour of the law.

On the other hand, if free and full remission of sins had been granted unto man, it would not have been seen, how such an act of grace could be consistent with the rights of justice, and holiness, and truth. In either of these alternatives, the character of God would have been but partially displayed, and his creatures would never have seen him as he is. But in the method of salvation which the gospel reveals, not only are all these perfections reconciled, but they are all enhanced and glorified; and a tenfold lustre is thrown upon them from the gospel, beyond what could ever have beamed forth in any other way. We will consider some of these distinctly.

1. The gospel exhibits the *divine justice* far more gloriously than it would have been displayed in the condemnation of the whole human race. Behold the view of justice which it presents. The Lord Jesus Christ, "God over all," puts himself in the place of sinful man, and undertakes to endure for man all that the sins of the whole world have merited. But will justice venture to seize on *him?* Will it draw its sword against *him* who is Jehovah's fellow? Will not the sword of justice, stretched out against him, refuse to execute its appointed work? No. Sin is found on our incarnate God. It is true, it is on him only by imputation; yet being imputed to him, he must be answerable for it, and endure all

that it has merited from the hands of God. Behold, then, for the honour of God's justice, the cup is put into the hands of our blessed Lord, and the very dregs of its bitterness are given him to drink; nor is he released from his sufferings until he can say, "It is finished. I have finished the work thou hast given me to do." Contemplate this mysterious fact. The God of heaven and earth becomes man. By his obedience and death, he satisfies the demands of law and justice, in order that God may be just, and yet the justifier of them that believe in Christ Jesus. With nothing less than this could justice be satisfied. It could not consent to the salvation of a single human being on any other terms. Behold, then, how exalted is its character! how inalienable are its rights! how inexorable are its demands! In all that it inflicts upon men and angels, it is not so highly glorified as in this stupendous mystery.

2. But if the gospel so gloriously exhibits divine justice, see how it displays the *divine mercy*. This attribute would have been displayed, if man, by a mere sovereign act of grace, had been pardoned. But it would then have triumphed over the concealment of all other attributes of the Deity. It shall be brought to light, but only in such a way as shall consist with the honour of every other attribute, in a way by which God may be "a just God and a Saviour." God's dear Son shall be substituted in the place of sinners. The Creator of the universe shall become a man. He shall have the sins of a rebellious world laid upon him, that man, worthless man, may be spared. Shall mercy be exercised with such a sacrifice as this? Yes. Every thing but God's honour shall give way to it; and when *that* can be secured, no sacrifice shall be esteemed too great to save a perishing world.

Go now to Bethlehem, and see that new-born infant, your incarnate Lord, "God manifest in the flesh." Who sent him thither? Who brought him from his throne of glory into this world of wretchedness and sin? It was mercy struggling in the bosom of Almighty God, and prevailing for development in this mysterious way.

Go again to Gethsemane and Calvary; behold that innocent sufferer prostrate upon the earth, bathed in a bloody sweat, suspended on the cross, agonizing under the load of his creatures' guilt, crying, in the depths of sorrow, "My God, my God, why hast thou forsaken me?"

Who has brought him to this state? It was mercy. Mercy would not rest; it would break forth; rather than not exercise itself towards mankind, it would transfer to God himself the penalty due to them; and write, in the blood of an infinite and holy Saviour, the pardon it designed for sinful man. How glorious is this display of mercy; and where but in the gospel of Jesus could it be beheld so honourably and so clearly exhibited?

3. Add to this glorious exhibition of justice and mercy, the manifestation which the gospel makes of *divine faithfulness and truth*, and you will see sufficient reason why, in answer to the prayer of Moses, "Show me thy glory,"—God should preach to him the unsearchable riches of Christ.

God had surely threatened death as the punishment of sin. When, therefore, man had sinned, what remained but that the penalty denounced should be executed immediately? The word had gone forth; it could not be revoked, nor could its sentence be reversed, consistently with the sacred rights of truth. What then shall be done?

If the sentence be *executed* on man, the veracity of God is undoubtedly displayed and honoured. But how can man be *spared*, and God's truth be preserved inviolate? In no other way than the substitution of God's own Son in the sinner's place. This proposal truth willingly accepts, gladly transfers the penalty to him, and joyfully inflicts on the voluntary sufferer the sentence denounced against the offender. Here "mercy and truth have met together; righteousness and peace have kissed each other." All the perfections of God are made to harmonize in the salvation of man, and all are displayed in a more clear and glorious manner than they could be in any other method. Justice is exercised in a way of mercy; mercy is exercised in a way of justice; and both of them are manifested in the way of holiness and truth.

This is one view of the glory of the gospel as a divine dispensation;—the clear and sublime manifestation which it makes of the character of God. While all his works praise him and his saints give thanks to him, it is this dispensation which proclaims his name and his honour: "The Lord, the Lord God, merciful and gracious, long suffering, and abundant in goodness and truth; keeping mercy for thousands, forgiving iniquity, transgression and sin;" and for this revelation of his character, it is well called "the glorious gospel of the blessed God."

IV. While this glory of the gospel should lead *us* to speak with all boldness, and never to be ashamed to declare its power and its worth, it should lead *you* to remember how worthy it is of all men to be received. This faithful saying is worthy to be accepted with all readiness of mind; worthy to be welcomed, like the star of the wise men, with exceeding great joy; worthy to be enamelled in the crowns of princes, and to be written in the soul of every Christian with a beam of the sun, "that Christ Jesus came into the world to save sinners." The faithful have ever been ready to unite in the exclamation of the inspired prophet, "How beautiful are the feet of him that bringeth good tidings, that publisheth peace, that bringeth good tidings of good, that publisheth salvation, that saith unto Zion, thy God reigneth." What man of sorrow would not open his heart and welcome the embraces of that messenger who was coming to him with more lovely and acceptable news than the very wishes of his heart could have framed for himself?

When Joseph was sent for out of prison to Pharaoh's court, and when Jacob saw the chariots which were sent to carry him to his long lost son, their spirits were revived and comforted after their long distress. When Caligula, the Roman emperor, sent for Herod (that Herod who was afterwards smitten by an angel of God,) whom Tiberius had bound in chains and cast into prison, and placed a diadem upon his head, and for his chain of iron gave him a chain of gold of equal weight, the historian says, "Men could not believe the reality of a change so wonderful." But what are all good tidings to the gospel, which is a word of salvation, which opens prisons and releases captives, and gives a joy with which the world intermeddles not? "Your joy no man shall take from you." O how worthy is such a gospel to be accepted and improved!

If we suffer the loss of every thing for Christ, godliness is great gain after all. In a shipwreck, I throw my goods overboard, and count myself happy to get my life in exchange. O how willingly, then, should the man who is convinced of the danger of his soul, cast off every thing which presses him down; and rejoice, with unspeakable joy, to have his soul saved from an eternal shipwreck, and to be brought before God in peace.

Have *you* no desires to see the glory of God displayed in the face of Jesus Christ, or to enjoy the presence of God, made peaceful and happy for you by the sprinkling of the blood of Jesus? Can you deliberately make the choice, that while hereafter myriads of ransomed sinners rejoice in the glories of a full salvation, your souls should see God only as an avenger of blood? It is a painful alternative which is presented to you, but it is the only possible one.

God is dwelling among you in the riches of gospel invitations and in the fulness of spiritual strength. In the persons of the Son and the Spirit, he would be received into your bosoms, and rule over all your affections and purposes. But if he be rejected by you to the end, you will be constrained to see him appearing in the glory of his government, "to take vengeance on them that know not God, and obey not the gospel of our Lord Jesus Christ."

The glorious gospel which is offered you now, forms the highest honour of your souls. It brings you a king having salvation, and makes you with him, kings and priests for ever. Happy are the people that know the joyful sound, they shall walk in the light of his countenance; and blessed will you be, though in the midst of reproaches and tribulations, if you are led to welcome this salvation to your hearts, and to wash your robes and make them white in the blood of the Lamb.

LECTURE IX.

THE GLORY OF THE GOSPEL FROM ITS METHOD OF PUBLICATION.

How beautiful upon the mountains are the feet of him that bringeth good tidings, that publisheth peace, that bringeth good tidings of good, that publisheth salvation, that saith unto Zion, thy God reigneth.— ISAIAH, LI. 7.

No one would be led to doubt, probably, in the most cursory reading of this text, that it was intended to refer to the publication of the gospel of our Lord Jesus Christ. But if there should be such a doubt, St. Paul has decided the proper application of the passage, in his epistle to the Romans, by adducing it as a reason for sending preachers of the gospel throughout the world. Speaking of the messengers of the gospel, he says, "How shall they preach except they be sent?" as it is written, "How beautiful are the feet of them that preach the gospel of peace, and bring glad tidings of good things."

It is then the gospel of Jesus, the ministry of which is said to be so excellent and desirable. This gospel, in its very name, is glad tidings; it is a publication of peace between God and his alienated creatures. It is good tidings of everlasting good, through the mediation of a crucified Redeemer, to those who return unto God and live. It is salvation,—full, free, eternal salvation,—to every one who accepts its tidings with a thankful heart; salvation from present despair and misery; salvation from everlasting sorrow and punishment, the just wages of sin. It is a glorious annunciation to Zion, or the people of the living God, that their God, an incarnate God, a justifying God, reigneth for ever more.

He who proclaims to a ruined world that Jesus reigns as a Prince and Saviour, to give repentance and forgiveness of sins, in the proclamation of this one great truth, tells the whole system of gospel grace, publisheth salvation, bringeth good tidings of good, publisheth peace. The people who hear the joyful sound, are a highly privileged people; the heart that embraces the glad intelligence, is a converted and thankful heart. The man who welcomes the precious truth, finds it all his salvation and all his desire. And the community and nation upon which its beneficial influence is exerted, is converted from a wilderness into the garden of the Lord, a place in which the Lord delights to dwell.

In the text the prophet rejoices in a view of their happiness and glory who are allowed to minister this gospel of peace. He derives the figurative expression, "how beautiful upon the mountains," from the local situation of Jerusalem. That city was surrounded by mountains, which were considered alike its glory and its defence. The Psalmist adduces this peculiarity of its location, as an illustration of divine protection to the people of God. "As the mountains stand round about Jerusalem, so the Lord is round about his people, from henceforth, even for ever." From whatever direction a messenger came to this city, his path crossed the mountains. In the text the prophet is carried forward to hear the publication of gospel mercies; and in the glorious prospect of this publication of grace, the circumstances of his own city furnish him an illustration of the emotions of his own heart.

As the sight of a bearer of any joyful tidings to Jerusalem was delightful to those who watched him crossing the surrounding mountains, so in a still higher degree, beautiful upon the mountains, *i. e.* beautiful at the most distant point from which they can be seen, are the feet of him who comes with more joyful and valuable intelligence to men than they have ever heard before; who comes to proclaim to the waiting people of God, the tidings that their God, Emmanuel, reigns as the Author of salvation, and the Prince of Everlasting Peace.

The text contains an extensive exhibition of the excellency and glory of the gospel, as a dispensation of God's goodness to man. The particular view of this glory, however, which it leads me to propose to your present consideration is,

The glory of the gospel arising from the method of its publication.

In considering this subject, I shall speak

I. Of the character of its various preachers.

II. Of the providence which has attended its publication.

III. Of its triumph over every species of opposition.

I. In speaking of the preachers of the gospel in various ages, the exclamation, "how beautiful, how glorious," may be most equitably applied. The gospel has been at all times highly glorious and exalted in this aspect of its publication.

God himself, who commanded the light to shine out of darkness, who created the world, visible and invisible, by the word of his power, was the first preacher of these good tidings of good. On the very first day of man's transgression he descended with a promise of grace. In that promise he held forth to view a Saviour who should be miraculously conceived as man, and should be a bruised, and yet a finally triumphant Saviour. This promise contained the elements of the whole gospel dispensation. And while Adam, as a sinner trembled before the visible glory of his Creator, as a believer he was enabled to see with rejoicing, a glory in this exhibition of the gospel far more excellent.

Through the whole patriarchal and prophetic ages the gospel was administered to the faith of men, by those who spake as they were moved by the Holy Ghost; and was glorious in its ministry from its being the peculiar subject and end of all intelligence from God to man.

In the personal ministry of Jesus, a Saviour miraculously born, Jehovah incarnate for man, the most exalted glory was connected with the gospel. "Never *man* spake like this man," said they who were sent to apprehend him for punishment. All wondered at the gracious, or becoming and ennobling words which proceeded from his mouth. All creation listened to his voice and obeyed his irresistible commands. Things animate and inanimate alike yielded to his control; the sea heard him, and was still; the earth heard him, and opened; the dead heard him, and awoke to life; the blood-thirsty multitude of the Jews heard him, and went backward and fell to the ground; the spirits of darkness heard him, and departed from men. All this exercise of power elevated the character of the gospel dispensation, because it displayed his rank and glory who had come to the earth solely to declare it. Jesus appeared simply as the great preacher of gospel grace, and all the honour which appertained to his character as a messenger, was reflected upon the message with which he was charged. And highly glorious and excellent indeed was that dispensation which brought the Deity to earth, as a preacher of its truth.

His ministry was honoured by the annunciation of angels, and by the proclamation of a divinely appointed herald; and though he was despised and rejected by a portion of men, yet honour was paid to him in his humiliation by heaven and earth. But during his earthly ministry he was comparatively in a cloud. His real glory was eclipsed by the burden of man's afflictions, temptations and sins; and it was in the subsequent ministry of his apostles that his divine power and sufficiency were really displayed.

Then, when the gospel was preached with the Holy Ghost

sent down from heaven, and the Lord confirmed his word with wonders and signs following, the honour of the Son of man was gloriously exhibited. The apostles acted in the name of Jesus of Nazareth; and this name was every where the signal of divine and unlimited power. The miracles which Jesus wrought in person, while on earth, they wrought in his name after his ascension to glory. And in addition to all these mighty signs and wonders, the conversion of myriads of immortal souls from the power of Satan unto God, did honour to that dispensation of the gospel which had been committed unto them.

How beautiful, *then*, in the eyes of the multitudes throughout the earth, who were asking the way to life, were the feet of those who published with such authority and effect, glad tidings of peace and salvation through the merits of a crucified Lamb! And how glorious in their ministry, was that gospel of the blessed God, which triumphed over error, pardoned sin, consoled the disconsolate, and gave life from the dead, in the name of our great God and Saviour Jesus Christ, to every believer in its truth.

But while through all these periods of time, the glory of the gospel was displayed in the character and rank of its preachers, can we adopt the same assertion of the present ministry of the gospel? Now, the excellency of this divine treasure is committed to fallible, weak and sinful men; they have no miraculous powers entrusted to them; they have no signs and wonders to follow their utterance of the name of Jesus; they have no power to overrule or punish the disobedience of those who obey not the gospel; and, generally speaking, they have no excellency of speech or of wisdom to command the attention of those who cannot be attracted by the truth.

Is the gospel still glorious in the character of its preachers? And are the feet of those who publish it still beautiful upon the mountains? Yes, for there is still a preacher of the gospel among men, without whose influence, signs and wonders would be powerless, and the tongues of men and angels utterly unprofitable. He follows the sinner with a boldness which is always undaunted, and tells him hourly to his face, "thou art the man." He carries glad tidings with a forbearance which will not be wearied, and beseeches, "to-day, after so long a time, if ye will hear, harden not your hearts." He grasps the conscience with a hold which cannot be shaken off; and awakens the transgressor with a solemn cry, "escape for your life." He binds up the heart which he has broken, with more than parental tenderness, while he leads the soul to Jesus, and says, "believe, and he will give you rest." There is none who teacheth like him; and while we preach the gospel with the Holy Ghost, and with much assurance, its ministration is glorious, and brings honour to the truth which it declares. This divine Spirit will be the great preacher of Christ crucified unto the end of the gospel dispensation. His power is unceasingly displayed,—in the instant conversion of many who come under the word, cold and ignorant and careless; in the extensive revival of the power of godliness, in the community which has settled down into a dark and lifeless state; in the spreading before an individual sinner the startling view of his own iniquities, and in causing great searchings of heart among those who have held the truth in unrighteousness. And while the ministry of the gospel has such power, though the earthly minister be weak and ignorant, the gospel is glorified in the character of its preachers.

For nearly sixty centuries God the Father, God the Son, and God the Holy Ghost, have united to publish these glad tidings of peace, of good, and of salvation. In this divine ministry, great honour has been brought to the gospel dispensation, and it has been made glorious in the method of its publication.

II. The glory of the gospel in the method of its publication is exhibited in the *Providence which has always attended it.*

It is perfectly evident from Scripture, that the existence of the human race, after their apostacy from God, was permitted only as a display of God's grace in their redemption; and the whole divine government of man has been a comment upon that promise, which was given to Adam, of a coming Saviour. Four thousand years were employed in preparing for this manifestion of God in the flesh. During this period the Divine Providence was unceasingly displayed in watching over the great purpose of redemption, and making provision for the fulness of time.

The division of nations in preparation for the final triumph of truth and grace; the call of Abraham to be the father and spiritual representative of all believers, the depository of that everlasting covenant, which was in all things well ordered and sure, and the head of the earthly line from which the desire of all nations should be born; the separation of the Israelites, to keep those precious truths and promises, which constituted so much the treasure of the world; the various dispensations and revelations which were made to them, all pointing to more excellent things to come; the diversified events of their history, and their relations to other nations of the earth; all these were arrangements of Divine Providence, to prepare the way of the Lord and a highway for our God.

When the fulness of the appointed time was come, the same Providence was displayed, in the subjugation of the temporal power of the Jews, that there might be no rival to that kingdom not of this world, which the Lord God designed to set up among them; in the universal empire which Rome had been permitted to establish through the known world, giving such free course to the divine word, and such opportunities and protection to the preachers of the gospel, as no age before or after could have afforded; in the establishment of a general language through all civilized nations, and that the language in which the New Testament was written; in the great literary cultivation and wisdom of that period, affording the most certain and scrutinizing examination of the claims of the new religion, which made such large demands upon men; all these also are remarkable arrangements of that Providence which was ordering events to co-operate for the establishment of the kingdom of Christ among men.

In the whole period of time which has since elapsed, all human changes have been made to work together to promote the same intended results. The gospel of Jesus, its progress, its establishment, its triumph in the world, have formed the all-sufficient reason for the most wonderful alternations among the children of men. In the embracing and cultivation of this gospel, savage nations have been raised to civilization, prosperity, and temporal happiness and power. In the neglect and contempt of it, civilized nations have been reduced to degradation, barbarism, and ignorance. All desirable earthly blessings have been made to follow in the train of the Redeemer's gospel; and while no nation has been exalted without it, the sin of its rejection has been a permanent reproach to every people who have been guilty of it.

The great commotions of the world, the wars and tumults which have agitated the sons of men, have all been made to prepare the way for Jesus, as the fire, and the wind, and the earthquake in Horeb, introduced to Elijah the still, small voice of divine commands. The present overturnings of the nations of the earth, though so dark and trying, in their prospect and their immediate results, are overruled to establish the more widely the kingdom of the Saviour. Men fill the atmosphere with noise and confusion to gratify their own ambition. God rides upon the storm, and makes the clouds the dust of his feet, to bring to pass his great designs. They think to destroy nations not a few; he purposes to establish a dominion under another King, one Jesus, from sea to sea, and from the river to the ends of the earth.

This same Providence is to carry on the gospel to a final triumph. The north and the south are to give up the victims of ignorance and idolatry, that they may be made the children of God; and even now commerce has for this purpose brought together the ends of the earth, and the peaceful galley of the merchant has carried the ministers and the books of truth to most of the remotest nations of men. This continued providence of God, watching over the gospel, preparing the way for its propagation, establishing it upon the ruins of human ignorance and vice, has thrown unceasing honour upon it as a dispensation from God to man. That God, by whom and for whom all things were made, is exhibited a glorious God, and that gospel for which the earth has been preserved and governed, and the promotion of which among men has been the object of a sleepless Providence, is for this reason a glorious gospel, and is honoured and made beautiful in the method of its publication.

III. The glory of the gospel, in the method of its publication, has been displayed in *its constant triumph over every species of opposition.*

In every age Satan has sought to destroy it among men, and to defeat the divine purpose to redeem and to bless them. His triumph over our first parents led to the promulgation of this glorious scheme of grace; and from that period his purpose has been to pervert its operation, and to destroy its saving efficacy. He buried the nations in ignorance and vice in the antediluvian world, until the Creator was provoked to cleanse it with an universal deluge. He involved the Israelites in the deepest and most degrading idolatry, until sometimes, as in the reign of Josiah, the divine law had become quite forgotten. He led them to a repeated forsaking of God, and despising of his ordinances, that he might annihilate the truth which had been entrusted to their keeping. But notwithstanding all his power, the purpose of God to accomplish man's redemption kept on a steady and undeviating course; all things were made ready for its development in the appointed time; and though the heathen raged, and the people imagined a vain thing, God did set his King upon his holy hill of Zion.

When the Saviour was manifest in the flesh, he attempted to destroy him. He excited the jealousy of Herod to cut him off in his infancy. He attempted to persuade him to his own destruction. He arrayed against him the whole power of Jewish and Roman governors, so that in the expression of the apostles, "against the holy child Jesus, both Herod and Pontius Pilate and the rulers of Israel were gathered together." He finally succeeded, as he supposed, in his destruction, by nailing him to the cross. But still the gospel triumphed; and the very death which was to shew the weakness and falsehood of the professed Messiah, was his full and perfect triumph over the gates of hell, and his open spoiling of the principalities and powers of darkness.

Foiled and defeated in this attempt, the enemy has pursued the gospel in every succeeding age like a flood. He raised against it the arm of temporal power and wealth, so that the most dreadful and bitter wasting of human lives was exhibited in the persecution of the apostles and all its succeeding preachers. But the gospel triumphed over his power, and in the reign of Constantine seated itself upon the very throne of the persecuting empire. Millions of lives have been sacrificed by the enmity of Satan because they were Christians, and yet increasing millions have risen up to supply their place.

He has inspired the wisdom and genius of man to write down the religion of Jesus in the books of infidelity, so that some of the mightiest efforts of the human mind which the world has ever seen have been, displayed in hostility to the gospel. Age after age has furnished the same display; and yet this despised gospel has triumphed over the arguments and writings of infidelity, and still stands the monument of God's Almighty power, while the names and the actual existence of many of these opposers, are known only by the answers which Christian writers have made to them.

He has in different ages thrown corruptions and heresies in practice and doctrine into the body of the Church; has raised up secret enemies in the very camp, until the word of God has appeared almost buried under the wickedness of men. But the gospel has thrown off successively corruptions and heresies, and still stands, after all these attempts, precisely the same living and life-giving truth, as when it was first revealed.

He has sent his agents and ministers to assume the Christian garb; to array themselves among the followers of Jesus, and thus to betray the cause which they professed to espouse. But though the tares have grown together with the wheat, there have been continually succeeding harvests in which they have been separated, and the gospel is still offered in its simplicity and purity to man, and embraced in its true character by thousands, while these false pretenders and preachers have gone to their own place.

No species of opposition which could have been aroused has been omitted. Every possible instrument has been called in requisition, and every instrument in its highest possible power; and yet over all, truth has prevailed. The gospel has set its foot upon the necks of its enemies; and still triumphs, and still will triumph, until its full dominion has been attained.

Opposition probably was never stronger or more serious than in the present day. The truth is every where spoken against. The doctrines and ordinances of the gospel are reviled by thousands. Bitter terms of reproach are appended to the names of those who maintain its truth, and the most unfounded calumnies are circulated in reference to their character and conduct; and yet the gospel establishes its throne in the very midst of those who hate it, and converts its enemies into friends.

Such triumphs reflect high honour upon the gospel of Jesus, and show its glory in the method of its publication. Men may raise insuperable difficulties, as they suppose; but beautiful in their triumphant march over all these mountains, are still the feet of those who publish the gospel of peace and preach glad tidings of good things.

From this view of the glory of the gospel, we may learn,

1. That whatever men may think of the dispensation of the word, the rejection of the gospel is really a rejection of God himself. Whoever may proclaim to you this message of grace, and however weakly and infirmly he may proclaim it, provided he be faithful, he speaks the word of the Lord; and he that despiseth, despiseth not man but God. From God himself to you is the word of this salvation sent; and let all take heed that they receive not the grace of God in vain. In his name we demand the submission of your hearts to him. We offer you the fulness of mercy for perishing sinners, which is laid up in the Lord Jesus Christ; and by his authority we require you to repent and believe the gospel. We must leave it to your own choice whether you will accept the provisions of divine mercy or not. You may reject them indeed, but you will reject them to your eternal ruin. Brethren, Almighty God demands his own. He made you not to be destroyed; he has bought you with an inestimable price; he commands you to return to him and live; and you will answer it before him in a solemn, final judgment, how you have received and improved the precious opportunity of salvation which he has so long allowed you.

2. The way in which you should receive it, is not as the

word of man, but as it is in truth, the word of the Lord, which worketh effectually in you that believe. The word of God profits you not, if it be not mixed with faith in them that hear it. Listen to the gospel as a personal message to yourselves; hear it describe your necessities, and offer you a full and perfect remedy, with the humble acknowledgment of your want, and a cordial embracing of the mercy proposed; appropriate with thankfulness the privileges which God offers here to sinners, and learn to come with your whole heart, to the fountain of blessedness and mercy which he has laid open. The Lord Jesus invites you in great kindness to receive his love. By his ministers he calls you, and by his Spirit he strives with you, that you may not be permitted to destroy yourselves. Believe in him with your hearts, and it shall be well with you; he will pardon your unrighteousness, and your iniquities will he remember no more. He brings you this day good tidings; he publishes to you peace and salvation. O let your thankful hearts rejoice that there is a Saviour so worthy to be received, admired and loved, presented to your embrace; and come unto him and he shall give you rest.

LECTURE X.

THE GLORY OF THE GOSPEL FROM THE SUBJECTS WHICH IT PROCLAIMS.

How beautiful upon the mountains are the feet of him that bringeth good tidings, that publisheth peace, that bringeth good tidings of good, that publisheth salvation, that saith unto Zion, thy God reigneth.— ISAIAH, LI. 7.

SUCH we have seen is the divine description of the ministry of the gospel of Christ. Whether men justly appreciate their office or not, they are sent as messengers of God's chief blessing to a fallen world. Coming with intelligence of pardon from on high, to the penitent and contrite their approach is welcomed, their feet are beautiful. God is pleased to put high honour upon their office, and to show himself personally interested in the acceptance and respect which they receive.

But why are they thus styled beautiful? Not for any personal merit or worth in themselves. They are infirm and imperfect. Not for any dignity or power which they possess, or which they can exercise. They are like other men, altogether weak, sinful and unprofitable. God honours them, and they are welcomed by believing man, altogether on account of the message which they are commissioned to proclaim. This message contains the highest possible benefit to man, and reflects unceasing glory upon God. The text exhibits this message at large, and introduces to your notice the subject of the present discourse.

The glory of the gospel, arising from the intelligence which it communicates to man.

1. It brings " good tidings." This expression is a general designation of the revelation made by our Lord Jesus Christ. It is the title by which we know this glorious system, and which is thus called the gospel, because it is altogether a communication of good tidings to man.

The good tidings of the Christian system of truth involve many particulars, adapted to all human circumstances and conditions. It appoints every where to them that mourn, to give them beauty for ashes, the oil of joy for mourning, the garment of praise for the spirit of heaviness. It speaks in language of consolation to all who suffer, of security to all who are in doubt, of encouragement to all who fear, of promise to all who seek for mercy. There is no condition of man under the Providence of the God of Truth, for which the gospel of Christ will not bring relief and comfort. He cannot be placed under such circumstances as shall shut him out from security and hope, if he be willing to accept the offers which are here made. Whenever the sinner is destroyed, he has destroyed himself, though God has offered him abundant help.

But the good tidings of the gospel may all be comprised in its one offer to man of universal pardon for sin, and perfect righteousness for justification with God. It exhibits a Saviour, who has accomplished in his own person a full salvation for the sinful posterity of Adam, and the riches of whose grace are truly unsearchable; and it offers simply through him, and in the acceptance of him, universal forgiveness and life to those for whom he died. I say *universal* forgiveness, for not a single sinner is personally excepted from the offer which it makes. Whosoever will, may come and drink freely of the water of life. Jesus has offered himself once for all. And there is not a man living who can say with truth, "for me there is no redemption, God has shut me out of life." No, brethren, we do injustice, great injustice, to the free and unbounded grace of God, if we suppose that it is not honestly proposed to all, and proposed with a sincere desire on the part of its great author that all should partake of it and live. Whatever theoretical difficulties may be imagined, in reconciling God's purposes of love defeated, with his unlimited and resistless power to do his will, we cannot lay the blame of man's destruction upon him. Nor in searching through the whole catalogue of offenders against him, can we find one to whom we are authorized to say, that no atonement has been made for him, and no pardon is offered upon his return to God.

This offer of forgiveness is *universal* in regard to the transgressions of each individual. No sinner can be too guilty to be pardoned. No man can have fallen to a depth which is beyond the reach of Almighty grace. Is he the *chief* of sinners? Has no one *ever* passed beyond the limits of his transgression? Then is the faithful saying true for him, that Christ Jesus came into the world for his salvation, and is able to set him forth as a pattern of divine long suffering. All the offences of previous life are forever pardoned, when a sinner embraces the provisions of grace in Christ Jesus. One act of divine mercy restores him to the favour of his God, and removes forever all charge of guilt against his soul. It is true that the sinner's forgiveness is dependent upon his return to God. If he continue in a persevering rejection of the Holy Spirit, and determine to sin because grace abounds, he commits indeed a sin for which there is no forgiveness, either in this world, or in the world to come. None in this world, because he thus casts finally away the only possible means of pardon. None in the world to come, because all exercise of pardon is confined to the present life. This sin against the Holy Ghost cannot be forgiven, not because its guilt is too great, but because it is final impenitence; and no impenitent sinner can be pardoned. But for all classes and degrees of guilt, if the sinner truly repent and submit himself to God, there is forgiveness offered in the gospel. And thus the gospel is a message of good tidings to man, bringing him back to God and restoring him again to the divine favour and love.

2. It "publisheth peace." The transgressions of men have excited the just anger of God against them, have exposed them to necessary punishment, and made it the inflexible rule of his government, that there should be no peace to the wicked. This is the relation in which by nature you stand to God; your souls are forfeited to his divine justice. Should he carry forward his anger against sin to final execution, and cast you all into everlasting ruin, no one of you could have the right to complain. Your own consciences would unite with his holy determinations, and proclaim that God was just though he thus took vengeance. You could make no offering to him which should purchase peace, or deserve the remission of the punishment denounced against sin. Under such circumstances the worth and glory of the gospel are displayed. God has accomplished and proposes reconciliation, and his gospel declares it to you in his name. It is an offer of peace altogether worthy of God; it compromises not the justice or integrity of his character, but confirms and glorifies his whole government of man.

Peace between yourselves and your Creator is thus proclaimed. You are allowed to come before him with your prayers and offerings without fear. He looks upon you in the righteousness of his Son with acceptance and favour. He invites you to become united to him in the spirit of new and holy obedience, and to forget that there has been any separation between you, in your experience of the future manifestations of his love. The gospel exhibits the character of God to you under the most attractive aspect. It shows you that he is desirous to pardon and save you; and invites you to commit all your cares and ways to him, in the assurance that he will be a friend and beloved to you forever.

Beside this relative peace between your souls and God, the gospel publishes peace in the experience of your own hearts. When you receive by faith the Saviour whom it offers, and he is allowed to dwell in your hearts as your hope of glory, there is then bestowed upon you the peace which passeth understanding. Your troubled and anxious minds have rest. Tranquillity and assurance forever establish their dominion in your souls. The accusations of guilt are hushed by divine testimonials of pardoning love. Your hope is fixed calmly and surely upon the promises of God; and resting thus in love for him, and in his love for you, you are filled with peace in believing through the power of his Spirit. Peace is thus thrown over all the changes and prospects of mortal life. All things work together for good to those who love God; and he keeps them in perfect peace whose mind is stayed on him. There is real worth, beloved brethren, in this gospel offer of peace to the sinner's soul, and you will exhibit true wisdom in embracing it for your own comfort in the present world, and your eternal joy in a world to come. God makes it his glory to pass by transgressions, and gives glory to his gospel, in constituting it the instrument of proclaiming his riches of love, to every sinner truly repenting and believing in his Son.

3. The gospel brings " good tidings of good." It not only restores the sinner by the offer of free forgiveness to the condition of an innocent man, removing all penalty, and rescuing him from condemnation, but it adds also positive and infinitely valuable benefits. It offers him in the righteousness of God his Saviour everlasting life and glory. It bids him lift up his eyes and his hopes, for God hath provided for

him such good things as pass man's understanding. The present good which results from a cordial acceptance of the gospel is important, but it is partial. The following of Christ may involve, with all the peace and comfort which it promises, the endurance of much suffering and trial. The Christian may pass through many and great tribulations in entering into the kingdom of God. But the future good which is set before him is all-sufficient and entire, and the final result of his obedience will make abundant reparation for any conflicts by which he must be here tried. But what is this future good? What offers are made to be fulfilled in a world to come? Continuing life to beings who deserve to die. Unceasing enjoyment for those who merit only sufferings and woes. Perfect acceptance with God, for rebels against him, with whom he was justly angry every day. Everlasting honour and glory for those who have been degraded and destroyed by sin. The fellowship of Jesus and his saints, the society of all who are holy and perfect, the approbation of the Ruler and Judge of all, for beings who were cast out in their sins ready to perish. Such is the good which the gospel offers. It is a spiritual and permanent good, which, like its author, has no variableness nor shadow of changing. Such honour, such recompense have all his saints.

This everlasting provision of good answers all the reproaches of the world, while it shows that the Christian, in counting all things as loss for Christ, acts with wisdom and prudence; that he lays up his treasure securely where moth and rust do not corrupt, nor thieves break through to steal; and builds his house upon a rock which shall stand the assault of every tempest, and abide firm forevermore. It answers all the temptations of the world, while it presents more than a counterbalance for every sinful joy, and excites a faith and hope which shall overcome every allurement to transgression. It applies itself to all the changing circumstances of life, bringing encouragement and treasure from God, wherever its possessor may be placed. It is so satisfying, that its messenger is always welcome to those who understand its worth. To the poor, the afflicted, the sick, the dying, the glorious gospel brings always good tidings of good. It takes man by the hand when all others forsake him. It can speak with power when all others are silent. And shows itself thus useful and desirable, however low and desperate may be the condition of the individual to whom its gracious offers come.

4. The gospel " publishes salvation." It proclaims to every believer final security from the punishment of sin, and from the power of Satan. It encourages him with the assurance of victory, even while he is in the midst of his warfare. It bids him remember the Almighty power which is engaged upon his side, and under whatever circumstances of danger, to be not faithless but believing.

The salvation which the gospel offers is a salvation already finished and completed. Man is invited to partake of that which God has freely provided for him; and the great office of the gospel is to publish to man this glorious salvation, and to invite him to an enjoyment of the bounties which have been thus prepared. This salvation it proclaims in exhibiting an all-sufficient sacrifice for sin and an all-glorious righteousness as a title to eternal life, offered by God's dear Son. It shows that the burden of human guilt was actually laid upon him, and that his death upon the cross was borne as a required punishment in the sinner's stead.

In such an exhibition of the death of Christ, it displays a full and final atonement made to God for human transgressions, and publishes salvation in the assurance that every barrier which unexpiated guilt interposed to the acceptance of man has been thus removed. It proclaims this salvation in displaying the resurrection from the dead and the subsequent exaltation of the glorious Redeemer who had humbled himself even to this death upon the cross for man, and thus shows that Almighty power is enlisted in behalf of all who come to him, and that he is able to save them unto the uttermost, seeing he ever liveth to make intercession for them. While the gospel proclaims the united exercise of the power of God, and the sufferings of man, in the person of Jesus Christ, the Lord our righteousness, it publishes salvation in a method which removes every difficulty, and commends itself to the enlightened judgment of man as perfectly adequate to his wants, and precisely suited to his condition as a guilty and helpless being.

But though it thus publishes to man a complete salvation, it does not leave him to obtain for himself, and by his own power, a personal interest in this salvation. It comes to him attended by the same Spirit who has proclaimed its intelligence to the world, as a personal gift to his soul, to enable him to see his dangers, and to take advantage of the mercies which are offered to his acceptance. It brings this Holy Spirit to dwell within his heart forever as a comforter and guide, to encourage and to lead him in the path to life eternal. By the ministration of the Spirit, it applies to him the salvation which it publishes abroad, and thus completes the gracious design of God of bringing sinners whom he hath chosen for himself, from the power of Satan, to glory everlasting.

It displays the Father, the Son, and the Holy Ghost united in the work of man's redemption; shows the office which each person of the Deity exercises to attain this end; and having proclaimed the whole scheme of grace, it publishes as the result, a full and eternal salvation to all who believe the intelligence which it communicates.

5. The gospel "saith unto Zion," to the people of God, "thy God reigneth."

This personal designation of God as connected with his

people, shows us that Emmanuel, God manifest in the flesh, is especially referred to. Of him, the righteous are by the same prophet represented as saying, " Lo, this is our God, we have waited for him, and he will save us." The God of Zion is an incarnate God, our " great God and Saviour Jesus Christ." The gospel declares his reign, his everlasting dominion as God over all blessed forever. It proclaims his exaltation as head over all things for the church, as LORD OF LORDS AND KING OF KINGS, making his enemies his footstool. It declares this reign of Christ as joyful intelligence to his people, assuring them that their cause is safe under his extensive and resistless dominion.

He reigns in the government of the present world ordering all things according to the counsels of his own will, and constraining all beings and all events, to promote his glory and the good of his people. In this assurance Zion rejoices, in the prospect of a final victory for his truth, and fears not but his cause is safe, whatever may be the assaults of the ungodly. However men may fill the earth with confusion and sin, he rides upon the whirlwind and the storm, and makes the clouds the dust of his feet. He brings light out of darkness, and makes crooked things straight. And he will accomplish his purpose of the universal dominion of righteousness and peace among men, through whatever opposition and conflict he must pass to gain the end.

He reigns in the heart of every redeemed sinner, and will keep each one, therefore, to the enjoyment of his eternal glory. In this intelligence, too, his people rejoice. They have put on the Lord Jesus Christ, and they stand complete in him. Whatever may be the temptations of sin, and the difficulties of obedience, while he reigns in their hearts, they shall be made more than conquerors through his divine power. The world shall be overcome, Satan shall be bruised under their feet, self shall be crucified and destroyed, and grace shall triumph finally and eternally, because Christ rules in those whom he has redeemed.

He reigns amidst the hosts of heaven, and Zion rejoices in the prospect of reward which his dominion there ensures. His presence constitutes the happiness and glory of his people. They look forward with delight to another world as an everlasting home, because he is there. The single promise of recompense which the gospel makes, is an enjoyment of his favour and a dwelling together with him. In the hope of this the believer's heart rejoices with joy unspeakable and full of glory; and having counted all things as loss for Christ's sake, he looks forward with triumph to the day when he shall be like him and see him as he is. Jesus reigns in heaven, and, therefore, for those who love him, heaven must contain a desirable and ample reward.

He will reign in visible glory among his saints upon the earth, when he shall return, according to his promise to them, without sin unto salvation. He has now, as it regards his visible presence, gone to receive for himself a kingdom and to return. When the appointed hour arrives, the Son of man shall appear in his glory, and all his holy angels with him. In this reign, Israel converted unto him, by looking upon him whom they have pierced, shall rejoice. The fulness of the Gentiles shall be brought under his dominion, like new life to a world that has been long dead. The wickedness of the ungodly shall have come to an end, and he shall establish the just. To this blessed kingdom of the Son of God, multiplied prophecies of the Scripture bid us to look forward continually, and it is our blessed privilege to live in unceasing expectation of the happy day, when angel voices shall thus announce unto his waiting Zion, "thy God reigneth."

Such is the glorious intelligence which the gospel brings you; such are the communications whichs it makes to a world of sinners. It brings good tidings, it publishes peace, it brings good tidings of good, it publishes salvation, it declares to Zion, thy God reigneth. These gracious communications throw a glorious light over the whole message, and constitute it, by their excellency, the glorious gospel of the blessed God.

How important is the obligation which arises from such intelligence to constrain sinful men to accept with thankfulness these heavenly offers! The immediate duty required of you all is the reconciliation to God which the gospel proposes, and for which it has made provision. All things are ready for the return of sinners unto Christ, and I would beseech you, brethren, to welcome the ministers of reconciliation, to receive the pardon which is offered, and to place yourselves under the dominion of this glorious and merciful King. Kiss the Son in token of your cheerful submission to him, and let not his wrath be kindled against you, even but a little, lest you perish from the right way, and lose for ever the hopes which are offered you through His grace.

How important also is the obligation upon Christians to press upon all others the acceptance of these messages of divine love! To you who have believed, the Lord has committed the treasure of his grace, that you may offer it to others. In your conversation and your conduct, and in direct efforts to lead sinners unto Christ, much influence is to be exerted to publish this salvation, and to spread abroad the knowledge of the truth. The worth of this glorious intelligence marks the amount of your responsibility; and while it teaches you what Christ has done and suffered to open the way of salvation, it impresses upon you, how much you should be willing to do and to suffer, to make this way plain and profitable to others. Let no effort be spared by you which he has appointed and which can be made effectual to bring men from the darkness of their sins, to the light of the glory of God which is seen in Jesus Christ.

LECTURE XI.

THE GOSPEL MAGNIFYING THE LAW.

The Lord is well pleased for his righteousness sake; he will magnify the law and make it honourable.—ISAIAH, XLII. 21.

We have considered the different aspects and operations of the Law and the Gospel, through a long series of remarks; —and we may now profitably reflect upon the actual connexion between these two great departments of divine truth, and their mutual influence upon each other. Faithfulness and immutability are attributes inseparable from the divine character. With God, there is no variableness, neither shadow of turning. He illustrates this entire unchangeableness of his own character, by contrasting with it, the passing nature, and temporary existence, of the most magnificent of his visible works. The earth with all its apparent stability, shall perish, and the heavens with all their uncounted, and apparently, unchangeable glories, shall wax old, and like a garment or a curtain shall be folded up, and changed. But God, who is the Creator of the heavens and the earth, remaineth the same forever, and his years have no end. This immutability of his nature and purposes, constitutes the foundation of all the hope of his creatures in him,—and the reason of his forbearance towards them. "I am Jehovah, I change not. Therefore ye sons of Jacob are not consumed." "I will not execute the fierceness of mine anger, I will not return to destroy Ephraim, for I am God, and not man." The same unchangeable character is declared of him, when he is revealed, as "God manifest in the flesh." "Unto the Son he saith, Thy throne O

God is forever and ever, a sceptre of righteousness is the sceptre of thy kingdom." "Jesus Christ is the same yesterday, to-day, and forever." The Saviour asserts also this entire immutability in his own word; "heaven and earth shall pass away; but my word shall not pass away." This immutability of God is exhibited in all the divine revelations, and connected with all the divine purposes and plans. He is from everlasting to everlasting, the same wise and holy being. He changes not the purposes which he forms; nor is he frustrated in the accomplishment of his designs. He has made different revelations of his will and his truth to man; but they are all parts of his one mind, which none can turn, and are all known unto him from the foundation of the world. These revelations have placed men, under different dispensations of light, and in different circumstances of responsibility. But they are not contrary the one to the other; nor is the unchangeableness of God affected, by their apparent differences of communication. Those differences are only apparent. The perfect unity of the truth of God becomes manifest to those who understand and love his word. The law is not against the promises of God. Nor do we make void the law through faith. They are designed not to destroy, but to confirm and establish each other. The grace and truth which comes by Jesus Christ, fulfils and honours the law which was given by Moses. The consideration of this fact, is now before us.

Our text declares that God was perfectly satisfied with that everlasting righteousness, which the divine Saviour accomplished and brought out for man, under the glorious revelation of the Gospel. The Father, the Son, and the Holy Ghost, are perfectly united in the provision, and in the acceptance, of this glorious work of merit as perfected and offered by the Great Redeemer of man. And in the acceptance of this perfect righteousness for man, it is declared, the law also to which it was offered, was magnified and made honorable.

The subject which the text leads us to consider, is *the honour which the Grace of the Gospel reflects upon the holiness and authority of the law.*

I. In considering this subject, we may first recall some of the clear and important views which we have taken of the several characteristics and operations of these two dispensations.

1. The law of God is simply the revealed will of the Creator. It was first proclaimed, when the first intelligent creature was formed. It required in every such being who should be called into existence, unqualified and instant submission to the Creator's will, whenever and however that will should be proclaimed. By all the angels in heaven, who remain in their original holiness, and delight still to do their Maker's will, it is fully obeyed. It was communicated to man at his creation, requiring from him, this simple and unquestioning submission to God, and fixing the trial of his obedience upon a single and comparatively unimportant precept,—in which the single question was, would he be freely and entirely obedient to God? It was revealed anew to the Israelites from Mount Sinai, bringing out again this single principle, branching out in many additional and subordinate precepts, some of which were wholly national and local. It was renewed and confirmed by the revelation of God's dear Son, who established its authority over his Church by new motives of gratitude for redemption from its curse,—and fulfilled for them, a perfect and justifying obedience to its commands. Its single principle of simple and entire obedience to God is as binding upon every soul whom he hath redeemed, as upon those who stand in the obedience which they render for themselves. This holy law governs throughout the universe, and must govern forever. There can be no intelligent creature exempted from obedience to its commands; nor can its authority ever be annulled. While the Creator reigns, every subject of his dominion must

be held under the obligation of unconditional obedience to his holy and perfect will.

So soon as any being disobeys this law, he comes immediately under condemnation, and is at once a lost and ruined being. He is subjected to immediate punishment for his transgression, and is at once without protection and without hope. His guilt has turned God against him, and none can be upon his side. Thus it was with angels that sinned. Thus it was with man in his transgression. And thus it is with every man now born into the world. None of the race of Adam are keepers of the law, and therefore the whole family of his posterity, in every generation, have come under the curse, and are in condemnation under the law, as transgressors against God. The holiness and faithfulness of this law cannot be set aside or annulled. It demands an obedience and satisfaction completely adequate to its own character, and perfectly spotless and unlimited in itself; and it will not release from condemnation, any transgressor who does not produce them. If no such obedience and satisfaction can be produced by sinful beings, whether angels or men, no fallen creature can be restored or justified by any operation or power of the law. That this cannot be done by such beings, becomes indisputably evident; and from this fact flows the solemn and everlasting testimony, " by the deeds of the law, shall no flesh be justified, for by the law is the knowledge of sin."

This is the view which we have taken of the divine law. It is not the law of Moses, nor the law given to Adam merely. It is the original, divine will of God however revealed, requiring simply unqualified submission in every creature, under all the circumstances in which his Creator shall see fit to place him. It was proclaimed in some precepts to Adam, in others by Moses, and in others still, by our Lord Jesus Christ. So far as it is revealed and written for us, it is contained in the Holy Scriptures, which are given by inspiration of God. But it may be made known in new precepts to the creatures of God throughout eternity. And to whatever labour or duty God shall ever direct, this universal law will require from every creature, instant and unconditional obedience. Neither the gospel then, nor any other dispensation from God, can make void, or annul this law, because whatever is revealed or commanded by him, becomes from that moment, a part of his law, and comes to man with the same authority which has proclaimed and established all previous revelations of the divine will. They cannot be inconsistent with the law, because God cannot deny himself. He is always the same, he changes not, nor can his purposes and plans ever contradict or thwart each other.

2. The gospel of the grace of God, is simply a free offer of actual, finished salvation, to man under the condemnation of the law which he has broken. It is designed as a remedy for existing, actual evil, and was intended to restore the transgressor of the law, to his former condition of security and peace, not by annulling, but by fulfilling the law for him. It makes this gracious proposal of salvation to man, through the obedience and sufferings of a divinely appointed substitute for him. It is the annunciation of a Saviour who has assumed the sinner's place, and rendered for him, the obedience and satisfaction which the divine law required. It is not a system which has originated from another being, than the one who gave man his law, and which was intended in its operation to set this law aside. But it is one which has flowed from the Divine Lawgiver himself, designed to restore the violated majesty of his own government, and to provide for man, that answer to the law, without which he could never be rescued from condemnation in sin. This intelligence of the gospel was first revealed to man, immediately after his transgression, as his all-sufficient remedy. It proclaimed to him, the fact of a provided salvation, and offered this salvation to him freely,

as a lost and helpless creature. But it did not and cannot give him salvation in opposition to the demands of the law. It first shews the law satisfied, and made perfectly whole; and then it freely justifies and completely saves, the sinner whom the law had condemned. There is here no opposition, but a perfect unity of action, and cordial mutual agreement. "What the law could not do, in that it was weak through the flesh, God, sending his own Son in the likeness of sinful flesh, and for sin," did accomplish,—"that the righteousness of the law might be fulfilled in us, who walk not after the flesh, but after the Spirit." If a creditor should imprison his debtor for failure in payment of his claim, and another individual should come forward, voluntarily to discharge the debt, and set the prisoner at liberty, the latter could not be said on this ground, to be opposed to the former, or in any way to destroy or disparage the legal justice of the claim which he thus freely meets; but both would unite in releasing the man whose obligations had thus been completely and honourably discharged. So while the law of God held man in bondage, as a transgressor of its precepts, and the gospel provides and proclaims a full discharge of the penalty, and bids the ransomed soul go and sin no more, it does not on this account shew itself opposed to the justice of the law's demands. It honours the holiness of the law by presenting a perfect obedience to its claims, and in no degree lessens its authority.

The same Divine Being has given the law as the rule for his creatures, and the gospel as the hope and salvation for fallen man. In both these dispensations, he is the same, and there is in him no shadow of turning. When he first created man, he placed him under his law, as he had done all other intelligent beings whom he had formed. When man transgressed the law, and sinned against him, and was of necessity, immediately condemned by the law, he revealed his gracious purpose to save him, in perfect consistency with the majesty and holiness of the law which he had violated. He provided and offered a righteousness in the Lord Jesus Christ, his Son, God manifest in flesh, with which he was well pleased, and which would forever magnify the law, and make it honourable.

II. We may consider the direct assertion of the text. God was himself well pleased with the righteousness which the appointed Saviour finished, and now offers in the gospel. This righteousness magnifies the law and makes it honourable. This fact deserves very particular attention. In preaching he gospel of our Lord Jesus Christ, we are sent to offer a free and full salvation, to those whom the law condemns ; and that salvation wholly in Christ without any dependance upon human works, to be obtained simply by a faith in his word, which accepts and confides in the work of merit thus revealed. In such an offer of grace, we seem to many, to set the law entirely aside. We declare that the law cannot justify any man; that it is not to be obeyed with any view or hope of obtaining justification by it; that men must not lean upon it in the slightest degree for this purpose ; that the least dependance placed upon this obedience to it, will invalidate their whole interest in the system of the gospel. In these assertions we are supposed by some, to give instruction of an unholy tendency, and to teach doctrines which are subversive of moral obligations. The apostle Paul was obliged to contend with the very same difficulties ; his doctrines were obnoxious to the very same reproach ; and against this reproach, he was compelled to vindicate the gospel which he preached in repeated instances.

But let us consider the real ground which we occupy in this matter. The law requires perfect obedience to all its commandments. It denounces a curse against every one who shall violate them in the smallest degree. But it is undeniably manifest, that every man living has violated them in ten thousand instances, and is consequently obnoxious to all the judgments which they denounce. And yet in preaching the gospel of the Lord Jesus Christ, we say to those who believe in him, and are thus walking not according to the flesh, but according to the Spirit, that they have no ground for fear, for there is no condemnation to those who are in Christ Jesus, and neither the law in its punishment, nor sin in its power, shall have dominion over them. Now do we in this preaching, set aside the law, and act or teach, in contradiction to its established and unalterable principles? We answer, by no means;—we establish, confirm, and honour the law by this instruction, to the utmost possible extent. We announce a salvation which God has provided; in which he is well pleased; which satisfies every legal demand; makes the sinner honourably and perfectly secure;—and at the same time infinitely glorifies the majesty and character of God.

1. The Gospel honours and magnifies the law, by the voluntary *obedience* of the Lord Jesus, which it announces. The law would have been honoured by the obedience of man, had he continued upright, as it is honoured by the obedience of the holy angels in heaven. In the universal submission to God which is there displayed, the cheerfulness with which all unite to glorify the divine Creator, and the love and communion which is maintained among themselves, the purity and glory of the divine law are unceasingly beheld. Had man remained in his first estate, such would have been the character of the earth; and here, in all the intercourse of men with each other, the perfect law of God would have been the controlling authority, and been completely and continually honoured. This obedience would have magnified the law and have displayed its excellence and worth. But the voluntary obedience and submission of God the Son to its commands, has magnified it far more highly. He, over whom it had no control, and whose will constituted the law itself, yielded

himself to be commanded by the law, for those who were under its condemnation. His perfect obedience to every precept is the righteousness with which God declares himself well pleased. As man, he fulfilled every command. From his childhood to his death, he was constituted under the law. He thus wrought out a spotless righteousness, by which the majesty of the law is perfectly sustained, while the redeemed subjects of its condemnation are released and set at liberty. How can the law be more glorified, or set upon higher ground, in the view of the intelligent universe, than by this voluntary humiliation of God himself? With what peculiar authority and reverence, must it have pressed itself home upon the thrones and dominions, and principalities, and powers in heavenly places, when they beheld such regard paid to it, by the Creator himself! The personal obedience of the Lord Jesus honours the purity and holiness of the law, in its undefiled and spotless character, shewing how holy is that rule, in obedience to which such perfection was brought out by one who was entirely conformed to it; and it honours the majesty and authority of the law, as it is the voluntary submission of a being so elevated and so glorious, over whom the law could have had no necessary or just control. And the Gospel by proclaiming this perfect obedience, magnifies the law, whose excellence and authority it thus acknowledges.

2. The Gospel magnifies and honours the law, by its proclamation of the voluntary *sufferings* of the Lord Jesus Christ in enduring the penalty denounced against transgression. The righteousness which the law required from man, was not only a righteousness of obedience to its precepts, but also of satisfaction for transgressions. Had the law been violated, and the transgression remained unpunished, its authority would have been wholly overthrown; and instead of being magnified and made honourable, it would have been dishonoured and despised. Had all the transgressors of the law been pun-

ished, it would have been honoured, and the Creator would have been displayed as a Being glorious in holiness and justice. But it is far more highly magnified, when the mighty God himself consents to bear its penalties, rather than its honour should be compromised, or its authority despised. The sufferings which he sustained, were a satisfaction to the violated law. They were the penalty which the just anger of God must inflict upon transgression. They must be regarded as the same sufferings in their nature, which unpardoned sinners must endure for themselves. The bodily pain, the darkness of mind, and the violent agony in death, which the Lord endured, were certainly the penalty which the law had denounced as the wages of sin; though the abiding hatred of God, and the unquenchable despair, which are also included in this penalty, as condemned transgressors endure it, were not found in the sufferings of the Son of God. But the infinite dignity and power of the divine Saviour affixed a worth, and gave an extent and depth to these sufferings of his, which made them an ample equivalent for pardoned men. They met the demands of the law. They made it whole and honourable, and thus opened a way indispensable for the salvation of a single sinner, and sufficient for the salvation of all sinners, as one or all should accept the offers of his salvation and be made partakers of his redemption. Thus the Lord Jesus magnified and honoured the justice and fidelity of the law, in submitting both to obey, and to suffer for man, under its holy requisitions. And the Gospel in proclaiming this twofold righteousness for man, magnifies the law, from which it releases him.

3. The Gospel honours the law, by requiring *every sinner* upon whom it bestows a pardon, *to acknowledge his guilt in its transgression, and his desert of condemnation under its sentence.* The honour which the Lord Jesus gave the law, is but a part of that which it receives from the dispensation of the Gospel. The mercy which these glad tidings

announce to man, compels every one who receives it, to confess the justice of his condemnation, before he can partake of the gift thus presented. The sinner who asks for pardon must confess himself a sinner deserving to perish. He must not only declare in words, but he must feel deeply in his conscience, that he deserves to be cast into outer darkness, amidst weeping and gnashing of teeth; and that God would be just and right, in avowing that he has no pleasure in him, and in refusing to accept or aid him. He must go to Christ, as one who feels himself exposed to imminent and awful danger, and cry to him for mercy, as a cast-away sinking into everlasting destruction. He is to plead nothing for himself, but the full satisfaction which the obedience and sufferings of the Lord Jesus have made to the demands of the law, and must found his whole hope upon the perfectly sufficient and honourable offering which has thus been made for him. He must not desire that the demands of the law should be lessened or dishonoured, even for his salvation. And while he feels himself condemned, and acknowledges himself to be condemned, he must still proclaim that the commandment which destroys him is holy, just, and good. He must acknowledge, that without a righteousness which fully answers the demands of the law, he cannot be, and ought not to be accepted before God. And while he acknowledges and laments his own inability ever to render this righteousness, he must plead the merit of his Incarnate God, as all his salvation and all his desire. Thus in the very entrance of the way of salvation which it opens, the Gospel provides for the honouring and magnifying of the law, in the confessions which it requires the redeemed sinner to make. It will save none who do not feel, and who will not confess, this guilt and danger under a previous just condemnation. There must be a deep humiliation for sin, and a deep conviction of his lost estate, in the sinner's mind, before he can hope for pardon in the

Lord Jesus, and obtain the gracious blessings which the Gospel offers. Where this state of mind is found, and the sinner comes to plead the obedience of his divine Redeemer in his behalf, the Lord is well pleased for his righteousness' sake, and the law is magnified and made honourable. No precept has been set aside, and no principle has been overturned. The sinner acknowledges the justice of God in his condemnation, while he sues for the exercise of mercy in his forgiveness. God is consistent with himself, in hearing and answering the penitent's supplication,—and the Gospel which proclaims forgiveness magnifies the law which denounces condemnation.

4. The gospel honours the law in the *new obedience* through which it leads every one whom it has thus pardoned and renewed. It allows none to sin because grace abounds; but while it forgives all who seek for pardon, it leads them as the result of their forgiveness, to serve God in newness of life, and to walk according to his holy will. It is true, the man who has embraced the offers of pardon does not expect perfectly to obey the commands of God; still less does he expect by any such obedience to commend himself to the favour of God. But he has the love of holiness, and the desire for holiness implanted in his heart, as a divine gift. He approves of the precepts of the law in his inner man. He has the law written upon his heart by the Holy Spirit, and the grace of God which has brought him salvation, teaches him to deny ungodliness and worldly lusts, and to live soberly, righteously, and godly, in this present world. His whole effort and object in regard to himself, is made by the Holy Spirit which has been given to him, the desire that he may perfect holiness in the fear of God, and walk in all the commandments and ordinances of the Lord blameless. This is the abiding and secure purpose of his heart and life, and the law is thus magnified and made honourable in all his experience and in

all his character. He has been made free from guilt, that he may be a servant to holiness. He has been delivered by the grace and righteousness of the gospel, from the condemnation of the law, that he may obey and honour this very law in all its precepts, in a new and eternally holy life. And while he is accepted solely for the righteousness' sake of God his Saviour, and glories only in him, his whole life is an unceasing exertion to be holy as he is holy,—meet to be a partaker of his inheritance with his saints.

Under these four aspects of the work of the Saviour *for* the sinner, and of the Spirit *in* the sinner, we see how perfectly united, are these two holy dispensations from God, and how completely the one has established and honoured the other previously revealed. These considerations may form a just conclusion to the instructions which, under the blessing of God, I have attempted to give you upon the great subjects of divine truth which have been successively brought before us. The importance of these views cannot be overstated. The more you study the communications of the Holy Scriptures upon these subjects, and reflect upon their instructions, will you become convinced that the views which have been thus set before you, are the revelations of the truth of God. I trust you will also find them to be, more deeply and permanently, instruments of divine power in your own souls.

These are the truths which the apostles preached in the demonstration of the Spirit, casting down all man's native pride and wisdom, and exalting the Lord alone, as the sinner's righteousness and salvation. These are the truths for which the venerable reformers of the Church in the sixteenth century willingly offered their lives as a testimony under the cruelty and hatred of anti-christian bigotry. These blessed truths were embodied by them, in all the formularies of the whole Protestant Church, as the doctrine of the oracles of God. In every land in which the power of the Reformation was felt, this same system of doctrine was simultaneously drawn from the divine word, as the faith of God's elect. These are the truths which all real and faithful preachers of the gospel in every Christian Church now proclaim. They are the truths, by the proclamation of which alone, the gospel of Christ can triumph among men, and sinners be saved in a real conversion to God. They are the truths which our Church teaches, in all her standards of doctrine, and in teaching of which she shews her peculiar worth to us, and the honour which she gives to God. These are the truths, by which alone, and a faithful adhering to which, we are to stem the torrent of popery in all its varying shapes, as it is flowing down upon us in these last days. Prize them as your treasure. Cling to them as your hope. Proclaim them as the word of God. And may God, even your own God, cause them to bring forth for you, the everlasting fruits of holiness and peace. And all the glory be to the EVER BLESSED TRINITY, the FATHER, the SON, and the HOLY GHOST, ONE GOD, world without end. Amen.

LECTURE XII.

THE GUILT AND DANGER OF REJECTING THE LAST REVELATION FROM GOD.

He that despised Moses' law, died without mercy under two or three witnesses. Of how much sorer punishment, suppose ye, shall he be thought worthy, who hath trodden under foot the Son of God; and hath counted the blood of the covenant wherewith he was sanctified, an unholy thing; and hath done despite unto the Spirit of Grace?—HEBREWS x. 28, 29.

No principle of government can appear more just and reasonable, than that every increase of privileges should be attended with a corresponding increase of responsibility. From those, who in the wise arrangements of the divine Providence, have been placed in a state of comparative ignorance and darkness, more will not be demanded than is in due proportion to their means of information and improvement. God will undoubtedly be found, to make, in his final dealings with mankind, whatever distinctions shall be proper and just, between the heathen and the nominal Christian,—between the idiot, and the man of intelligence and reason,—and between all involuntary ignorance, and despised and neglected means of knowledge. This just principle of proportioned responsibility is repeatedly acknowledged, and dwelt upon, in the sacred Scriptures. Our Lord declares that the men of Nineveh, and the Queen of the South, shall rise up in the judgment, for the condemnation of those who had listened without effect, to the invitations of the gospel as proclaimed by him; and that even the dreadful punishment of the inhabitants of Sodom should be found more tolerable, than that of those who rejected his gracious invitations and offers. Upon this principle, he assures us, that "to whom much is given, from them also shall much be required." A high attainment of holiness, an ardent thankfulness for divine blessings, and an eager endeavour to do the will of God, must be expected from those who have received the amazing privileges of the gospel. And a fearful aggravation of guilt, and an exposure to extreme danger and punishment will attend a continued disregard of the truths which it proclaims, and the offers of mercy which it makes.

The application of this important principle to ourselves will be readily perceived. Our privileges are great and peculiar, beyond even the most of those to whom the gospel has been preached. The glory of divine truth shines around us. The provisions of the kingdom of grace invite our universal participation. No one of those who have listened even to the discourses which I am now concluding, can be necessarily ignorant of the way of life. If in the case of any one in such circumstances, transgression results in the final wages which are threatened against it, the condemnation must be altogether wilful, and the aggravation of the guilt will fearfully increase the terror of its recompense.

This principle of comparative responsibility is now brought before your view, and forms an appropriate practical conclusion to the lectures which you have heard. The text presented to you, assumes the point, that it is the same Divine Being who speaks both in the Law and the Gospel; and that he will manifest himself in each, the same inflexibly holy and just being; and that so far from mitigating the strictness and purity of his demands upon men, under the latter dispensation, he will visit their voluntary disobedience with a far sorer punishment. It will be impossible for those to escape, who neglect so great salvation. The apostle in this text illustrates the fearful condition of those who reject the gospel, by a comparison of it with the condition of men under the law. The parts of this comparison, and the conclusion which he derives from it, it will be our purpose to consider, as an illustration of *the guilt and danger of rejecting the gospel.*

I. "He that despised Moses' law died without mercy under two or three witnesses." The law as revealed by Moses contained a great variety of precepts, of different importance and influence. Under its provisions some transgressions might be pardoned through the offering of an appointed sacrifice. For others the prescribed and inevitable punishment was death. If a soul had sinned through ignorance, or inadvertence, there was a way opened, by which the evil results of this involuntary deviation might be avoided. But if a man wilfully disobeyed a high and important moral command, there was no provided means of expiation. The life of the transgressor was to be certainly forfeited to the violated majesty of the law. It is probably with particular reference to this distinction, that the apostle employs the term "despised." There was a pardon for unintentional transgressions. But no contempt of the divine authority, no wilful disregard of a known prohibition, no voluntary rebellion against the majesty of the lawgiver, could be passed over with impunity. For such offences the immediate retribution was death without mercy. The law had been given in the clearest and most positive terms. It could not be misunderstood. When man was accused of its intentional violation, the plainest evidence of guilt was required. By the concurrent testimony of two or three eye-witnesses at the least, every word must be established. But after the fact of the crime was thus satisfactorily and clearly established, there was no remission; no one had authority to interfere; none could sue for pardon, or for further trial. Such a man had despised the law, and there was no provision for mercy. There remained nothing for the rulers of the people, but the infliction of the prescribed punishment; and nothing to the transgressor, but the fearful expectation of the death denounced. The hour of mercy had passed. The criminal must be dragged even from the horns of the altar, to his merited condemnation. The hands of the witnesses must be first upon him, to put him to death. The high authority of God had been despised, and the despiser must perish without mercy.

II. This extreme severity of punishment is employed in our text to illustrate the far higher measure of indignation, which must recompense a similar contempt of the gospel revelation. The law of Moses was a dispensation of vastly inferior privileges, and with far more limited means of light and knowledge for man. And in the same proportion in which the gospel has enhanced the privileges of mankind, must it also aggravate the guilt and the punishment, of their voluntary disobedience and contempt. Accordingly the Holy Spirit demands in the text, " of how much sorer punishment, suppose ye, shall he be thought worthy, who hath trodden under foot the Son of God, and hath counted the blood of the covenant wherewith he was sanctified, an unholy thing, and hath done despite unto the Spirit of grace ?" It will be allowed that such expressions describe an extreme degree of human guilt. But to whom can they with justice be applied? Are these the acts and attributes of men, who were known only during the short period of the apostolic ministry, and who have had no successors since, around the Christian Church ? Or are they the practical characteristics of many with whom we now associate? How extensively this description applies to different classes of mankind, it is proper to consider.

1. There is manifestly here, a description of those who have become apostates from a religious profession, and of those who

have voluntarily driven away from them, serious impressions of truth by a subsequent course of unbelief and sin. The apostle connects it with those who "draw back unto perdition." Though once awakened by the Holy Spirit, to see, to acknowledge, and to follow after, the excellence and the promises of true piety, they returned again to their former pleasures and sins,—they "walked in the counsel of the ungodly, and stood in the way of sinners, and sat down in the seat of the scornful," and thus denied the faith, and brought upon themselves a swift destruction. To all such persons, the solemn demand of the text is applicable, to the end of time. It should awaken them to the danger of resisting the convictions of the Holy Spirit. It should arouse them to consider the alarming difficulty of their ever regaining any spiritual benefit, when they have thus deliberately torn themselves loose from the merciful intreaties of the Son of God. It is not that any sins of men are in their actual guilt beyond the reach of divine forgiveness. But it is, that the very nature and necessary tendency of a backsliding spirit, is so to harden the heart, and to sear the conscience, that no means are found adequate to rouse its victims from their apathy, and to bring them again humbly to seek for mercy at a Saviour's feet. Rarely can they be renewed to repentance. Their course of sin, though possibly under the influence of a strong temptation, has been a voluntary and deliberate course. Having willingly rejected the one great only sacrifice for human sin, there remaineth no other sacrifice, but the certain, fearful expectation of judgment and fiery indignation which shall devour the adversaries.

2. The solemn description of the text must be applied to those who are avowedly unbelievers in the truth of the Gospel. Such persons are generally disposed to claim peculiar indulgence, by the allegation, that their faith is not within their own power. But is this true? If the infidelity of man

amidst the privileges of the Gospel were wholly an error in the judgment, and it could be proved, that the man had used all the means of information and knowledge within his reach, without effect, there might be possible room for the urging a plea like this. But the fault with men in such circumstances, is not in the head, but in the heart. The carnal mind hates the humiliation, and the purity, which the Gospel requires, and the wrath which it denounces against the darling sins of men. And when conscience enlightened by the truth of God, checks the commission of sin by the threatenings of the divine word,—to soothe and still this unquiet monitor, man will rush into the boldness of unbelief. He will proclaim the falsehood of a book, of which he knows nothing. He will retail the impiety and sophistry which other opposers have handed down to him. And in the ardour of his hostility, will imagine himself actually overturning the foundations of that truth which God's own Son hath revealed to men. But whence arises this zeal for propagation? Is not its source in that corrupted heart alone, which would tread under foot the authority of God? Mere mental doubt or hesitation would be quiet, and rather be disposed to envy, than desire to overturn, the confidence and comfort of believers in the Gospel. But the spirit of unbelief is hateful and hating others. If you should separate from the Gospel, its sacred laws of conduct, and remove its humbling doctrines, and its solemn warnings to the guilty, and leave its professors, to indulge the appetites of corrupt nature, and still to look for impunity and peace, all the opposition of infidelity would be removed. O, how fearfully does the description of the text apply to such! They are thus warring with the best interests of man, and pouring contempt upon the authority of God. And what can be the result of their impiety, but death without mercy, and that eternal?

3. But the text must have a broader application than to these two classes of despisers. It actually describes the course

of every heedless and ungrateful transgressor against God, under the abundant privileges of the Gospel. To every man, whose proud and guilty heart rejects the power and love of an offended Saviour, do its alarming characteristics apply. He is treading under foot the Son of God, and counting the blood of the covenant wherewith he was sanctified an unholy thing, and doing despite unto the Spirit of grace. Among those to whom the Gospel has been faithfully proclaimed, a rejection of its spiritual, renewing influence cannot be a sin of ignorance. The disobedience and heedlessness of a worldly mind is in such circumstances, persisted in, against all the means of light and knowledge which men can have. The continuance of an unpardoned and unconverted state is therefore always the certain evidence of a voluntary rejection and contempt of God's abounding grace. The Gospel has established one plain and simple distinction, between those who gather with Christ, and those who scatter abroad, in opposition to his gathering. To this latter class, without reference to any minor differences of character, the solemn description of our text is justly and wholly applicable. Their rejection of the Gospel in its invitations and offers of mercy, goes to the utmost extent of which they are capable, in rebellion and ingratitude against the Saviour of men from whom its privileges come, and by whose sufferings and death, they have been purchased.

"They have trodden under foot the Son of God." God has been pleased to send his own Son, as the personal substitute and offering for guilty man. But glorious and exalted, as this Almighty Being was amidst the heavenly host who worshipped before him, by guilty men for whom he came, his authority and love have been treated with disregard and contempt. In all ages, the greater portion of those who have heard his word, have refused the benefits of his gracious interposition, and rejected his messages of kindness, with the most rebellious and fatal indignity. In their actual personal intercourse with him, the generation of men to whom he was first offered, crucified the Lord of Glory; and every sinner who has since rejected the pardoning and transforming power of the Gospel, remaining impenitent under its merciful invitations and warnings, has crucified the Son of God afresh,—set his seal, and given his approbation, to the stand which they assumed,—and thus in deliberate contempt, trodden him under his feet. He has gone to the utmost extent which his circumstances would allow, in taking part with those who hated him. And upon the just principle of our text, that conparative privilege is the proper measure of comparative responsibility, they who now assume this ground, justifying and following out the first rejection of the Lord of life, are far more guilty, and deserving a far more dreadful puishment, than the generation who actually stained their hands with his blood. To you, the Son of God comes anew, in every invitation of his Gospel. "He that receiveth you," said he of the ministers of his word, "receiveth me, and he that despiseth you, despiseth me." His own divine authority is connected with the solemn messages which you hear. When you receive these messages of mercy, you receive him personally, you accept him as your Lord, and he dwells within you, as your hope of glory. When you reject his word, it is his personal worth which is despised,—and his authority which is the object of your disregard. This is not the fact in a remote and secondary degree merely, as the contempt of earthly ambassadors insults the authority by which they are commissioned. For the very blessing we are sent to offer, is Christ himself, a personal interest for you in the atonement and righteousness of the Incarnate Jehovah. The thing therefore which you reject, is Christ himself. And this rejection, perfectly voluntary and deliberate, flowing only from a disregard of Christ himself, and resulting in a contempt of him, is declared to be a treading of him under foot. All that you can do in the spirit of hostility against him is thus done. The army of the aliens, the hosts of rebellion and unbelief claim you, as acting with them to the utmost of your influence to promote their dominion, and to overthrow the kingdom of Christ. And the Saviour mourns over you, as shutting yourselves out of eternal life,—and as scattering to the utmost of your power, what he gathers.

But it is not merely in the character of a Creator and Ruler, that you tread the Son of God under your feet. You "count the blood of the covenant wherewith he was sanctified, an unholy thing." He comes to you, as a Redeemer, suffering in your behalf, clothed with a vesture dipped in blood,—bearing your iniquities, and enduring the chastisement of your peace, and making his soul an offering for your sin. It was thus to heal you by his stripes, according to the everlasting covenant with the Father and the Holy Ghost, which gave him as a Saviour to a lost world, that he died for sinners. By the shedding of his blood, he was sanctified, acknowledged, and accepted, in the accomplishment of this work of mercy. And by rejecting his offer of divine atonement, and refusing the exercise of its cleansing and pardoning power upon yourselves, you treat it as an unholy and worthless thing. You proclaim it to be unnecessary and useless, and thus despise him though standing in the very attitude of gracious entreaty, and distinguished by the most affecting testimonials of divine compassion.

How affecting and painful is this view of human guilt! How awakening ought it to be, to the consciences and affections of sinful men! The Saviour stands in the sinner's path to ruin. He stops him in his madness. He extends his arms to him, beseeching him to stay. He points him to the wounds which have bled for him, and entreats and pleads with him to turn and live. The ungrateful man looks upon him with anger, or with unconcern. He still entreats him: "Turn ye, turn ye, for why will ye die?" The infatuated rebel thrusts him from his hold, treads under foot, all his offers and love,—scorns the sorrows which are thus inflicted upon him afresh,—and hardly looking at him, or thinking of him again, presses onward in his chosen path to death. Thus have many of you done, again and again. And yet the gracious Lord has not forsaken you. Through all the changes of life, his voice still calls upon you; and when at last, you are sinking into eternity, unpardoned and without hope, the accents of his pity still echo in your ears, as the melancholy evidence of his despised love, and of your increased and fearful guilt. "O that thou hadst known, even then, at least in this thy day, the things which belong unto thy peace! but now they are hid from thine eyes."

But this rejection of the Saviour is not all. "They have done despite unto the Spirit of Grace." The whole Adorable Trinity is despised and rejected by the unconverted soul. By the operations of the Holy Ghost, sinners are drawn to submit themselves to the righteousness and dominion of the Son of God. All who are the children of God by their union with Christ, have been made partakers of this blessed liberty, by the same Divine Spirit. And they who remain in their condition of carelessness and sin, are resisting and despising the gracious influence by which he operates upon the hearts of men. The Holy Scriptures represent this resistance to the Spirit by different terms of progressive strength. He is *quenched*, when in the first awakenings of conviction upon the conscience, he arouses the sinner from his folly. He is *grieved*, when still putting forth his power with unavailing affection, to draw the sinner with cords of love, he is driven from him with unconcern. He is *despised*, when still unwilling to cease his strivings with men, he makes his solemn appeals to their conscience, with the fears of woe,—and to their affections, with the exhibitions of divine compassion, and yet is obstinately opposed, and finally compelled to leave the sinner, to follow out his own devices, and to eat of the fruit of his own ways. Through this process of increasing opposition to his power, many who listen to me have already passed, quenching, grieving, despising the Holy Spirit of God; until perhaps he has left them to their own folly, and withdrawn the hope, and the offer of mercy from their souls forever.

To set before you, the full course of wickedness you have thus run, and the guilt and dangers which you have thus assumed, I must be able to open the register of heaven, and to give you the knowledge of yourselves which belongs to God alone. There you would see the early fears and warnings which were spread before your youthful hearts; the many awakened determinations to a renewal of life, which marked your maturing years; the solemn convictions of truth with which the messages of the gospel have been often impressed upon your minds; the tears of sorrow for manifest sin, which have marked your cheeks; the desires of deliverance from the burden of sin which have agitated your bosom; the thousand times in which you have acknowledged to yourselves, that it was high time to seek the kingdom of God, and his righteousness, and to have secured to your possession, some good part which should not be taken away from you. All these, and many other occasions and instruments, would be to you the evidence, that the Spirit of God had been long striving with you, with the utmost tenderness and patience. And why then, are you still unpardoned, and without God in the world? Simply because you have done despite to the Spirit of grace. You have despised the riches of his long-suffering, not willing that the goodness of God should lead you to repentance. These unsearchable riches of grace all testify against you. The Father's love, the Son's redemption, the Spirit's power, have all been equally in vain, and wholly in vain, for any spiritual benefit to you. And though you are ruined forever by this course of folly,—your ruin is but the measure of your guilt.

III. How solemn and awakening, is the appeal which the text makes to you? "Of how much sorer punishment, suppose ye, shall he be thought worthy?" The Almighty Jehovah appeals to your own decision in this fearful crisis. What higher guilt can attach itself to man, than is here described? "Death without mercy" recompensed the rejection and contempt of far lower means of light and knowledge. Is there any sorer punishment than death without mercy? None, save in that unchanging woe, where men desire to die, and death flees far from them. And what character or conduct in man shall be thought worthy of this dreadful retribution, if this rejection of God's own Son is not? Your single violations of moral precepts are but atoms to this globe of iniquity, which is thus heaped upon your souls. This sin of scornful unbelief puts all other sins in an eclipse. They are not counted in its presence. "This is the condemnation, that light has come into the world, and men have loved darkness rather than light, because their deeds are evil." This has cast the talent of lead upon the ephah of wickedness. This has stopped every mouth, and counted every unconverted soul guilty before God. "See then that ye refuse not him that speaketh. For if they escaped not who refused him that spake on earth, much more shall not we escape, if we turn away from him that speaketh from heaven."

The Christian Ministry
The Office and Duty of the Gospel Minister
Stephen H. Tyng

These outstanding lectures were delivered from September - October 3, 1873 at the School of Theology in the Boston University, and were subsequently published at the earnest request of the students and the faculty who heard them delivered. One reason for the value of this work is that the lectures were delivered by a man who had been serving Christ in the Gospel ministry for more than half a century.

The Christian Pastor by Stephen H. Tyng is very personable and pastoral and sound." - **Dr. Tom Nettles**

Lecture One -
Introduction to the Series, The Personal Object of the Pastor:

Lecture Two -
The Qualifications required for the Christian Pastor:

Lecture Three -
The Instruments to be employed for the pastor's work:

Lecture Four -
The Agencies and Opportunities prepared for the pastor:

Lecture Five -
The elements of Power and Real Attainments of the Pastor:

Call us Toll Free at 1-866-789-7423
Visit our web site at solid-ground-books.com

www.ingramcontent.com/pod-product-compliance
Lightning Source LLC
Chambersburg PA
CBHW022049160426
43198CB00008B/170